# Headbutting in Academe

# Also by Robert Anderson

*The Vanishing Village: A Danish Maritime Community* (with B. G. Anderson), 1964

*Bus Stop for Paris: The Transformation of a French Village* (with B. G. Anderson), 1965

*Traditional Europe: A Study in Anthropology and History*, 1971

*Modern Europe: An Anthropological Perspective*, 1973

*Denmark: Success of a Developing Nation*, 1975

*Conservative Care of Low Back Pain*, (Editor and author, with Arthur H. White), 1991

*Magic, Science, and Health: The Aims and Achievements of Medical Anthropology*, 1996

*Alternative and Conventional Medicine in Iceland: The Diagnosis and Treatment of Low Back Pain* (monograph), 2000

*The Ghosts of Iceland*, 2005

*The Labyrinth of Cultural Complexity: Fremont High Teachers, The Small School Policy, and Oakland Inner-City Realities*, 2008

# Headbutting in Academe

## An Autoethnography

**Robert Anderson**
**Mills College**

*iUniverse, Inc.*
*New York   Bloomington*

**Headbutting in Academe**
An Autoethnography

iUniverse books may be ordered through booksellers or by contacting:

iUniverse
1663 Liberty Drive
Bloomington, IN 47403
www.iuniverse.com
1-800-Authors (1-800-288-4677)

ISBN: 978-1-4401-6053-0 (sc)
ISBN: 978-1-4401-6054-7 (ebk)

Printed in the United States of America

iUniverse rev. date: 07/28/2009

# Celebrating 50 Years as a Professor at Mills College

# 1960-2010

## Dedication

What a Joy and Privilege
To Work With and Learn From

Fellow Professors, All Brilliant and Dedicated*
Administrators, Always Supportive and Generous*
Students, The Best of the Best, Our Pride and Our Joy*
Support Staff: Office, Computing, Facilities, Controller, Grounds

*With a few exceptions, of course, but ever so few and far between

I have been told that the first fifty years are the hardest.
I will get back to you on that in 2060, if I am still at Mills.

# Contents

# Part I

## Autoethnography as Method and Lifestyle

# Chapter One

## The Matrix *versus* The Labyrinth, More or Less

### School Ethnography

*Headbutting Teachers in Academe* is about how we butt our heads against institutional demands and constraints as we do our best to become effective teachers and creative scholars. It's our scream to the outside world from a cage we call the classroom, the lecture hall, or the laboratory, aching to be free. It's our plea for release to fly unhindered in the glorious universe of learning, discovery, and knowledge - to soar into those heavens with fellow teachers and learners, our colleagues and students. But our urge to do our best, to be free, to fly unhindered, to soar, is compromised. I repeat, compromised. It is Horace's Compromise (Sizer, 1984).

So, I write to protest the demands and constraints that clearly benefit us in some ways, but in major ways clip our wings and rattle our cages. I write as an anthropology professor in two academic institutions, Fremont High School and Mills College, located just two miles apart, the one an inner-city school in the flatlands of Oakland and the other an elite college for women in the prosperous foothills.

Anthropologists typically do research by immersing themselves in a society, learning the language if need be, spending a year or two observing, asking questions, getting involved, photographing, videotaping, filming and writing copious notes on how people live their lives. We call that ethnographic research method "participant observation." Ultimately, our most valuable achievement as cultural anthropologists is that we document how people lived their lives while we were with them. In that way we create contemporary descriptions that eventually become historical treasures. Yes, we are treasure hunters. But we especially dedicate our work to the betterment of society in our own time. We call that applied and practicing anthropology.

To a greater or lesser degree as circumstances permit, anthropological documentation will be holistic. Unlike any of the other social sciences, we investigate a school or college, for example, as part of a larger universe, such as a school district (Fremont High) or an state-wide accreditation region (Mills College), or sometimes as part of the city, state, or nation. But the holistic approach may also penetrate the small, hidden away, ordinarily inaccessible corners and crevices of a society. Within a school or college we want to know how work gets done in a committee meeting, how a specific teacher or professor transforms teaching into learning, what transpires in a lunchroom, or at a faculty party. We also aim for historical depth. In holistic ways we create lasting documents that can impact the present and endure to become irreplaceable archives of the past.

However, although ethnographic documentation constitutes the pivotal practice for every cultural anthropologist, there is, in fact, a second methodology that is equally important (and I refer here only to cultural anthropology, setting aside biological and linguistic anthropology for another time and a different book). The second method is comparative analysis. It is the method that shapes how we look for ways in which a culture documented by participant observation is both similar to and different from other cultures equally well described. Anthropological theories for the most part take shape as statements about regularities, about commonalities that emerge from those comparisons. Thus, in what follows I will describe teaching and learning in two educational institutions (ethnography), and on that basis will identify similarities and differences (comparative analysis) suggestive of broader regularities in academic administration, and specifically in the design, implementation, and assessment of educational policy (ethnographic theory).

Ethnology is importantly humanistic, qualitative as we say, although we also do statistical work, since quantitative analysis can be important for zeroing in on how societies and cultures can be both alike and different. It's a part of what Alfred Lewis Kroeber had in mind when he was reported to have said, "anthropology is the most humanistic of the sciences and the most scientific of the humanities."

## Autoethnography

What I have to say about headbutting is consistent with what I would be reporting had I done ethnographic research in East Oakland, except that I am not reporting on research as such. I am reporting on what I experienced and observed as a professional volunteer at Fremont High School and as a professor at Mills College, as an involved member of those communities who happens to be an anthropologist. So this report does not derive from a research-based ethnography, yet it is identical with what in-depth research would have produced. It is what sociologist Carolyn Ellis writes of as the method of autoethnography (2004).

That's what I rather awkwardly tried to say many years ago when the opening sentence of my little-noticed textbook read, "Anthropology is more than a science. It is a way of life" (1971: 1). Although I never defined my involvement at Fremont as a formal research project, it is an inevitable part of my personality that I am an anthropologist, and in everything I do I think and act as an anthropologist, or more specifically as an ethnographer. It's a way of learning about the world and learning about oneself at the same time. In a reflective mood, Adam Fish refers to his personal "practice of everyday ethnography," adding,

"I am always an ethnographer in praxis. . . . My subjectivity drives the discussion towards things I want to know about" (2007: 6). In a similar way, Robert O'Brien asserts, "I claim [anthropology] as a 'worldview' through which I interpret my experience and base my actions," which nicely states what I tried to say 35 years earlier (2007: 54).

Melford Weiss captured that idea especially well in a publication released this very month as I write in May, 2009. "Reviewing my career, I now realize that . . . I saw anthropology more as a perspective on life's events rather than the study of a . . . particular people." His own personal/professional concern for elementary school teachers and their pupils began in conversations with his wife, who was struggling to teach in an impoverished neighborhood school. Looking back on his career he realizes that his ethnographic understandings and writings grew out of what he calls "following the family." From his wife's classroom, to the Parent Teachers Association, to the high school gymnasium (where his older daughter became a champion gymnast), to the university (where his younger daughter pledged a sorority), and ultimately to his own career as a university professor. He recently documented early retirement programs and how they impact one's identity as a professional scholar. Having followed his career from early to late, it seems to me that Mel has been an unusually successful practitioner of autoethnography, although he has never said that and he might well disagree, since not everyone defines the term my way (Reed-Danahay, 2009; Chang, 2008; Pratt, 1992). What he says is that, "For me, work, home, family and community have always been part of the same system making up my life experience" (2009: 47). I might well say the same for myself.

## To Fremont High as a Volunteer

Pure chance and remarkably good luck brought me to Fremont High in the fall of 1999. At the time I didn't know anything about educational theory and was only dimly aware of public school problems, since my children in Oakland had long since completed high school and my grandchildren resident in Oakland were still just little kids. At that time my teaching, research, and writing at Mills College were centered on totally different matters as I put the finishing touches on a monograph about the diagnosis and treatment of back pain (Anderson, 2000).

My unexpected new interest in public education – it grew into a passionate commitment – began when two Mills College sophomores who had graduated from Fremont, Cristina Rosas and Brenda Orosco, invited me to tour their alma mater and introduced me to several of their former teachers, including Steven O'Donoghue and Michael Jackson, co-directors of the Media Academy, where students produced the school newspaper, the *Green and Gold*. I also got to know María Domínguez, Erica García, and four other seniors whom I chatted with individually over coffee in the weeks that followed, drawing them out on what their school experience had been and discussing their plans to go to college. (All four of those former Fremont students eventually graduated from Mills College.) What I encountered overall at Fremont High were some really nice young people and some very hard-working teachers, all of whom were struggling to succeed in an educational system that was failing them.

What was lucky for me was that the students and teachers I met stimulated my interest in the school and welcomed me when Fremont was at a low point in its history, yet poised for momentous change. As I will explain below, I was present in 1999 to witness destitution and I continued on into the spring of 2000 when the first formal efforts to implement a new educational policy took place. I remained deeply involved until 2006.

## Starting from a Low Point

It was a quick two-mile drive to get to the school from Mills. On arrival for my appointment with Cristina and Brenda I parked and walked along Foothill Boulevard, the heavily trafficked thoroughfare that edges the fenced-in campus. The neighborhood scene was dismal. Across the street the school fronted on a row of small boarded-up stores, including a couple that now serve as dwellings, as well as a closed-down car wash still in use, I learned later, for dealing drugs. The collective image of abandon and decay was not at all offset by two small liquor stores at opposite corners of the block from which an occasional individual emerged clutching an open bottle or can in a small paper bag.

The school side of Foothill Boulevard just beyond the school itself was occupied by shabby, rundown houses and an empty corner lot where I passed a couple of truant boys smoking joints, not yet chased off by José García, the disabled neighbor and eventual good friend who later made it his practice to keep an eye on my parked car while chatting on his front steps with neighbors, including one local resident who didn't want his picture taken because, as he explained, "I'm a wanted man." José never gave up trying to alert me to the basic "street smarts" I ought to acquire for safety in that part of town until even his house was abandoned and boarded up.

Residential streets on the other three sides of the campus are built up with multiunit dwellings, small houses, a couple of storefront residences, and two small churches. Visible just one block from the school is a beautifully maintained mosque and alternative school (madrassa), formerly a Baptist Church. The residential neighborhood projected a mixed message because, while many of the buildings were seriously in need of renovation, trash pickup, window washing, curtains, and gardening, others were neat and well-maintained by families defiant of decay.

The school itself, glimpsed from the street through a 15-foot high chain link fence, looked like a prison in need of paint. Walking from the gate to the office revealed very little vegetation but a lot of clutter, graffiti, cracked walls, and boxlike portable classrooms. In the absence of a parking lot, cars were scattered around on walkways and an asphalt surface fronting the gymnasium. Plastic turf had long ago replaced real grass on the football field at the far end of the school where the wind-blown detritus of carryout fast-food containers and dirty napkins fluttered like small flags of despair against fences behind the goal posts.

Along the way I stopped to glance at two different inoperative drinking fountains, both filthy, while simultaneously taking notice of how classroom windows were protected with the kind of heavy screens typically found in high crime neighborhoods. Inside the main building I pushed open a door to enter and quickly retreat from a half-dark boys restroom equipped with soap and towel dispensers, but not with soap or towels. Along two walls to the side and rear, the room was furnished with cracked porcelain urinals, broken stall doors, and unflushed toilets that, by some logic incomprehensible to me, youngsters had tagged with their artistically designed initials, an immature imitation, I suppose, of the highly qualified professional adult whose name and title are painted on the door of an office. Could I ever penetrate the mindset of such a boy and his youth culture? Would I ever come to understand a status system in which respect was enhanced by marking territory over a urinal? In retrospect more than ten years later, I must confess to only limited success, in spite of the teaching efforts of students who befriended me, of Mills students, many only recently out of high school themselves, who worked with students and teachers under my supervision, of faculty like Steve and Mike, and of parents and neighbors like José.

Yet, what impressed me the most occurred after that first day when awareness of the neighborhood and the campus receded as mere background to the pushing, shoving, shouting mass of 2,300 students who walked by – Latino, African American, Asian, Pacific Islander, and mixed, in contrast to most of their teachers who were white. When I got to know Fremont students as individuals I found them to be intelligent, talented, inquisitive, playful, bright, hormonally challenged, hyperkinetic, loud, absurdly dressed, individually unique, mostly delightful, and with high potential, just like my own children and grandchildren as teenagers.

I taught a course on anthropology in the Media Academy each of my first two semesters at Fremont High, after which I served as a community representative on committees tasked with working on educational policy changes. Over a five-year period of time, 169 Mills students joined me (around 15 each semester) to assist teachers and to tutor for "service learning" experiences related to courses I taught at Mills. As often as I could I sat in on the Fremont courses in which they served as teaching assistants, since my responsibilities included supervising their service learning on site. In observing them I also observed overall classroom activities. And not the least, in weekly e-mail exchanges with me, Mills students reaffirmed my own mixed first impression. They, too, were distressed by the dilapidated physical plant and yet impressed with the basic goodness and promise of students they got to know.

This was apparent in an e-mail report of first impressions sent me by Brieann O'Flaherty, a recent high school graduate herself, who spent the semester assisting once a week in an English class. "What stood out most to me was the surrounding area of the school and the school's physical appearance. The harsh feel of an urban campus was definitely out of my frame of reference. I can't even fully grasp what a large impact this must have on the school and it's students. And while I am familiar with security on school campuses, the reasons must be enormously different. I know I would personally feel trapped, exacerbating the mind-set that school is like prison, which I'm sure is what many kids feel. . . . Vandalism takes place in all schools with all kids. In my own high school it was rare, but not a surprise; and when it did occur it was chalked up to boredom and mischief. But in this case I would think that there is probably a lot more behind it. I'm sure these kids feel a lot of frustration, resentment, fear, and hostility, and one way that is expressed is in destruction of property. Yet, in the class I was placed in I found these kids to be very sweet and receptive. There were problems of disinterest in the work at hand and distraction by classmates, but once their focus was redirected they were very genuine about learning the material."

Laraine Downer, the middle-class mother of a college graduate and a Mills student herself who luxuriated in finally pursuing her own college education, extended Brieann's characterization. "I just don't know what keeps staff and teachers going. I'm aghast at what a difference 'class' makes in our society." Joan Callahan, a full-time executive secretary by day and an evening degree student after work, returned from an evening planning meeting for school reform with the principal, teachers, parents, and members of the community (Joan and me) to write, "It's heartbreaking that so many kids are in such a negative environment. It's crowded; it's understaffed; it's depressingly in need of beautification, and it has somehow missed out on the Bay Area's economic boom of the past several years."

## Autoethnography at Fremont High

At times I have referred to my involvement with Fremont High as an example of immersion or embedded ethnography, or, in more expansive postmodernist moments, community-based participatory research and action, except that research was not my conscious intent. But for those characterizations to make sense I need to explain more fully how I ended up at Fremont High School in 1999.

I was born in 1926 and grew up just a 20-minute bike ride from the school. One of my closest and most loved relatives, an uncle, enrolled at Fremont in 1907, shortly after it was founded in 1905. He graduated in 1912. Close cousins graduated in the 1920s and 1930s. I was a Fremont student myself from 1941 to 1944, as was my brother Stan from 1942 to 1945 (Anderson, 2008). I continued to call East Oakland my home while I was in other parts of the world studying and doing ethnographic fieldwork, but I returned for good when I joined the faculty at Mills College in 1960, where I have taught ever since.

On rare occasions I drove by my old high school when I was on my way to other places, but it never occurred to me to drop in for a visit. In 1994 I received an invitation in the mail to attend the 50th reunion of my graduating class. I had no interest at all in attending, but for several months I received newsletters updating me on reunion plans. Later I purchased a videotape of interviews with old grads. "Humph," I thought. They met in a nice convention center in the suburbs. With two or three exceptions they were all white like me. They had great fun talking about the old days, when a nickel would get you a cup of coffee and a donut and a movie cost only ten cents, but nobody had anything to say about the school of today. They invited the old football coach from the 1940s, but not the current principal. And what really bothered me, not one word was said about doing something for the school. I thought a class gift would have been appropriate, but apparently it wasn't even thought of.

Five years later my wife Edna Mitchell, Professor and Head of the Department of Education at Mills, was invited to her 50th high school reunion in Independence, Missouri. She was excited about seeing dear old friends, having me meet people she has told me about, and showing me where she grew up. Now, being an anthropologist, I love doing comparative studies, the technique of qualitative comparative analysis mentioned above, looking for how cultural traits can be alike and different in different societies. So, when I got an invitation to my own 55th reunion, scheduled to take place just two weeks before Edna's 50th, I decided to participate. I thought it would be interesting to compare my class and school experience with hers. So with Edna at my side I attended, and it was just as I expected. They were very nice people, but nobody gave a thought to Fremont students and teachers of the present or to the possibility of doing something for their old alma mater. "Humph."

A week or two later we flew to Independence and I met Edna's old friends. They toured their school and presented a class gift to benefit today's young people. As we left to return home it hit me. I had crossed the line from being an outside observer and self-righteous judge of my former classmates to being no better than they. I had celebrated with them but had done nothing for today's school. Within two weeks I returned to

Fremont High for the first time in 55 years with Cristina and Brenda as my guides and with my conscience sorely bruised as motivation.

So how different is autoethnography from going native or carrying out indigenous research, or participatory research and action, or embedded ethnography? Only subtly so, I would say. All of those designations are quite similar insofar as they refer to intensive, usually long-term community involvement. I attach no great importance to the terminology, but I do want to convey an awareness of how this book is autobiographical as much as it is anthropological, and personal as well as professional. I have been deeply immersed in East Oakland from the day I was born. In spite of sojourns abroad as a student, researcher, and teacher, I remained an Oakland resident, lucky for the unique good fortune to have lived and worked most of my life where I grew up, with my children and grandchildren living nearby.

## Autoethnography at Mills College

With a first doctorate in anthropology from the University of California at Berkeley and a second doctorate in sociology from the Sorbonne in Paris, I joined the faculty at Mills College to build on the excitement for sociology that the Rev. Dr. George Hedley stimulated in the 1950s by teaching a couple of sociology courses each year for several years, along with his highly popular activities as the college chaplain. I was hired because I was qualified to formally establish a program that expanded Hedley's offerings in sociology and added others in anthropology. In 1977, with a leave of absence to complete a PhD-to-MD program, my specialization in research and writing shifted from the anthropology of complex societies to medical anthropology, a subfield in which I was very active for a quarter of a century (See, *Magic, Science, and Health: The Aims and Achievements of Medical Anthropology*, 1996).

Beginning in 1999 with intensive community service at Fremont high school, I shifted my major area of specialization for a third time. In the spring of 2009 I deleted medical anthropology courses from the college catalog to be replaced by a new course titled Educational Anthropology. The capstone of my first decade in anthropology and educational policy shaped up as a 2008 book, *The Labyrinth of Cultural Complexity: Fremont High Teachers, The Small School Policy, and Oakland Inner-City Realities.*

Just as the Fremont campus is separated from East Oakland by a high fence, Mills, too, is separated by a fence, but at Mills it is ivy covered and entered between tall polished-stone columns displaying bronze lettering that welcomes visitors to a formal gate house where uniformed security staff direct cars and pedestrians along tree-lined avenues past buildings designed by famous architects and landscaping coiffed by a diligent crew of gardeners.

When I joined the faculty half a century ago almost all of our students came from well-to-do families. I will never forget my third year on staff when for the first time I discovered a young woman in one of my classes whose mannerisms and dress were clearly working class. She dramatized for me how elite the institution was. I had signed on in the waning days of what had begun a century earlier as a finishing school replete with formal tea parties, May Pole festivities, and a spring celebration in which seniors in white dresses and big smiles stepped through a giant wreath of flowers to formally announce that they were engaged to be married, often kept a secret until that moment to enhance dramatic effect. I was told by the Dean when I joined the faculty that we were educating an American elite, women who would marry powerful men and who would, by virtue of their academic training, be well positioned to do much good in the world. That's how it was in the early sixties, but transformation was already well under way. Today the college graduates women who are prepared to enter any and all professions, to hold power themselves if they choose.

In subtleties of language, dress, and demeanor that working class student dramatized for me how different family cultures at Mills were from those of Fremont High, which was still 80 percent white in 1960 but dropped off precipitously to 25 percent ten years later and continued to plummet (Anderson, 2008: 61). The Mills student body was white, but with a number of Asian students, also from privileged families, reminders that Cyrus and Susan Mills were missionaries in the Far East before they purchased the Young Ladies Seminary founded in nearby Benicia in 1852. And the faculty was white.

However, the college was poised for change, and while it is still a women's college, 35 percent of our undergraduate students (2008-2009) are now women of color. They are also very diverse in terms of socioeconomic class. Most (97 percent) now depend on financial aid in the form of grants and loans, the average award amounting to $30,835 (against a full-time tuition charge of $34,170). As a matter of equity in hiring policy, the faculty was always more than 50 percent female (it is presently 61 percent), but almost without exception the entire faculty was white. Now 26 percent are people of color.

All of the students at Fremont high when I returned in 1999 were boys and girls of color, with no more white students than could be counted on one hand. Most of their teachers were still white, although that was changing. Over 68 percent of the children were classified as economically disadvantaged. Yet their school was grossly underfunded. California spends $1,900 per student less than the national average, which ranks the state 46th nationally in per-pupil spending.

## The Use of Metaphor and the Value of Aphorism

*Metaphor*: A word that literally denotes one kind of object or idea but is used to suggest a likeness or analogy to something else that is quite different, as in my use of the words labyrinth and matrix.

*Aphorism*: A pithy observation that communicates a basic truth, which is how I use the statements, *less is more*, as well as, *more is better*.

During those years, 1999-2009, contrasts between the two schools, Fremont and Mills, were enormous: a public secondary school versus a private college, boys and girls versus women only, an underperforming educational program versus a top-ranked degree-granting institution, the flat lands versus the hills, poverty versus prosperity. And yet, the two institutions were similar in one very important sense. They struggled in comparable ways with governance issues of power and control, the high school with the Oakland Unified School District (OUSD) and the college with the Western Association of Schools and Colleges (WASC).

That similarity makes comparative analysis worth doing. The two institutions provide ethnographic support, I will argue, for a model of binary oppositions in policy analysis. I find it useful to examine teaching and learning in those two very different educational institutions as similarly challenged by an opposition of powerful bureaucratic dominance characterized by narrow organizational rigidities, symbolized as a matrix, in defiance of the fluid, convoluted, open-ended world that teachers and students must navigate by the use of imagination and creativity, symbolized as a labyrinth.

*Matrix*: Defined mathematically as a rigid, rectangular array of rows, columns, and boxes, I use it to symbolize any structuring of formal organizations that subordinates or overrides cultural and social complexities and attempts to manage human relations as though people are interchangeable units distinguished predictably by uniformities of age, gender, race, ethnicity, class, education, status, and role. In the domain of a matrix, less is more rules.

*Labyrinth*: In Greek mythology the Labyrinth was created by Daedalus as a gigantic tangle of dead-end and branching tunnels that trapped whoever would hope to escape. It baffled the Minotaur, a bloodthirsty half-bull, half-man. Theseus cut down the monster, after which he escaped the Labyrinth by the simple expedient of following a trail of string he had spun out as he entered. A small ball of string defeated the purpose of an enormous tangle of tunnels. Again, less is more. I use the image of the labyrinth as a metaphor for how infinitely complex human societies and cultures are at the level of people living their lives from one day to the next, and as a symbol of how frustrating it can be for social scientists who struggle to identify regularities and to forecast events at that level.

*The Concept of Culture*: Much more in the past than in the present, anthropologists have described lifestyles in terms of a theory of culture as learned and shared beliefs and behaviors that implied a massive sameness within any one society, downplaying real-world complexities. Cultural analysis in that way was conceptualized as a domain of homogeneity. It was a domain amenable to descriptions that ignored misfits, controlled research variables, and accommodated broad glosses. Both for good and for ill, culture as a domain of homogeneity made it easier for anthropologists to develop theories of functional integration and cultural change. It continues to be useful at times in discussions of educational policy (Cushman, 1994).

Ultimately, however, theorizing culture needs to characterize it as a defiant domain of complexity. "We no longer see what is learned and shared as a lifestyle of conformity," I wrote in *The Ghosts of Iceland*. "On the contrary, we theorize cultural traits as options that one may activate or ignore, as constraints that one may conform to or resist" (Anderson, 2005: 13-14). Ann Swidler implicated complexity in stating that culture is "a 'tool kit' of symbols, stories, rituals, and world-views, which people may use in varying configurations to solve different kinds of problems" (1986: 273). Lawrence Hirschfeld captured the domain of complexity well in his observation that, "At any given moment the cultural environment which an individual inhabits is fragmented, fluid, noisy, and negotiable" (2002: 615).

*Bricolage and Adhocracy*: In the domain of complexity - in a labyrinth - on the level of children in school, undergraduates in college, teachers in their classrooms, and families in their neighborhoods, coping strategies often work better if circumstances permit what Claude Lévi-Strauss (1966) termed bricolage (to "fiddle," "to tinker," to be creative and resourceful). In a comparable way, Alvin Toffler (1970) coined the term adhocracy, later described by Robert Waterman as "any form of organization that cuts across normal bureaucratic lines to capture opportunities, solve problems, and get results" (1992).

*Bureaucracy*: In a contrasting way, the matrix symbolizes a bureaucratic management style and it's requirements of conformity (Weber, 1979). It can work quite well for social stability, especially for large and complex organizations, but it can also devastate policy initiatives when resorted to inappropriately in a labyrinth.

In what follows we will explore the interplay of that two-system model for policy analysis. For analytical purposes, ethnographic descriptions will be presented as binary oppositions of a number of metaphors and aphorisms:

- rules *versus* bricolage
- bureaucracy *versus* adhocracy
- rigidity *versus* fluidity
- less is more *versus* more is better
- domain of homogeneity *versus* domain of complexity
- a matrix *versus* a labyrinth

As a teacher I know that I write in this book for many fellow teachers and their students who at times want to shout: Get out of the way! Set us free from the constraints of the matrix. Free us to negotiate the labyrinth. But it isn't that simple at all.

# Part II

Less is More as Educational Policy

# Chapter Two

## Fremont High School and Mills College
### Less is More as Educational Policy

I take as my underlying theme a very broad and rather elusive recommendation that originated with the architect and furniture designer Ludwig Mies Van Der Rohe, Director of the Bauhaus Movement from 1930 to 1933 in pre-Nazi Germany. His architectural style was characterized by extreme clarity and simplicity, exemplifying a design principle captured in the now well-known aphorism that he coined, less is more. A couple of generations later that design principle got acculturated to educational policy on the initiative of Theodore Sizer, who was a professor of education in 1984 at Brown University when he founded the Coalition of Essential Schools (CES), a national network of like-minded institutions dedicated to whole system reform.

Less is more in education advocates searching for clarity and simplicity by pursuing depth over breadth. Students should take fewer courses so they can pursue well-chosen fields of knowledge more profoundly. "Serious use of the mind takes time," Sizer insisted. " If you have really high intellectual standards for kids, the curriculum overloaded with stuff has to give way. . . . Practicing any art or any science means circling around a subject, trying this and trying that, asking questions that simply cannot be answered in a trivial way" (cited in Cushman, 1994). I take it also as favoring an open administrative system of minimal demands and constraints that support each student's freedom to explore deeply and widely as much as is consistent with the maintenance of order. On rules and regulations as on curricular plans, less is more when judiciously applied.

To educate one's mind a student has to figure out how to negotiate a labyrinth. As students we like to think of an educational goal as a map and it is indeed a map insofar as we plan which schools to attend and which career lines to consider. But knowledge itself cannot be laid out as a map, because you cannot map a labyrinth. Science, the humanities and the arts will lose you at times as you take off in unexpected directions ("circling around"), get lost in blind alleys ("trying this and trying that") and seek a goal that leads in unexpected directions ("asking questions that simply cannot be answered in a trivial way"). In short, in classrooms where every student in some ways is different from every other student in physical body, personality, capabilities, and interests, where every teacher is gifted or lacking in diverse ways, where each school differs from every other school in the opportunities it offers or fails to offer, and where one semester is different from another – in other words, to the extent that every class, every student, every teacher, every school, and every year is different from every other of its kind, less is more is a way to talk about sacrificing the predictability a matrix can provide in exchange for the unforeseeable surprises of a labyrinth. And that reality holds true as much for high school kids as for college undergraduates, as well as for their teachers and administrators.

The problem is that educational policy design tends to follow a contrary rule captured in the contrary aphorism, more is better. However, before exploring the more is better policy, let's use our two case studies to explore how "less is more" can work well when given a chance.

# Case Study I
(Adapted from Anderson, 2008)

## The Career Academy Policy at Fremont High (1985-2003)

### Design of the New Policy

Despair in Oakland and throughout the nation deepened over the failure of high schools such as Fremont to educate minority and low-income children. A downturn in average Scholastic Aptitude Test (SAT) scores in the late 1960s plunged into a tailspin in the 1970s, making it apparent to all that inner-city schools in the United States had reached a disastrous nadir of academic dysfunction (Steinberg 1997: 31-46; Ogle et al 1991: 40). At the federal level in 1983 a committee of experts published *A Nation at Risk*, a widely influential assessment documenting "a rising tide of mediocrity that threatens our very future as a nation and a people" (National Commission on Excellence in Education, 1983: 5).

One major policy recommendation was that teachers be trained to a higher level of professional excellence, in response to which a teacher reform movement gained momentum. In 1986 the Carnegie Task Force on Teaching as a Profession published *A Nation Prepared: Teachers for the 21st Century*. In that same year, The Holmes Group (made up of university education deans) released their report, *Tomorrow's Teachers*, and in 1990, John Goodlad published *Teachers for Our Nation's Schools*. The upshot was, as sociologists Alan Sadovnik and colleagues recently recalled, "If the schools were not working properly, then teachers and teaching - perhaps the most important piece in the puzzle - had to be looked at critically" (Sadovnik, et al 2001: 511).

That challenge impacted the Oakland Unified School District. In 1990, community activists, education professionals, and district representatives organized the Commission for Positive Change in the Oakland Public Schools to ask more than 800 people what they thought the public schools ought to provide. Their intent was to create a long-range plan for the district. To that end the 19 commissioners, including the Head of the Department of Education at Mills College, Professor Edna Mitchell, divided themselves into six fact-finding panels. Edna served on the panel that examined the teaching profession in Oakland based on a teacher survey.

In an unpublished written summary of survey findings the panel described a demoralized profession. "Teachers and others perceive that District support for their needs is unequal, insufficient, non-systematic, poorly planned and [poorly] implemented. During the school day there is insufficient time for teachers to confer with one another, to plan and prepare lesson plans, to develop curriculum, and to meet with parents." They further agreed that the teacher evaluation process failed to identify good teaching, and they complained that staff development opportunities were a low priority in the superintendent's office, which lacked any kind of long term plan. To this day, almost two decades later, good teachers still struggle to teach well under adverse conditions that include salaries inadequate to the high cost of living in the Bay Area.

As concerns students, by the mid-1980s some policy theorists were insisting that the practice in comprehensive high schools of tracking selected students into college preparatory courses while the majority enrolled in less demanding vocationally-oriented programs was unfair to low-income and minority children. Jeannie Oakes argued convincingly that approximately 60 percent of high school seniors were counseled into non-academic coursework, not because they were uneducable or without potential for post-diploma studies and professional careers, but in effect on the basis of their race, ethnicity or socioeconomic class (1984; 1985; Maran, 2001: 39-53).

Additionally, across the nation members of the business community in the 1980s articulated concerns about high school graduates who did not possess minimum skills for employment in a modern economy. They urged the creation of school-business partnerships that would align educational goals with the needs of business enterprises, as occurred in Boston in 1982 and in other cities where schools were adopted by businesses (Sadovnik et al, 2001: 507).

Not the least, a growing coterie of educational policy theorists were worried about failing school discipline in large comprehensive high schools and a lack of student commitment (Steinberg, 1997: 28, 66-69). Some explored the possibility that unmotivated students might be energized if they could attend academies, houses, magnet schools, schools-within-schools, or other variations of small schools organized around themes. Linda McNeil, reporting on her ethnographic study of a small Midwestern magnet school, articulated the widely held belief that centering schools on programs in the arts, health, business, and so on could improve student performance (McNeil, 1988).

In Oakland as far back as the early 1970s, a succession of school superintendents experimented with small, specialized, set-apart schools. In collaboration with the Urban League, OUSD superintendent Marcus Foster together with his assistant superintendent and successor, Robert Blackburn, founded The Street Academy for struggling students. They also made plans for three arts-centered schools. Between 1975 and 1981 their successor, Ruth Love, advocated for five specialty schools "to reward success, not failure," and her successor in turn, David Bowick (1981-1985), followed up with a proposed strategy for creating small theme schools that included the concept of small schools within large schools. He hoped to reorganize Castlemont, a comprehensive high school not far from Fremont High, planning to incorporate two magnet schools, one for computer technology and the other for performing arts (Yee, 1996).

Those policy initiatives relating to the importance of teachers, the insidious downside of tracking, the benefits of business-school partnerships, and the appeal of small theme schools, influenced the California State Legislature to propose an experiment. In 1984, Assembly Bill 3104 provided funds to enable a limited number of schools to plan and organize career academies that would start up in the fall of 1985, with the promise that they would receive $50,000 a year in state funds. Those special (categorical) state funds would have to be matched by additional direct and in-kind matching funds, either from the district or from community sources.

Under the provisions of AB3104, a career academy was thought of as a way to salvage failing students who were dropping out of comprehensive high schools. Academies would attract, support, and energize excellent teachers, it was argued. They would create school-employer partnerships (which later gained additional support from the federal School-to-Work Opportunities Act of 1994). And they would end the practice of tracking by integrating academic and vocational courses that would enroll academically successful students together with those who were at-risk. In principle, every graduate would be qualified to continue on for college-level academic or technical training or to enter directly into the job market. It was a plan calculated to preserve the strengths of large schools by enrolling students simultaneously in small learning communities. It seemed just right for Fremont High.

## Implementation of the Career Academy Policy

Steven O'Donoghue grew up as a San Francisco boy, attending Catholic schools and graduating from San Francisco State University with a major in history, a minor in English, and a teaching credential. After graduation he continued to reside in San Francisco, but worked in the Oakland Unified School District. From 1973 to 1976 he taught social science at Castlemont High School. That early professional experience became his initiation into a reality that was not adequately taught in his university education. In the classroom he learned that good teachers can be demoralized by uninsulated authoritarianism. He had to learn how to navigate episodes of rigid institutionalism. He also experienced the joy and creativity of teaching under good leadership that accommodated diversity and reflexivity.

During his three years at Castlemont he worked under three different principals. That experience is illustrative of what succeeds and what fails. The first principal was a weak and inflexible man who enforced regulations in counter-productive ways. At that time, Castlemont facilities extended beyond the main building into an area where dozens of portables were laid out on a grid. As a new member of the faculty, O'Donoghue was assigned to a portable at the outer edge of the grid.

"I was on one of the last streets, approaching the football field. That was OK, because I was young and new on the faculty. But it wasn't OK that I didn't have enough desks, so I went to the head custodian to ask for more. He said nothing, but at sixth period that very day I got a note to meet the principal after school. When I got there he chewed me out for not following procedure.

"No one told me the procedure, and what I learned later was that the head custodian was also head of the custodian's union. So the principal berated me because he felt threatened by the custodian, who was telling him what to do. At first I was afraid, but then I got mad. I was doing this for our students. They need seats, and I'm getting chewed out.

"I survived that first year, and fortunately the principal was transferred. He was inadequate in many ways and needed to go. He was replaced by Rosemma Wallace. She was great. She had a good touch with people. You wanted to do things for her. She didn't feel threatened, which was fortunate for me. This was before collective bargaining. Castlemont had a strong faculty and I became a faculty rep. Instead of being confrontational, when we approached her on an issue she would say, 'How can we solve it?'"

Curious to know more I asked, Can you give me an example?

"Sure. That year the school got money for new textbooks, but the need was great and the money was not enough to take care of everybody. Instead of teachers fighting over it, leaving the principal to make unilateral decisions, she held a conference for all of us and we negotiated. Now, the two biggest users are English and social science, so they cut a deal. The first year English got all of their books, and the next it was the social science turn. Or maybe it was the other way around, but the point is, we agreed among ourselves how to handle the problem.

"Unfortunately, she was too good. After that year they brought her downtown and she became a higher administrator. In my third year there the third principal was a former army officer and a former police officer. That tells you right there what he was like. He was the total opposite of Rosemma. He concentrated authority entirely in his own hands. He saw the union as an adversary.

"I enjoyed the courses I was teaching, U. S. history and the history of minorities, but the atmosphere of the school was bad. Prior to that last year, the staff was strong and united. Teachers socialized with one another. We had a strike, and out of 110 or 120 teachers only two crossed the picket line. But the district started setting up TSA positions [teachers on special assignment] for curricular development. Several of our top people were transferred downtown. The most successful teachers were department heads and such. They were replaced by new people just learning their way. I decided I had to get out of there."

So you moved to Fremont in 1976. How did that happen?

"I signed up to teach in summer school at Fremont, where I saw a social studies job announcement. In the interview they kept working on me to sign on to teach journalism. Later I realized they had a really fine social science teacher in the wings, so I never had a chance for that position. But I resisted journalism, and then agreed to it. It meant lots of work to change from social sciences. I had to learn all new things, like teaching English, training kids to do photography, producing the school newspaper and the yearbook. What made it possible was that Fremont had a great principal, Harold Zuckerman. He was 100 percent for the school. He fought for it, and he was fearless. He had been a teacher and he had served on the school board. He didn't care if his efforts for Fremont made people mad. And the vice principal, Donald Holmstedt, was also a good man. Later he became principal in his own right."

How did the principal help you get started as the journalism teacher?

"He bought copies of this book, [enough to supply a whole class]. It took me a couple of years to realize how important that was, Robert F. Kennedy's *Captive Voices*. [Subtitle, *The Report of the Commission of Inquiry into High School Journalism*, 1974, Jack Nelson, author, but frequently referred to as the Kennedy Commission Report.] It dealt with censorship, racism, and all of the other major issues. Above all, I knew that I could go to Harold or Donald when I needed backup, and they would be there for me."

O'Donoghue's journalism program offered a basis for creating a school-within-a-school with an added attraction, because teaching could be oriented to creating a product. Students would publish the school paper. O'Donoghue and his willing accomplice Michael Jackson took up the challenge.

In a conversation with O'Donoghue during a lunch break I asked, How did it happen? I was accustomed by then to how rapidly he moved from one computer to another, a ham sandwich in one hand while the other was precisely booting up programs for a room-full of students soon to arrive, and yet demonstrating that he could simultaneously respond thoughtfully to any and all of the questions I posed as I shadowed him around the room. O'Donoghue, Jackson and many of the other teachers I have observed closely work long, hard hours in what amounts to a daily multitasking marathon that always leaves me breathless, but seems not to faze them at all, except that they are exhausted by the end of the day. It is a labyrinth. I repeated when O'Donoghue paused to cast a quizzical glance in my direction, How did it happen? We grabbed two chairs at random and sat down while he explained.

"One day the principal came to me. He said, 'Hey, we're starting up these new programs.' I hadn't even heard about them. He said journalism would be really great. How about building a career academy around journalism? He said it was supposed to be for at-risk kids, and we had a lot of kids who had difficulties with language arts."

So the principal talked it over with you and offered to back you if you wanted to go for it. "Right." What was his name? "That was Don Holmstedt. He gave me time off the semester before to plan it. That was the spring of 1986. I attended some meetings. The District helped set up an advisory board, and that got me connected with the city."

What do you mean, "connected with the city?"

"Business and professional people were supposed to work with us, so we needed help to get that organized. Robert Maynard was in on it from the start. He was the first African American to be publisher of a major city newspaper, the *Oakland Tribune*, and did a lot to help us as long as he was alive. I had met him before and always had his support in teaching journalism, but with a career academy he needed to be more formally involved, and he agreed to that, arranging for our students to visit the Tribune Tower, meet with reporters and editors, things like that."

How did Mike [Jackson] come into the picture as co-director with you? "Mike started teaching the English part right away. It was an evolutionary process. We started one class at a time, beginning with the entering sophomores."

Oh, that's right. Until 1997-98 Fremont was a three-year senior high school, so there was no freshman class.

"Right. So Mike and I worked it out over the next several years. Mike and I learned to work closely together. That first year, for example, we took the sophomores to Yosemite National Park as a way to get them to bond to one another, to us, and to the Media Academy. We did it together. It worked. And I have been taking the kids to Yosemite every year since, always with one or several other teachers."

What I hear you saying, Steve, is that developing the academy was an unfolding process for you and Mike as co-directors. Whatever the plan, it took time to make it a success, to get all of the pieces in place.

"Yeah. At first, the academy classes were just part of a teaching day, because most of my journalism students were not in it. Over the next three years the academy got bigger and bigger, but also in many ways, more and more complicated."

A research team led by Professor Gary Wehlage of the University of Wisconsin-Madison came to Oakland to evaluate the new Media Academy the very first year of its existence, 1986-1987. That year he and his associates carried out blitzkrieg ethnographic research on fourteen promising small learning communities in different parts of the United States, which led them to visit Fremont three times that year for a week at a time (Wehlage et al, 1989: 155, 258).

Tell me about your experience with that study, Steve.

"Oh, it was great. They flew Mike and me to Racine Wisconsin. We got to hang out at Wingspread, the house that Frank Lloyd Wright built for the Johnson family, you know, the people who made millions from Johnson's Wax. It had a nice pool, amazing furniture, comfortable meeting rooms. That was one of the best deals we ever were in. We were eating with this silverware, also designed by the architect. Anyway, Wehlage invited people from nine of the academies that were in his study. They came from all over the country. There were a few he didn't invite because they weren't doing well."

What did you and Mike get out of it?

"Sharing ideas with other teachers. We stole all kinds of stuff. You know, what I mean is, it was OK to take their ideas and apply them to our academy. We were all doing it, because we were all working with at-risk kids, but with varying levels of success."

Wehlage wrote that up to fifty students were expected to enroll in the program the next year when they arrived at Fremont High in the tenth grade, and that writing, critical thinking and public speaking were emphasized. He was favorably impressed with the academy's efforts to collaborate with professionals in the community. As Steve said to me, "Many members of this [professional] group gave students access to their employees and work sites. Some of these professionals came to the school to teach about the media, and students are invited into local television and radio stations, advertising agencies, and newspaper offices to experience first hand the range of opportunities in the media. In addition, students wrote for their school newspaper, the yearbook and a Spanish-English paper distributed to local residents." (Totally different and more stimulating, I thought to myself, than narrowing the curriculum to preparation for high stakes testing in English and mathematics, a practice in which less is not more, it is only less.)

By the time I showed up at Fremont High in 1999, O'Donoghue had long since turned the yearbook over to other non-academy teachers, and the Spanish-English paper was short-lived, to be replaced by *Teenage Magazine*. A few years after the Wehlage research, the academy began to add student options additional to those in the print media. Jackson developed first radio and then TV courses. Later still other teachers added video production.

The manner in which the Media Academy underwent its developmental process contributed to its success organizationally because the less is more principle was activated. Funding was provided up front. The principal demonstrated leadership skills in the way he granted a measure of autonomy to the co-directors. The founding co-directors for their part learned to collaborate, which was not at all easy. The two men are very different in temperament, and conflicts were not infrequent, but they always worked through them by compromise, demonstrating mutual respect and easily agreeing on their shared ambition for the academy.

It was important, too, that they began in a small way, with an entering class of 10th graders who were new to Fremont High and optimally malleable for enculturation to emergent academy values and goals.

Beginning with about 25 students, the cohort was small enough for intimacy both among themselves and with their journalism teachers.

Not the least, field experiences bonded students and faculty with each other, including site visits to publishing houses and participation in conferences relating to journalism. The most important field trip of all was an annual fall event early in the school year when new students were loaded onto a chartered bus to spend a week in Yosemite National Park. Inner-city youngsters whose world was shaped by asphalt and cement canyons walled in by featureless buildings and telephone poles were introduced in Yosemite to the beauty and sensuousness of grass and trails beneath their feet, the challenge of cautiously venturing into a snow-fed river, and the drama of looking skyward in awe at a high green canopy of redwood trees and filtered sunlight as well as at Half Dome and the mountain range.

Girls and boys alike tested their bravery and physical endurance against each other and against short, middle-aged, but trim, O'Donoghue, as he challenged them to keep moving on long, exhausting hikes up trails to mountainside waterfalls and higher still to long-distance views of a forest that stretched to a horizon of surrounding mountains. They discovered that they could keep going even when they were frightened and exhausted, and they learned to help and encourage each other. After returning to their classrooms, as they laughed and reminisced over their photos, O'Donoghue could see that they had bonded; that they were committed to giving the academy a chance to be important in their lives. They were ready for their imminent three years in high school.

## Implementing Wall-to-Wall Academies

On a beautiful day in May when it would have been tempting to slip away for a walk in the hills, O'Donoghue and I were talking in his room during his conference period. He was sitting at a computer and there were no students around, so he was vulnerable to my questions about recent history.

"The Media Academy was by itself for several years," he told me. "But soon others got interested in looking at alternative ways to organize the school. [Some of our Fremont High] people visited schools all over the country between 1989 and 1991, including Central Park East in Harlem and other East Coast schools. They found other academies or similar [including small learning communities called houses]. So we tried 'houses.'"

On another beautiful spring day two years later I showed up for an after school meeting to discuss small learning communities in the library only to discover it was empty except for Tom Scott, a teacher on special assignment to work with kids in trouble. As he and I waited to see if anybody else would show up (and no one did), Scott reminisced on how Fremont parsed itself into houses a dozen years earlier (1992-1993).

"There was money from the state, AB1274, granting $75,000 to personalize education by organizing a [small] school within a [large comprehensive high] school [like Fremont High]. We checked into it; did a year of planning to find an infrastructure that would work.

"We looked at different models. We studied three approaches. One was the Bay Area Coalition of Essential Schools [BayCES]. Another one was from Stanford on accelerated learning. Finally, we arrived at a consensus and went with the Comer Model. We voted, and 87 percent of the faculty was in favor of it, but it turned out to be hard, because every decision had to be based on consensus."

James Comer, M.D., had developed an approach centered on the importance of communication and active collaboration with parents in order to involve them in the education of their children. Additionally, a Comer School was required to support the ongoing professional development of teachers, acknowledging in that way the central importance of excellence in teaching. Not the least, Comer identified the need for each school to organize a mental health team tasked with fending off the prevailing culture of violence, substance abuse, and crime (Johnson et al, 2002: 482-483).

Recalling that year of planning, Scott continued, "We all agreed on the infrastructure. Folks came from Comer [that June] to advise us on how to set up site-based management. You have to have at least three parents and three students at every meeting, along with teachers and staff," he told me. The guiding principles are "No Fault," consensus decision making, and collaboration. As Scott put it, "we had to work on solving problems by consensus, no fault, no blame. It was a headache to get consensus, but the campus was united. It was a joy.

"Before that we had terrible gang problems. Children's Hospital got involved. They sent Dr. [Barbara] Staggers to provide guidance and facilitate meetings. She taught us how to triage when students got unruly, and we had a full-time nurse and psychologist after the clinic got started." The leadership of an outstanding principal added an essential ingredient, Scott added.

"[Principal] Richard Durand was the motivating force in getting small houses in place. For four years he kept us motivated and on track. Then he left for a better job as superintendent in Southern California. When Durand left the unity ended. Under the principals who replaced him, [the school fell into] chaos."

Under Durand, a reorganization called the Fremont School in Houses (FRESH) program was introduced. Math teacher Ellen Salazar told me that FRESH began with a pilot project in 1991 when 250 tenth graders (half from a bilingual program) were enrolled in a house in which they all had the same teacher for English and social studies and, similarly, a committed teacher for math and science. Consistent with current theorizing that motivation improves if students are able to see how what they learn in class can make them more successful in the adult world, all students did community service one afternoon a week as tutors in elementary schools or as assistants in public agencies such as the Red Cross or Highland Hospital. While students were occupied off campus the faculty was able to meet to problem-solve and plan.

The following year Fremont won a state grant to fund the creation of four career-oriented houses plus an International House for students with limited English language skills. The Media Academy, already funded under an older state program, was to continue, and in 1993 was joined by an Architecture Academy that had newly won state support. After existing on campus since 1986 as a model of how a small school within a school might function, Media found itself incorporated into a consortium of seven small schools within the big school.

During a week of staff development in August, 1993, the faculty planned curricula for the houses, and that fall each student was scheduled into one or another of the following houses or academies.

- Business, International Relations, and Government House
- Health and Environmental Sciences House
- Humanities, Visual and Performing Arts House
- Technology, Mathematics and Engineering House
- ESL [English as a Second Language] House
- Architectural Design and Construction Academy
- Media Academy

In 1997 the houses were reclassified as academies. Salazar told me that the reclassification made Fremont the only all academy school in the nation. "Adequate funding is a fundamental prior condition for school improvement," Larry Cuban has written (2003:60). However, only Media and Architecture received additional support from the state, including salaries for two co-directors each. The Health and Bioscience Academy was awarded state partnership status in 1999, which added academy funding to a substantial biotechnology grant they had received earlier in 1996. The Arts and Letters Academy was granted state funding in 2000. That left the business and electronics academies unfunded, which partially explains the relatively poor quality of their programs, but only partially.

We need to look more closely at how academies worked to combine the benefits of being at once both very big and very small. By 1998-

1999 when I arrived the school was subdivided into the following six academies:

- Media
- Architecture and Construction
- Health and Bioscience
- Arts
- Business and Government
- Electronics

In reviewing that bit of school history with me, Salazar explained that implementation problems plagued them. It was almost impossible to arrange community service placements for so many students. It was hard for teachers to break away from the time-honored tradition of working independently of colleagues behind the closed doors of their classrooms, so a consultant was hired in 1994 to provide guidance in developing a cooperative learning curriculum. Not the least, it was very difficult to coordinate the master schedule for six or seven semi-independent schools sharing a single campus.

Additional adjustments were required in 1997 when, district-wide, a 9th grade was added for the first time since 1923. After a difficult first year as a four-year high school, with the freshmen class patched onto the master schedule on an *ad hoc* basis, by the second year a class of approximately 800 new freshmen was divided into three cohorts (called PODs) separate from the academies, each with core teachers who worked closely with them. The expectation was that the POD program would encourage students to bond to one another and would position them to get encouragement and guidance from their POD teachers. That year of enculturation should prepare them, it was hoped, to select academies that would be meaningful and appropriate for their last three years.

I was present in 2002 to observe freshmen enter the auditorium where each academy had set up a reception table and display. Recruiting took place on a student-to-student basis as representatives from each academy handed out brochures and answered questions. The process progressed quietly under the watchful eye of a vice principal, the only adult other than myself who was present. Surprisingly, only half of the 9th graders showed up to make their choices. Later, those who took advantage of their release from class to hang out or go truant, were assigned to academies by counselors in a largely arbitrary fashion, which suggests that the freshman experience had failed to excite much awareness or enthusiasm for academy participation. Yes, there were problems, most of which were district wide. But in spite of problems, the Media Academy was a big success.

## Assessment of the Academy Model

As noted above, the 1986 Carnegie Task Force rightly emphasized the enormous importance of placing highly qualified teachers in public school classrooms such as in those at Fremont High. At the other extreme of the bureaucratic hierarchy, as encountered in the Oakland Unified School District, the decision-making authority of superintendents was documented by Dr. Gary Yee, who wrote of the need for "miracle workers" at that administrative level (1996). My observations support both of those assertions. However, they also affirm the key role played by school principals at a middle level of power and responsibility.

Emery Roe and Paul Schulman, policy theorist at Mills College, argue persuasively that the knowledge and skills needed in a complex bureaucratic organization are not limited to those required at the extremes, as exemplified in schools, I would assume, by superintendents at the top and teachers at the bottom (Roe and Schulman, 2008). Because they are located between those extremes, principals need to possess skills as mid-level administrators whose worldviews are tempered by individual experience and whose abilities are enhanced by the discretion and improvisation needed to probe policy design. Given the inevitability of "paradoxes, dilemmas, and contradictions" in complex organizations, anthropologist Constance Perin draws attention to the importance of "middle managers" in coping with "an infrastructure of conundrums" (2005: 204-205). Middle managers accommodate limitations in a matrix to complexities in the labyrinth.

As I understand Schulman, Roe and Perin, policies promulgated at the highest but most remote levels of decision-making authority (as concerns Oakland schools, by the district superintendent, the school board, the city government, the state superintendent of schools, the state and local legislatures, the federal government) may be rational - as sociologist Max Weber theorized for bureaucratic management - but they are inherently incapable of anticipating all contingencies at the level of application (as encountered by teachers in their classrooms). Effective principals need the skills and experience it takes to mediate between formal policies at the top and real-life immediacies at the bottom, where teachers and children as abstract uniformities of ascribed social statuses dissolve into the achieved individuality of human beings who inevitably play their roles in highly variable ways.

The need for effective principals has undoubtedly always been a factor in the OUSD. Clear examples were evident in the memory of Steve O'Donoghue as he spoke of his early experience at Castlemont High, where he described the difficulties he encountered in working under two ineffective principals in contrast with his success as facilitated by Rosemma Wallace. Similarly, in initiating the academy policy at Fremont High, he spoke of how his creative energies were liberated by Principals Harold Zuckerman and Don Holmstedt. In a similar way, Tom Scott explained how implementing the Comer model of a small school within a school was achieved, in spite of difficulties, because Richard Durand was a skilled administrator. Conversely, Scott recalled how the policy fell into disarray under later principals who were inept.

"Theoretically," O'Donoghue told me, "every student should be in an academy because we had wall-to-wall academies." But, I countered, some I have talked with are unaligned students-at-large. "Yeah," he responded, because some academies [business and electronics] are doing so poorly."

He then went on to explain that failure of the two academies was only partly the result of not being funded as well as the other four. "When we began [the Media Academy in 1986] we started with the 10th grade, then [the next year] the 11th. We built up from the bottom. We built up a class at a time and gradually brought in more staff. With some of the other academies it was "boom," all at once - all three grades - no curriculum - no design. Teachers who were the most proactive tended to cling together [to form strong academies], but Fremont ended with [some] programs that had a lot of weaker teachers."

In a later conversation O'Donoghue elaborated. "When they set up the academies it was a free-for-all. "Who do you want to work with?" Better teachers and people with similar interests immediately formed their own programs. So some were successful and some not. The most academic is the Architecture Academy. They set everything up by math standards. They made it so tough that they got all the high-in-math kids. They recruited them [which was against the rules and unethical]. Each is supposed to be according to kids' interests, and you push them as far as they can go."

In the beginning the intent was to set up small, personalized magnet academies that would motivate students by recruiting on the basis of a lively potential interest in a particular field, such as journalism, business, or electronics. Unfortunately, they ended up accepting students without special interests, which detoured the plan.

How about the Business Academy? "It's a disaster. That and Electronics. They had the leftovers, teachers who had no one else to work with, [who] weren't ambitious, [and who] didn't like the idea. It was a real disaster [in terms of student recruitment as well]. For a while, Electronics was 90 percent African American male [students]. They had tremendous problems. Imagine a room all full of guys. In a Catholic school," he recalled from his Catholic childhood, "some priest would come in and [not literally] 'beat them up,' but you can't do that here. It was crazy. They ameliorated that, but Electronics is still not strong. You want to go for a teacher." He continued, "[The weak academies were] condemned [to failure] from the beginning."

From the time of Wehlage, The Media Academy has been identified in the educational literature as a model for change. "We get visited all the time by people thinking of starting up academies. [When visitors ask about what they should do] I just say "staff". I would throw away the money if I could just pick staff."

Unfortunately, academies were not granted the autonomy they needed to override disabling parts of the union-contract rules and of district-level prerogatives. Under the OUSD union contract, teachers have the right to choose where they will be assigned. A seniority rule grants a prior right to a new position to any teacher who has been in the system longer than any competing applicant, even though the principal or director may want to appoint a teacher who is better prepared to work in the collaborative mode that is essential for small school success.

"Curriculum is another unresolved issue," Steve explained. "In a way we have six little schools. Some [Fremont] principals, like the one we have now, [Brian] McKibben, he's pretty open to sharing responsibility and delegating authority, [a less is more approach]. But others - top down only - and that doesn't work well with these programs. You have to give some responsibility to the directors, because you're making decisions for the program that maybe don't affect [the rest of] the school at all. If everybody has to run to the principal for every single thing there would be a line out the door. You would never get in.

"Most of the flaws are design flaws: How to interact with the overall system. But the first thing I would want is the right to choose staff - to get people who want to do it."

From what I witnessed between 1999 and 2003, before all of the academies were shut down and the campus was taken over by six New Small Autonomous College Preparatory High Schools, I would say that the Electronics Academy was a failure and the Business Academy was only marginally functional, but the other four were succeeding quite well. The Media Academy, in particular, continued to enjoy a nation-wide reputation twenty years after Wehlage's visit. Until 2003, visiting educators showed up every year to meet with Steve and Mike and to see for themselves how a career academy model could succeed.

The success of the Media Academy for seventeen years was a tribute to what can be achieved when principals and teachers are encouraged to confront challenges in the labyrinth by freeing them from the constraints of a matrix. The Media Academy succeeded because, in school administration as in classroom teaching, there are times when a policy of less is more can be the best policy.

# Case Study II

## The Accreditation Policy at Mills College
## (1960-2009)

## Design and Implementation

For well over a century after 1885, when Mills transformed from a finishing school for young ladies to a chartered college for women, educational goals were high-minded and liberating, well-suited to a world that is a labyrinth. When I arrived in 1960 I felt I had gone to anthropology heaven where "intellectual curiosity" was the mantra, as was clearly articulated in the catalog for that year, and complexity was alluded to in stating, "A College like Mills is composed of hundreds of very different individuals, about whom any generalization is rash."

At Mills we believe that the essence of a liberal education is learning to penetrate any specific problem or conflict to discover what basic issues lie inside it, and what human values are involved. Some American colleges seem to conceive of education as the storing up of factual information, others as the development of skills, either at the purely technical level or at the level of logic and language. Mills values the well-stocked mind and the person skillful in its use. But ours is, at its core, not an education just for information or an education just for skills but an education for insight, which presupposes both knowledge and skills but is more difficult.

That profile still informs my approach to teaching. However, it was becoming an ongoing struggle for the college to stick with less is

43

more in a world of policy fads that repeatedly impacted colleges and universities throughout the nation. Three years after I arrived, explicit "College Objectives" were articulated at Mills for the first time. I was only marginally involved in that decision. My joy as a newly tenured associate professor was in teaching, keeping up with developments in my field, doing research, writing, and participating in scholarly conferences (as well as in spending time with my young family). I left administrative chores to others as much as I could. I don't even remember being told that we would have to follow new and broader distribution requirements when advising students, because a few distribution requirements were already in place. Perhaps the vagueness of my memory is also because less is more, in fact, remained in force. Students exercised labyrinthine freedoms in selecting which courses to take to meet what are now called General Education requirements.

As explained in the catalog of that year, "on the theory that 'distribution requirements,' when summed up by a series of selected introductory courses, appear a hindrance to education rather than a contribution to it, Mills prefers to state its requirements . . . in terms of 'college objectives,' and when practicable to leave the attainment of those objectives to the student herself, in consultation with her major advisor" (emphasis added). For that reason, what amounted to distribution requirements were very loosely prescribed "to emphasize the flexibility that is possible."

In the catalog of 1968, the purpose of an education at Mills was said to be to "widen awareness," "improve judgment," "intensify creative spirit," and "deepen knowledge." (Note that to deepen knowledge is consistent with depth instead of breadth, a corollary of the less is more principle.) Additionally, students were also expected to learn how to "ask the important questions," "test underlying assumptions," "challenge stereotypical answers," and "sharpen perceptions of truth." Yet, the educational program at Mills was designed "to give the student maximum flexibility to find and pursue her own path toward competence and mastery" (from the 1976 catalog).

By 1984, those goals were restated to emphasize career possibilities remote from academe. "Actually, the skills students can develop through a liberal education are very important in the working world as well." By then we had come a very long way from the finishing school that educated women for marriage to wealthy and influential men, destined to mother their children and serve the nation in volunteer activities and community service. By the last third of the twentieth century Mills students were preparing themselves for the working world as actors in their own right by acquiring:

- A firm grasp of cultural, political, and historical issues
- An appreciation of the values that shape human behavior
- An understanding of how societies organize to produce goods and services and of the role of work in our culture
- The ability to express oneself, to make sure one's ideas are heard and understood, in person or on paper
- Leadership skills which help one understand other people and inspire them to help achieve mutually-held goals
- Independence and a sense of integrity, even in situations which require making difficult choices between conflicting "rights" or between immediate and long-term goals
- The ability to evaluate facts and ideas from many different perspectives, and to weigh conflicting voices of authority
- The willingness to accept responsibility and take action in order to achieve positive goals

In sum, a student educated at Mills would graduate knowing how "to act with purpose and conviction throughout her lifetime."

## Less is More in State Regulations

Although Mills College is incorporated under the laws of the State of California, the College is free to govern itself. As noted in the Catalog for 1972, "*The faculty* [emphasis added] determines the educational policy of the College and prescribes the requirements for admission, the courses of study, the conditions of graduation, the nature of degrees to be conferred, and the regulations for the conduct of the educational work of the College." Those laws support academic freedom, and the state on the whole resisted intrusive legislative control.

An exception did occur when an additional course requirement was mandated. As published in the catalog for 1964 for the first time, "The State of California requires that all students receiving a Bachelor of Arts degree in this state demonstrate a basic knowledge of American Institutions. This requirement . . . may be fulfilled in American History (HIST 67-68) or American Government (GOVT 85-86)." That, however, was the extent of state control over the curriculum. Less is more prevailed, although it is a reminder that the power of the state is great and its future potential for shifting to more is better is a reality.

## Less is More in WASC Accreditation

WASC: The Western Association of Schools and Colleges.

"Centennial Year" was boldly stamped on the cover of the Mills College Catalog for 1985. In my year-by-year examination of catalogs for the last half-century, beginning with 1960, I carefully leafed through each one searching for statements on accreditation, but found not a word. Then, inexplicably in the Centennial Year edition, a short statement in small print was published for the first time. "Fully accredited by the Western Association of Schools and Colleges," followed by a bit of legalese. "The documents describing this activity can be reviewed by a current or prospective student upon request."

Until the end of the 20th century the sole purpose of accreditation (from the Latin *credito*, meaning trust) was limited and explicit. It was to provide "certification to the public that the school is a trustworthy institution of learning" (from the WASC website, 2009). It was to clearly differentiate institutions "worthy of the trust placed in them to provide high quality learning opportunities" from for-profit degree mills and inferior programs. Particularly as students increasingly transferred from one school to another, accreditation facilitated the evaluation of transcripts and the acceptance of work done elsewhere. It validated the credentials of students applying to graduate programs or seeking postgraduate employment.

To be granted accreditation, Mills had to provide self-study documentation and undergo site inspections. That had been done many years before I arrived on the scene, and even before WASC was established as a regional accreditation agency for California in 1962. Re-evaluation was required every six years, but as an ordinary member of the faculty I was scarcely aware of it. It was undoubtedly a bit of a burden for administrators, including department heads, but it was largely routine and minimally threatening.

Less is more was at play, and it has worked quite well to this day. Mills has always attracted outstanding entering first-year students. Scholastic Aptitude Scores (SAT) have consistently been quite strong. In 2008, the average math scores were 543, well above the national average of 515 and substantially above the national average for women of 499. Similarly, verbal scores averaged 588, as contrasted with the national average (including for women alone) of 502. In terms of college rankings, note the following:

- Ranked fourth among colleges and universities in the West by U.S. News & World Report.
- Ranked seventh in the West by U. S. News & World Report in "Great Schools, Great Prices" for high academic quality relative to the net cost of attendance
- Named one of the "Best 368 Colleges" in the nation by The Princeton Review
- Named one of the 117 "Best Western Colleges" by The Princeton Review

- Ranked 75th among Forbes' best colleges, placing Mills in the top two percent in the nation
- Ranked 49 among 201 top liberal arts colleges by Washington Monthly (2007)
- Named one of the top producers of Fulbright awards for 2008-09 by the Chronicle of Higher Education
- Rated 92 out of a possible 99 green rating from The Princeton Review for environmental policies and practices

Since less is more worked so well for us, why would we want succumb to the temptations of more is better? Yet, the college started moving tentatively in that direction as early as 1997, and more aggessively in 2003, so that now, in 2009 - suddenly in terms of our awareness - we on the faculty discovered that we are required by WASC to depart the labyrinth on pain of losing our accreditation. Even though we triumphed for decades like Theseus over the Minotaur, we are required now to respond to a top-down command that we abandon the responsive give-and-take we find necessary to teach well in a complicated world, (bricolage, adhocracy) in order to conform to rectangular requirements laid out in rows, columns, and boxes, to turn our backs on the realities of the labyrinth in order to respond in lock-step to the demands of a matrix.

## Less is More at Fremont and at Mills

In what is to follow we are going to see how less is more in both institutions gave place to more is better. In this chapter we have seen that the Media Academy succeeded quite well on a less is more basis, thereby evading the potential down-side of attempting to innovate in a matrix. As we shall see in what follows, Fremont High moved on to pay a steep price between 2000 and 2005 for making a more is better shift that embraced a matrix more fully in order to replace career academies with what early on were called New-Small-Autonomous-

Interconnected-College-Preparatory-High-Schools. Prior experience should have served as a caution.

Mills also thrived under a less is more policy by appropriately embracing the labyrinth in order to implement the original WASC accreditation program. That minimal goal of accreditation served the needs of the College maximally for many decades. As we anticipate the new school year (2009-2010), however, the teaching program is under pressure to reconstitute itself in a matrix. The process is taking place with good intentions based on mistaken assumptions. Or, is it? Judge for yourself. But first, let us take Fremont High School as a cautionary tale.

# Part III

## More is Better at Fremont High (1999-2005)

### (Adapted from Anderson, 2008)

# Chapter Three

## Policy Design

### Less is More as a Small School Policy

Theodore Sizer and those who worked with him in the Coalition of Essential Schools demonstrated the benefits of sticking to essentials, of putting into practice the principle of less is more. The problem is that educational policy is endlessly tempted to follow a contrary rule that seems to say more is better. I give you the example of Fremont High School.

It is an irony of policy intent that efforts to rejuvenate Fremont high school, to turn failure into success, began with a successful effort based on a policy of less is more, the career academy policy. Nonetheless, for most of the 20th century, influential national leaders in educational theory advocated a more is better approach, the creation and perpetuation of large comprehensive high schools, and for defensible reasons. However, as time passed, the realities of cultural complexity demolished the certainties of those convictions. Scholastic achievement rates were low and drop-out rates high. By the 1980s, large schools organized into academies or similar small sub-units on a less is more basis appealed to many as a way to preserve the benefits of scale, both large and small.

Yet, as the year 2000 approached, many influential leaders in educational theory, influenced by sound logic and impressive case studies, and motivated by pedagogic principles enforced by the No Child Left Behind Act of 2001, advocated abandonment of large comprehensive high schools entirely in order to replace them with new, small, college preparatory high schools. When the small school replacement policy was put in place in Oakland it was carried out on the more is better principle, which forced the Oakland Unified School District precipitously into bankruptcy and placed it in state receivership. What began with high hopes became an emotional nightmare for everyone concerned, as we shall see, but first, let us appreciate how well the design of a small school policy was carried out on the district level when less is more was still the motivating principle.

## Parents as Policy Promoters

The new small schools initiative (in contrast to the earlier academy policy) got its start as a grass-roots movement of concerned parents and community activists brought together under the auspices of the Oakland Community Organizations (OCO). The OCO as a non-governmental, non-profit, family-and-community-oriented voluntary association was founded in 1977 to take action in favor of creating urban safety, economic development, affordable housing, neighborhood improvement, accessible health care, and effective schools. It was organized as a faith-based collaboration of 31 Protestant and Roman Catholic congregations, but individuals participated who were not church members and I personally never encountered any trace of Christian ritual in their meetings.

The OCO school initiative grew out of parental and community frustration over persistent inadequacies in the education of Oakland children. That concern moved beyond an early reading and discussion stage in 1998 when a delegation of parents and teachers from the Fruitvale District of East Oakland were funded by OCO to fly to New York to check out for themselves the much touted success of the small autonomous schools described in books and articles by Deborah Meier, Theodore Sizer, and others.

A decade earlier, William Friedkin and Juan Necochea demonstrated in California that large schools, which often worked well for affluent students, were counterproductive for those who were economically disadvantaged (1988). Their data confirmed an interaction hypothesis of size and socioeconomic status. Craig Howley, reporting on similar research in rural West Virginia, summarized that hypothesis even more forcefully in noting that "large schools would appear to compound the afflictions of the already afflicted, whereas they deliver modest benefits to the already blessed. Conversely, small schools mitigate the disadvantages confronted by impoverished students" (1996: 26). One mechanism for afflicting the already afflicted is tracking, because it insidiously diverts low-income students from college prep courses and thereby lowers career aspirations and contributes to dropping out (Oakes, 1985; Chun, 1987, 1988; Cooper, 1999). OCO activists grew increasingly committed to a restructuring initiative based, in effect, on the hypothesis of size and socioeconomic status.

In December, 1998, the OCO organized what they referred to as the New Small Schools Working Group that met once a month to explore and discuss plans for taking action in the Oakland Unified School District. Parents, teachers, and community members were joined on occasion by members of the Board of Education and representatives from the teacher's union, the school district office, and the Mayor's Commission on Education. Most significantly, after the field trip to New York, the OCO agreed to join efforts with an equally committed organization, BayCES, when it became clear in the context of those monthly meetings that the two organizations shared the same small school goals. From a small beginning in 1991, BayCES, the Bay Area

Coalition of *Equitable* Schools, was legally incorporated in Oakland in 1995. It functions as a Northern California branch of the Coalition of *Essential* Schools, but altered the wording of CES to emphasize a commitment to social justice.

As a voluntary association of concerned citizens the OCO has remained steadfast for decades in its commitment to work for community betterment. It does not appear to have a political or religious agenda beyond those limits and no other institution involves parents, teachers and other individuals from the community in such a substantial and consistent way. Their investigation of Oakland public school failure along with agitation for reform was critical because it publicized the need for massive change and how it might be achieved, given that the need was dire. They proposed a small schools policy when it seemed to them that massive institutional change was the only way success might be achieved. They continue to this day to participate and contribute in many ways, but they fell easily into granting the leadership role to BayCES as a voluntary association of skilled, experienced, and well-funded education professionals. Together, the two civic organizations were and are determined to transform substandard schools by advocating the small school policy.

## Education Professionals as Policy Advocates

Leadership in policy reform, that began with parents and community activists organized as a civil society organization, was entrusted to the professional educators employed by BayCES under the leadership of Steve Jubb as executive director. Salaries and expenses were covered by the Melinda and Bill Gates Foundation, supplemented with funds from other donors. The power of persuasion by experts, combined with the ability to fund expensive initiatives, positioned BayCES as an independent not-for-profit association to play a guiding role as the district moved to break free of the political and bureaucratic constraints that usually block radical programs of change. The Common Principles of the CES, based on decades of research and experience, endorse the following:

- Personalized instruction to meet individual needs and interests
- Small enrollments that facilitate trust and high expectations
- Assessments based on the performance of authentic tasks
- Democratic and equitable school policies and practices
- Close partnerships with the community

## Policy and the Superintendent

For this program of reform to become an effective public policy a third player needed to join the team. It was imperative that parents and community activists (the OCO) together with education professionals (BayCES) be positioned to collaborate effectively with city government at the level of a complex bureaucracy, the Oakland Unified School District (OUSD), under the leadership of the superintendent of schools. Ultimately, only the superintendent is authorized legally and fiscally to appoint principals, teachers, and staff, to approve student placements, to oversee the maintenance of buildings and grounds, and to fund operating expenses. In sociological terms, the commitment to a small autonomous school policy would place heavy demands on an inherently problematic hierarchy of the OCO (with grassroots political power), BayCES (with expert personnel and seed money), and the OUSD (with legal responsibility and tax-based funding). In retrospect it is remarkable and fortunate that the collaboration worked out as well as it did.

The Oakland schools had long been administered by well-intentioned superintendents who worked under difficult circumstances. In the post-World War II years they were blindsided by new challenges of unprecedented dimensions: by an overwhelming demographic and economic revolution, by city politics, by entrenched bureaucratic subordinates, by union contracts, by governmental regulations, by legal straight-jackets, and by anemic budgets. They were severely criticized for promoting and graduating students who could scarcely read and write.

They were also embarrassed by failed curricular decisions. The district was lampooned nationally in 1996 when, in a desperate move, the Board of Education ordered the superintendent to develop a plan for teaching black students in the African American dialect known as Ebonics (Perry & Delpit, 1998). The district was ridiculed again in the fall of 1999 when it promoted 7,000 truant students in spite of having notified them that they would be held back because they had not attended summer school.

Then, in February, 2000, the state Fiscal Crisis and Management Assistance Team (FCMAT) reported that the district had completely failed in every category of accountability: personnel, community relations, facilities, finances, and - most devastating of all - in student achievement. In June of that year, half (51 percent) of all students in the district who began high school four years earlier in the 9th grade did not graduate with their class that spring. (The dropout rate was 63 percent for Latino students, 54 percent for African American students, and 26 percent for Asian students.)

Formal organizational changes at the district level began in March, 2000. That was when Dennis Chaconas took over as Superintendent of the Oakland Unified School District. He didn't need the job. He could easily have stayed on in the neighboring Alameda district where his seven year administration was succeeding quite well. Yet, as much for personal as for professional reasons, he wanted to return to Oakland where he was born and raised and where he had worked for most of his professional life as a teacher, high school principal, and assistant superintendent. No doubt, too, he wanted the recognition and other benefits that come with administering a much bigger, more visible district, the sixth largest in the state, especially if he could succeed where others had repeatedly failed.

He was a strong applicant and the Board of Education hired him over objections by the mayor, who favored his own candidate, a man more qualified as a politician than as an educator. As Chaconas later explained, "I made a decision at that time that most of my friends think I am insane to make, [which] was to go to a school district that has gone through five superintendents in four years."

His friends were right. He lasted much longer than any of his immediate predecessors. Even so, he was fired at the end of his third year, but I will come to that later.

Before his precipitous crash he flew high for three years of impressive success and great promise. Eight months after he took office, while still in his taking-off phase, I was present with my video camera when he talked about his decision to apply for the job and his plans for transforming the district. Here is how that meeting came about.

Once every other month I occasionally join as few as fifteen or as many as ninety aging graduates of Fremont High for lunch in one or another of the suburbs located away from the grime and crime of East Oakland. Fremont High for those graduates exists only as what anthropologists would call memory culture. They never visit the campus, rarely inform themselves about ongoing school affairs, and do not donate money, skills, or labor. Only a very few, like myself, still reside or work in Oakland. The rest were part of white flight after World War II. Fremont High only exists for them as it was when they were young, like old photos to remind us that in our time we were also young, good-looking, and energetic. No active participant in the alumni association is younger than 60 and the oldest were in their nineties. It is age-graded because for the most part only retired people have the time it takes for a cocktail hour and leisurely meal in the middle of a work day. Almost without exception, they are all white.

Chaconas is himself a graduate of Fremont High. He grew up in a little house just a block from the campus. When I brought him an invitation to speak to the alumni he acceded with alacrity, and the old grads hung onto his every word. Reminiscing about "the old days" is a preferred activity for this crowd, so we were delighted when he told us the well-honed and carefully embellished story of his experience as an entering 10th grade student at Fremont.

"I had two older brothers that I think people would say that school was not what they were really interested in. So when I went to Fremont in 1962 I remember my counselor calling me in. He looked me in the eye and he says, 'You know, I know your two older brothers real well. And the oldest one just barely got out of here. The fact is, he was fairly active in the workshop. He made cabinets for all the teachers'" (knowing smiles in the audience and a ripple of chuckles). "And he said, 'Ted. Ted was a good kid and we really struggled to get him through (pause for emphasis). So why are you taking these college prep classes?'" (an explosive outburst of laughter).

The narrative continued. "When I got home that night I told my father about this story, and he looked me in the eye and he says, 'I really like that man'" (More laughter). "He said, 'You know, you keep talking about going to college. I think you need to lower your sights. A high school diploma is all you need.'"

"My mother was considered an advocate for me, and a fighter for me. [She] argued with my father the whole night. And eventually, her stubbornness and mine, I was allowed to stay in classes that my counselor told me I should not take."

Young Dennis lived up to his mother's expectations. In his time each issue of the *Green and Gold* featured a boy and a girl as the Tiger and Kitten (*sic*) of the week. As a senior, Dennis was Tiger of the Week in the issue of December 4, 1964. According to the school paper, he stood out for his spirit and enthusiasm, for being on the honor roll, and for being active in student government and club activities.

After high school Chaconas went on to graduate from San Francisco State University with a bachelor's degree. In his college years he demonstrated the work ethic and goal driven endurance that characterizes him as a professional man. "I carried 40 hours that I worked in the restaurant business and I went to school full time taking 18 units to get out in 4 years," he recalled.

## Strategizing Change from the Central Office

When the new superintendent went to the microphone to speak to us old alums that November day in 2000, his first words were, "Actually, on my way over here today I went to Fremont High. A part of my duties is to supervise six schools, and one of those schools is Fremont, and I'm on the campus at least twice a week, making sure that the school is operating appropriately."

Although Chaconas avoided obvious favoritism and worked hard to improve all schools in the district, precisely because he was a Fremont graduate he was keenly aware of the desperate needs of his alma mater. During his first summer in office, campus buildings got a new coat of paint. Some shabby interiors were extensively renovated. Gardeners cleaned up the scattering of small grass and ornamental bush plots that grace an otherwise concrete and asphalt landscape. The worst of the plumbing failures were fixed. With those and other improvements, campus morale improved. And he had plans for how to improve student achievement.

## Fully Qualified Teachers

Chaconas began his professional career as an Oakland public school teacher and he sincerely respected the professionalism and dedication of good teachers. He believed fervently in the importance of recruiting and nurturing the best. That dedication had roots in his own experience as a student.

"When I was a junior I had two teachers who thought I was" (pausing as if searching for the right word) "[that I] really should go to college. I don't know what they saw in me at that time. I was probably hyperactive. Anyone who knew of me at that time knew that I had a little mischievous side that was always figuring a way to have a good time. And these two teachers started coming to my house and talk with my folks about why I should go to college. And, out of a very small [teacher's] salary - it was about $6,000 a year - they paid for me to take the college entrance exam out of their own money. And then they paid for my application for college to go to San Francisco State. If it wasn't for those two teachers I would have never gone to college."

As the new Oakland superintendent he supported excellence in teaching and was determined to recruit new teachers who would be well trained and fully credentialed. In June of 2000, as his first major decision, he authorized a 24 percent increase in salaries for district teachers. The flip side of that pay raise was that he also believed, as he put it, "if a teacher can't teach, we need to pull'em out of the classroom."

Unfortunately, follow through on weeding out incompetence was hard to accomplish. Protections in the employment contract make it is almost impossible to fire an inadequate teacher, and there were limits on how many can usefully be re-assigned to non-teaching duties.

## Skilled Principals

Just as outstanding teachers were a major priority, Chaconas recognized the importance of empowering principals who are skilled midlevel educational leaders. As he explained that day, "you might have read [in the newspapers] that some of my principals were not doing the best that I thought they can do. And so, 35 of those individuals out of 90 have chose to do something different with their lives" (laughter and clapping). The fact is, they had no choice. They were demoted to other jobs, returned to classroom teaching, or left the district.

His decisions on principals seemed arbitrary and unfair to some, and his certainty in having made good decisions in every case was not as easily defended as he would have had us believe when he told us about them. "I still remember," he told us, "a whole group of teachers [from one school or another] coming down to me [at the district office] to tell me how nice the person was. What a great family they had. And how they were fun to be socially with. And I said to them, you should have met my mother. She had all of those qualities. But good schools have great teachers, and great teachers work for a principal that has a vision that makes schools work for those kids. And until we have that type of leadership at Fremont High . . . " (he delivered that incomplete sentence as if gyrating in a grammatical break dance to unexpectedly make a startling announcement) " . . . and I will tell you that I put in a new principal at Fremont High last night. His name is Brian McKibben." So we were among the first to know. McKibben came on board as the new principal a couple of months later in February 2001.

## Small Learning Communities

As he made plans that included revitalizing Fremont High, Chaconas let us know that the world today requires a different kind of institutional culture from that remembered by the old graduates he was addressing. Organizational behavior needs to be restructured by implementing a complete and complex overhaul. "People always tell me [at high school reunions] that when they went to school, schools were better. For some of us it was better. But I have a lot of friends that dropped out of school very early, like my folks. But remember, when you dropped out in 1962, 1952, 1942, 1922, you could get a job. There was a gas station or a drug store or someplace you could get a job. And you could join the army if you were a boy, because you didn't need a high school diploma."

"But in 2000 if you do not get a high school diploma your chances are slim of getting a job. We can't push 'em out like we used to anymore." He was right on that point. In the nation as a whole between October 1997 and October 1998, 28 percent of the half-million 16 to 24-year-olds who dropped out of high school were unemployed (Council of Economic Advisers, 1998). Having in mind young people like that who fall between the cracks in large comprehensive high schools,

Chaconas alluded to what was to be the keystone of his administration. In full agreement with the policy recommendations of OCO and BayCES he planned to replace large impersonal schools with new, small, autonomous, learning communities. "We need to figure a way of redesigning and reconnecting kids to teachers, to their families, to support them. We can't afford to drop out 40 percent of the kids at Fremont High School because they don't have the skills to compete."

He then recalled that his entering 10th grade class began with an enrollment of 785 students. Three years later, only 485 graduated. The rest, 39 percent, dropped out. Yet, for the most part, in the mid-sixties, they were still able to find work and raise families. In contrast, the class that graduated from Fremont in the spring of 2000, just before he took office, had a dropout rate of 50 percent, which was worse than district and national averages. The job prospects of those dropouts were dismal, he pointed out. "And so," he insisted as he raised his voice and lifted his hand for emphasis, "I'm telling you as alumni of Fremont High, we need to make sure that we fight for these kids that they have the opportunities that we had upon graduation."

## The Struggle for Systemic Change

Chaconas had a plan when he took on his new responsibilities. It would require a policy shift of major proportions. He was well acquainted with the district and quite familiar with its problems. He was confident he knew what needed to be done. A decade earlier he had twice served as assistant superintendent. He defined the challenge as the "need to make sure that we fight for these kids," and his way of fighting for kids was to set about to change the system of education as such. What was needed, he insisted was to transform big schools into small.

The tentative beginnings of a small school movement began to attract attention decades earlier in the 1970s. One such early venture took shape when East Harlem superintendent Anthony Alvarado and his deputy superintendent, Seymour Fliegel, supported the establishment of new smaller schools in New York City's Community District Four. At about the same time, Deborah Meier spearheaded the creation of the best known and most highly influential model of a small school as principal of the city's Central Park East Secondary School (Clinchy, 2000: 5; Meier, 1995).

Drawing on the experience of those and other pioneers, Theodore Sizer founded the Coalition of Essential Schools (CES) to organize and energize the small school movement in the 1980s (1984). At the same time, John Goodlad, a university professor, concluded from his survey of schools that small schools work better but conceded that, "*It is not impossible to have a good large school, it is simply more difficult*" (1984: 309, emphasis added).

Throughout the 1990s the small school movement gained momentum. Around the time that Chaconas came back to the Oakland District, the educational literature he was exposed to was trumpeting the benefits of creating small schools, including the policy I favored, which was to perpetuate a large high school such as Fremont but at the same time to claim small school benefits by perfecting small schools within the school.

As examples of what Chaconas was reading, *Education Week* published on the following themes in the months just before he gave his talk to the Fremont Alumni Association on November 30, 2000.

- February 9, 2000: In 1999 a new federal small-schools initiative began to partially pay the expenses of comprehensive high schools planning to downsize into small schools.
- February 9, 2000: Research demonstrates that small schools contribute to improvement in test scores for children of poverty.
- July 12, 2000: Attendance improves, dropout rates decline, the incidence of violence lessens, and grades improve in *small schools-within-schools* (emphasis added).

- November 8, 2000: The city of Oakland will soon affiliate [as indeed happened] with the nation-wide Cross City Campaign. Cross City encourages community support for small high schools and the attendant benefits of accountability, parent involvement, and improved school climate.

In all, Chaconas had good reason to believe that the way to lead the Oakland Unified School District out of its state designated status as a failing school system was to aggressively pursue a policy of creating new small autonomous learning communities. That could not be achieved for the district as a whole by merely tinkering with district policies and practices. It would require a massive transformation of the entire educational system. Systemic change is not for the faint of heart, but Chaconas was determined to succeed, and for three years he did. Remember, as a young man he was a Fremont Tiger!

## Sudden Termination

Like the tragic hero of a Greek play, in his third year Chaconas was felled by a fatal flaw. He invested almost all of his energy and skill in improving academics but failed catastrophically to control the budget. He should have seen the financial crisis coming. It was his responsibility. But he was blind-sided, and when it was revealed it brought him to his knees like a dagger through the heart. Moreover, in the heroic mode, he drove that dagger home by his own hand, because he was the first to discover the full gravity of the crisis, to reveal it, and to take responsibility for it. "My soul-searching has been," he is reported to have said, "What should I have known and when should I have known it?"

Perhaps he should have known from the very beginning. Just a week before his official appointment in the winter of 2000, FCMAT, the state-appointed auditor, gave that F in finances mentioned above. The F was for not giving heed to ominous warning signs. FCMAT reported that the district was cutting into mandated financial reserves. It was not planning in terms of anticipated reductions in state funding. It was not producing three-year budget projections as required by law. But FCMAT only pushed the warning buzzer and Chaconas seemed not to hear. He was fully occupied with teachers, principals, children, and massive systemic change that would replace comprehensive high schools with new small autonomous learning communities.

He probably would have survived his budgetary indiscretions, just as his predecessors had, were it not for the unanticipated costs of raising the salaries of teachers. That improvement in pay and benefits attracted fully credentialed applicants who were paid much more per year than the people they replaced. Better salaries also attracted applicants to a substantial number of long unfilled teacher slots, adding still further to salary expenses.

At the same time, Chaconas and his advisors failed to anticipate a large loss in revenue as families deserted Oakland in search of jobs, cheaper housing, and better schools in the suburbs. In the 2002-2003 school year the district calculated income based on an estimate of over 54,000 students, when in fact enrollments tumbled to about 48,000. That shorted district projections in a very serious way, because the single most important source of income was what the state paid the district for every enrolled student who attended classes.

Other miscalculations plagued the district as well, but what made most of them happen was an outmoded bookkeeping system that Chaconas inherited when he took over. Budget managers worked with an obsolete computer system that did not connect one department with another. Human resources hired new people without interfacing with the budget department, and neither the one nor the other included the controller's office in its calculations.

Not the least, Chaconas was blindsided by three independent audits that reviewed and approved his budgets: that of the office of the state superintendent of schools, another by an independent consulting firm, and a third by his own budget manager.

The whole mess was finally revealed in the summer of 2002 when the district converted to a new state-of-the-art computerized system. Getting the new system on line was slow and cumbersome. Because the old and the new systems were not compatible, tens of thousands of accounting codes had to be transferred by hand, one at a time. When a full accounting was finally placed on his desk Chaconas was shocked. He immediately reported his findings and accepted responsibility. As he later explained to the state Senate Education Committee, "there is no excuse, and I can't believe I'm in this situation, but everything that I, the board, the county and the auditors looked at said we were on target" (Meredith May, 2002: 28).

On several occasions, Chaconas reflected on the source of his miscalculation. "I concentrated on academics. I thought that was the most important issue facing the district." Revealed there is his fatal flaw. Rather than anger or disdain, most observers feel compassion for a man like that.

Chaconas was forced to resign at the end of three years because the district came up short by 82 million dollars. A year later it was said to have been 57 million. Different people estimated the amount differently. In all events, falling into debt was the immediate or proximate cause and Chaconas took the blame.

The ultimate or original cause, however, cannot be blamed on him. The foundational fault was a quarter of a century of failure by state politicians to adequately fund public schools in California. The foundational fault is attributable to citizens who voted against taxing themselves to support proper schools for minority and low-income kids. The denial of funds began in 1978, when the electorate voted Proposition 13 into a law that put a cap on property taxes. California now ranks among the ten most miserly states in the nation in its funding of education, even though its students are among the most needy. Thirty-three percent of all students in the state live at or below the poverty line, yet they attend under-funded, over-crowded schools.

Only one state in the union has larger average class sizes that the State of California.

Columnist Chris Thompson has an interesting way of looking at what I have referred to as the ultimate cause. "The Oakland fiasco debunks once and for all," he observed, "that you can't solve social problems by throwing money at them. Chaconas threw at least $62 million he didn't have at the failing public schools. And by God, it actually worked" (2003: 12). I hasten to add, however, that increased spending in itself has never been shown to improve student performance. What distinguished the way Chaconas used district funds was the way money was spent as part of fundamental policy changes that included offering better salaries to teachers (Lindseth, 2004).

## Policy Under the State-Appointed Administrator

June, 2003, the school year ended, seniors graduated, and Superintendent Chaconas resigned to join the Mills College faculty that fall as a visiting professor of education. The change was comprehensive and dramatic. As approved by Governor Gray Davis, Dr. Randolf Ward was appointed by the State Superintendent of Public Instruction, Jack O'Connell, to manage the Oakland Unified School District as State Administrator. He arrived on the scene as a well-intentioned, well-qualified, and highly-experienced dictator in suit and tie (and after a death threat, always accompanied by an armed body guard, also in suit and tie plus the requisite wrap-around dark glasses and stern posture). In that capacity Ward was empowered to make decisions unilaterally, subject only to the continuing approval of the state superintendent. The emasculated school board survived as an advisory body of so little interest to Ward that its only remaining function was to provide occasional commentary and criticism for the media.

Ward was commissioned to lead the district out of bankruptcy, but he was expected to preserve and improve schools at the same time. Many in the community were hostile. It didn't help that in newspaper photos he always looked haughty and even mean. (I acknowledge that appearances can be deceiving.) Ironically, fiscal realities forced him to close schools with small enrollments, which always resulted in bad press. Personally, I am not prepared to evaluate his performance given the complexities and difficulties inherent in his assignment. However, I must comment on his role in the small school movement.

He was prejudged harshly. As Meredith May recorded at the time of his appointment, "battle lines against the state are being formed by Oakland parents and school board members who fear that gains of the last few years – new small schools, rising test scores and an influx of experienced teachers – will wither under a state administrator focused on finances" (*San Francisco Chronicle*, May 11, 2003). Quite the contrary, Ward strongly supported the policy that was initiated by Chaconas.

## Success in a Matrix

I want to emphasize that central planning and professional administration are critical to success in any school system and for any policy change to work well. Educational policy design needs to be undertaken in full awareness that cultural complexity (the labyrinth) must be accommodated in all of its uncertainties. Bureaucratic organizational practices (symbolized by a matrix ) work well when informed from the bottom up (from the labyrinth). Design of the small school policy in Oakland – a less is more policy – showed great promise precisely because the matrix and a labyrinth were both accommodated. Regrettably, at the stage of implementation for Fremont High School, that accommodation collapsed into chaos.

# Chapter Four

## The Struggle to Implement: Matrix Year One

### A Belated Policy Suggestion

Less is more ruled when the Media Academy was established in 1986 as the first small learning community within Fremont High School. To establish that first academy, cultural complexities were negotiated, like Theseus escaping the Labyrinth, by keeping the process informal, simple and open-ended. Teachers were in control, at least for the first four academies, and the resulting structure of wall-to-wall academies was highly successful for those four. It is notable that those successful academies made good progress toward implementing the defining criteria of the more recent small school policy. They functioned as small, intimate learning communities. Students became well known to core teachers with whom they studied for at least two sequential years. They enjoyed significant (although incomplete) budgetary autonomy that allowed them to finance special programs (such as sending students to attend journalism meetings in other cities).

Rather than disband the academies to create totally new small schools, administrative and cost economies would suggest that the wall-to-wall organization of small schools within the comprehensive school should have been perfected. Fundamentally, what was needed was to reconstitute or replace the two failing academies and increase the autonomy of each of the remaining four. In addition to budgetary autonomy, the most desperate need was for autonomy to recruit fully qualified teachers and to organize programs for teacher development. Making the site management program work would constitute a challenge, but was at least as feasible for academies as for new small schools.

It not only would have made sense to build on what was in place, but it would have meant that the benefits of being part of a comprehensive high school could have been preserved: advance placement classes, programs of music, art, dance, and drama for all students, shared facilities such as the library, cafeteria, physical education and sports programs, ROTC and a motivating sense of identity as Fremont Tigers. Why give up the benefits of being big for those of being small when the basic organizational structure of Fremont High could have provided the benefits of both?

But that question seems not to have been asked. On the contrary, policy change was formalized as a matrix plan rather than as a labyrinth opportunity.

## Stymied by the Double Bind

The first year of small school implementation at Fremont High School began with high hopes at all levels, but high hopes mired in a swamp of double binds. Gregory Bateson, an anthropologist, introduced the concept of the double bind as a way to describe individual emotional and cognitive responses to mutually contradictory demands, orders, or requirements (1972). When caught in a double bind, a Catch-22 (Heller, 1999: 52), no matter how one might respond, it must inevitably be wrong, and that can result in disappointment, confusion, anger, and failure. Yet, that's what teachers encountered at Fremont during the 2000 - 2001 school year as they were asked to explain and defend proposals for creating new small schools to replace the academies.

One way in which district policy was framed as a double bind was that an academy, customarily defined as a "school within a school," was explicitly not a "small autonomous school." As explained in the policy statement, an academy did not qualify because it did not "have autonomous control over the key educational areas of decision making," which the Board of Education defined as possessing "the resources, authority and flexibility for staff and parents at each site to make the changes necessary at the school level." As we shall see, that vague and ineptly worded qualification made it painfully difficult for an academy at Fremont High to figure out exactly what was required to qualify for status as small autonomous high school, since it was qualified to make "necessary changes" in many ways.

As the process of implementation got under way in the fall of 2000 I realized that I could not completely immerse myself in efforts to create half-a-dozen different new schools all at once. At first it appeared that four academies would be reconstituted, but even those four were more than I could handle, and beyond reach in any case because their planning sessions were usually all held at the same time. Nor could I track on potential schools being planned independently of existing academies. Those efforts were in flux, often transient, and largely covert. Remember, I was there as a participant, not as director of a research program.

I concluded that I had no other choice than to limit the focus of my close attention to a single future school in its context of campus wide involvements. The decision to limit intense observation and participation to the Media Academy was a no-brainer, because from the moment of my return to Fremont in 1999 my entrée and main faculty involvements had been in that academy where O'Donoghue and Jackson, in particular, had encouraged me and served as mentors.

On reading the RFP (Request for Proposals) from the district office it was immediately apparent that to gain approval a written proposal had to conform to a strictly prescribed format, a matrix, that required detailed explanations as answers to a list of 16 goal-directed "proposal questions." Proposal writers were asked to identify the needs they promised to address, what the educational philosophy of the school would be, how the instructional program would be organized, how language minority students, African Americans, and students with special needs would be accommodated, how the achievement gap would be closed, how parents would be involved, how space on campus would be shared with other small schools, and so on. Those were needs they were already attempting to meet. It was a double bind.

Given that educational reform appears to thrive in the relatively new culture of constructivist leadership based on a free exchange of information and respect for all suggestions, socalled "distributed leadership," it should not have come as a surprise that the proposal approach turned out to be a frustrating and counterproductive double bind, especially for educators who had not benefited from workshops and experience in grant and proposal writing.

The dynamics of power, authority, and control worked against the Media applicants. "Shifting from traditional, hierarchical bureaucracies to participatory governance and decision making is a major theme in school restructuring" (King, et al, 1996: 245), and the approach to implementing the new small school policy in Oakland failed to make that constructivist shift.

"Governance is a can of worms" (Sarason, 2000: 200). What was missing in that first year was "reciprocal talk [that] becomes a flow of information" (Lambert, et al, 1997: 123, 136). To put it differently, instead of requiring design teams to compete for approval by answering questions, a constructivist approach would have scheduled conversations with OUSD, OCO, and BayCES administrators who possessed the power, authority, and control to approve or not approve. "[T]he open flow of information is vital to self-organizing systems," usually as structured but informal conversations (Lambert et al 1997: 135). "From a distributed [leadership] perspective, it is the collective interactions among leaders, followers, and their situation that are paramount" (Spillane 2006: 4, the author's emphasis). In the words of Michael Fullan, "the change process is so complex and so fraught with unknowns that all of us must be on guard and apply ourselves to investigating and solving problems" (1994: viii).

As another double bind, proposal writers were required to fill in the boxes of a matrix, but they were also encouraged to be creative and daring. One consultant, Dr. Jacqueline Ancess, downplayed the oxymoronic dilemma inherent in attempting to produce a rigidly structured proposal while also attempting to be innovative. "In asking people to submit proposals, and you can't just submit any old proposal, there have to be conditions and guidelines for a variety of reasons; but in asking people to submit proposals you are asking them to use their imagination, to use their knowledge to invent something that can be exciting for them, exciting for kids, and to get people to be more productive. And if you get enough people to do this . . . you'll have a vibrant intellectual community" (2003).

Participants on the design team did at times get excited about the opportunity to create the school of their dreams, but given that the proposal process was a Catch-22, rather than a constructivist exchange of information, it is not surprising that composing and writing was undertaken with a certain amount of cynicism and resentment. This was especially so for the Media Academy, which was already in place and, as it seemed to the design team, mainly only needed to be given autonomy over budget and hiring, along with the opportunity to fine-tune their program.

The preceding comment about cynicism and resentment is a reminder that I need to introduce some well-known sociological concepts in order to document the process. This is because even a well-planned and well-executed implementation plan will always be limited by constraints that are impossible to anticipate and difficult to evade.

The small school policy was promulgated in a collaboration of the Oakland Board of Education, the Oakland Unified School District, and BayCES, all of which are formal organizations. Moreover, the goal of the small school policy was to convert the formal structure of large individual schools into small schools: formal organizations again. All of this fits in broad outline with Max Weber's theory of bureaucracy (Weber, 1979), an institution constituted as a matrix. What is missing if policy is looked at only in this way is how the informal relations of individuals and small groups within a bureaucratic structure, the underlying labyrinth, modifies, distorts, inhibits, or otherwise impacts the implementation of policy mandates (Blau, 1963). The way a formal organization actually functions can end up being very different from what was intended because of the shaping impact of informal relations (Meyer and Rowan, 1977).

Having been influenced by the early work of Erving Goffman (1959), I find it helpful to distinguish the qualities of social interaction that characterize people in formal settings from the way they relate to one another - give voice to opinions and vent emotions - in informal settings, as when I encountered expressions of cynicism and resentment by teachers in the privacy of a classroom where they struggled to follow the formal guidelines imposed by the RFP. Goffman offered an analogy to theater as a way to contrast "discrepant roles" of this sort. An actor on stage performs very differently from the way that same person behaves when back stage. How Media and the other new small schools ended up being very different from what was intended, and very different as well from one another, can only be fully understood if we know what went on in the back regions. My immersion in the community provided an opportunity to participate in and observe behavior in back regions as well as up front, in the labyrinth as well as in the matrix.

## The First Request for Proposals

The wisdom of my decision to focus on the Media Academy seemed confirmed when we learned that the superintendent intended to move rapidly in order to transform one Fremont academy into a new autonomous school by the beginning of the next school year. Two academies were to compete for that opportunity. Health and Bioscience had a high quality program that made them a strong applicant. However, it seemed to us that Media was sure to get the nod given its status as the oldest and most experienced academy on campus and the only one with a national reputation. As it turned out, we were wrong, but our experience taught us a lot about the implementation process, including its often unpredictable and frequently inexplicable twists and turns.

A major failing in the first year was that the BayCES implementation program had not yet been put in place. A new principal of Fremont had not yet been appointed. The timeline was short for the two academies that were urged to compete to be the first independent offshoot. In less than three months, on December 15, a formal proposal had to be submitted to the district office. The selected school would be required to admit its first cohort of students at the beginning of the next school year in September 2001. For Steve O'Donoghue and Michael Jackson, the implementation process was reminiscent of twenty years earlier when they improvised to start the Media Academy, and of a decade after that when the implementation of wall-to-wall academies became what O'Donoghue called "a free-for-all."

As co-directors of the Academy, Steve and Mike would assume primary responsibility for writing the proposal, accepting input from all concerned. They would have to get this done while remaining fully occupied with their normal teaching duties, which required long hours of extra work. (It was very different from 1985, when Steve was relieved of his teaching responsibilities for a semester while he made plans to create the Media Academy.) The school that was approved would be given a check for $5,000 to cover development expenses incurred between February 15, when winners would be notified, and the beginning of September, when the school would open its doors to students. Under that timeline the additional workload would have to continue through the spring term and on into the summer vacation.

In the back regions, Mike and Steve resolutely plugged away at what one of them referred to back stage as "poop chasing," composing answers to the proposal questions that they thought would win approval. Yet, in casual chats with Steve I detected a kind of cautious excitement; cautious, because, like all experienced teachers, he had been asked numerous times in the past to invest his hopes and energies in reform programs that created excitement for a time only to fizzle out and leave little or no residue of lasting improvement.

At first, the Media design team thought they would form a new small school in partnership with Health. An extract from my journal for September 6, 2000, based on a backstage chat with Steve, reads as follows: "The Media and Health schools [together] will enroll a maximum number of students, 400. Grades 9 – 12. [Students will have morning classes in the new autonomous school.] Afternoons on the main campus for PE and all other school activities. 'We are prisoners of the system [the bell system], ' [he said].

"He told me again how they are looking forward to being identified as a small unit that will be semi-autonomous within Fremont. [A widely believed rumor attributed to the superintendent was that the district would purchase land on the other side of Foothill Boulevard to add to the campus, which eventually they did when they acquired the old car wash property.] 'We will move into new portables [and eventually a new building] across the street as a media and health program, with much more independence in administering ourselves. [That never happened. Instead, the newly acquired property was paved over to create a parking lot.]

"'We will control the program. Ninety percent of the time we will be in control." They have to make a proposal – to get this is competitive – but we think it will come to us. Steve and I will be on the advisory board."

I cannot emphasize strongly enough that what Media was proposing was to benefit fully from the being a small school while continuing to profit from what a reconstituted big school would be able to offer.

In short, the wall-to-wall academy model would get an upgrade that would preserve Fremont High as such.

October 19, 2000: "Steve is very excited. The meeting held yesterday on the small school concept seemed to support getting reconstituted as a small school. Chaconas said there is money for them, seven figures [for all new small schools in the district]. And he wants to improve high schools above all. Most of the people there were from elementary and middle schools. Steve said they are wondering whether they should go it alone as Media Academy, with about 250 students, or should join with Health and Biology and have 450. I advocated the latter [because] biology has money for biotech, so they should be capable of high standards."

So much for my opinion. The Media leadership decided it was better to apply alone, in effect, in competition with the Health Academy (or perhaps it was the Health Academy that backed out. I'm not sure). In retrospect I agree they were probably right.

## Approval Denied

The first discouraging indication that Media would probably not make the cut came in an e-mail message from O'Donoghue dated January 13, 2001.

"Subject: New School Roadblock. Message: As most of you know, the staff of the Media Academy applied with the school district to become what they are calling a New Small Autonomous School – The Robert C. Maynard Media Academy, an independent public high school with 250 students, Grades 9-12. We turned in our proposal on December 17. It is our understanding that none of the proposals were passed by the screening committee the first time. From conversations with the superintendent and others, we believe that one reason they may not have accepted our proposal initially was a concern we were not 'new' enough [emphasis added], that we just wanted to move a program off campus as opposed to start up a new school. And I suspect there is some prejudice against academy programs because many of the non-Fremont Oakland academies are not effective.

"Our view is we have an effective program and have had for 15 years, but we are handicapped within the current school structure and only operating at 40-50 percent of capability. We believe we could do a better job keeping students in school and preparing more students for university matriculation if we controlled our own fate. For example, last week we had our own open house for sophomore parents. We had 90 percent turnout. We want to do this for an entire school."

OUSD decisions on the proposals from Media and Health were supposed to be announced on February 15, but were postponed. What did that mean? Would both academies be approved? Neither? Approved but delayed? Growing uncertainty and tension overrode optimism. A week later my journal entry for Monday, February 26, 2001, reads, "Steve told me the plan to acquire land across Foothill Blvd is in trouble because it includes some private homes. Nobody looked to see if other space is available." That sounded ominous, and with good reason.

By e-mail earlier on February 8, Steve wrote, "We learned in January that our proposal for the New Small Autonomous School was accepted but would not be moving forward for next year. We were disappointed but are persevering. We are meeting with the BayCES team that read the proposals in a week or two for feedback. Apparently no high school level schools will open next year."

Steve was wrong in that last assumption. By the end of the month the news was out: one of the two competing academies would, indeed, open next year as an autonomous school, but it would be Health and Bioscience reconstituted as Life Academy College Preparatory High School. Media was told they needed another year for planning and revisions.

For a week or so, those who worked so hard in their attempt to create a new Robert C. Maynard High School were offended and dejected. Members of the design team experienced Kubler-Ross-like emotions of shock, denial, anger, bargaining, depression, testing, resignation (1969). Yet, to my surprise, teachers, and especially the co-directors, soon rebounded in acceptance as though nothing unpalatable had happened. During March, April, and May they focused on teaching spring classes and preparing 12th graders for end of the year presentations of their portfolio projects.

## A Summer Double Bind Imposed by the State

Media had been denied advancement to autonomous status on the district level that spring, but was fully expected to succeed in the next school year (or so we were led to believe). Then, with summer vacation looming on the horizon, some ten to twenty Fremont faculty and staff, including two or three from the Media Academy, were unexpectedly asked to serve as a "school reform committee" that would meet on five May and June evenings in the cafeteria (with catered dinners as an inducement) in order to elaborate a new and different state-wide policy that was even lengthier and more complex than what they had worked on for the district. (Along with interested parents, I was invited as a member of the community, accompanied by Mills students Joan Callahan, Beth Hoffman and Donna Martin.) The demands for writing this new proposal reawakened latent cynicism and frustration in faculty and staff. Some were "ticked off and tired out with being beat up by state mandates and high stakes testing," as Marilyn Hohmann aptly recalled from her own similar experience as a high school principal in Kentucky (cited in Cushman 1997: 5). We were confronted with yet another double bind.

In part the assignment was irritating because it was imposed as a top-down bureaucratic command authorized by state law as the Immediate Intervention/ Underperforming Schools Program (II/USP). But what was even more intensely infuriating was that it required developing a school-wide policy, a competing matrix, that was directly at odds with the kind of proposal Media had been required to submit earlier in the spring.

To avoid severe state penalties as an underperforming school, and to qualify for a $400,000 grant if the plan gained acceptance, Fremont as a comprehensive high school was required to explain the steps they would take to improve - to rescue - the very academies that were scheduled to be eliminated under requirements of the district small school policy. It was decreed by the state that the *Fremont High School would be required to "provide autonomy and accountability for all academies* [emphasis added], with all teachers dedicated to one [or another] academy, where feasible" (from a handout of June 4). That plan was perceived by some as oxymoronic, and was especially demoralizing for those from the Media academy who had been denied autonomy just three months earlier.

State politicians in good faith sincerely believed they could legislate school success from the state capital. A major provision of the State of California Public Schools Accountability Act of 1999 required that every school demonstrate a specified level of improvement each year based on how students rank on a so-called Academic Performance Index (API).

The API was described as "weighted," which means that the calculation of achievement was supposed to reflect a range of student performance measures based on a wide variety of assessments but with a major emphasis on written tests. To understand widespread teacher negativity, think of the implications of devoting hours and days to mentoring senior projects and portfolios to demonstrate a range of cognitive and performance skills not captured in multiple choice questions and fill-in-the-blank memory challenges, only to discover that the API ended up being based solely and exclusively on a standardized test, the Stanford Achievement Test, Version Nine (SAT-9).

The required improvement seemed unattainable on the face of it. To avoid severe penalties, the API scores by law had to improve by at least 5 percent every year for the school as a whole. Yet, of 1,909

Fremont students who took the Sat-9 test in the spring of 2000, only 168 (9 percent) school-wide were at grade level in reading. To raise that school-wide average to the 50th percentile, and in the long term to the 100th, seemed unrealistic, and as a downside would undoubtedly encourage schools to "teach to the test" at the expense of wider educational goals.

The year before the accountability act of 1999 became state law, Tony Wagner warned about the danger of emphasizing standardized tests in such a way. "More time spent going over multiple-choice questions and test-taking strategies means less time for real learning and fewer interesting things being done in school," he wrote. Teaching to the test will "lessen the amount of class time spent on challenging and interesting material, and undermine the development of real academic competencies" (1998: 516).

In addition to the API ranking of Fremont as a whole, each ethnic or special needs subgroup would also have to improve at a rate of 5 percent per year. Almost half of the total student population was Hispanic that year (46 percent), with only 3 percent in the 10th grade at grade level in reading on the SAT-9. The next largest ethnic group was African American (33 percent), with 11 percent at grade level in the 10th grade, followed by Asian (18 percent), with 7 percent at grade level. (Less than one percent of students were officially categorized as non-Hispanic white.) More than half of all students (62 percent) at Fremont were from economically disadvantaged families.

With that mandate as an inducement, the policy goals promised when the Fremont proposal was submitted specified "READING/ LITERACY" based on teacher collaboration that would emphasize reading and writing across the curriculum by means of aggressive intervention in English language development, including for special education students. (What happened to student-centered and inquiry-based learning? It was a double bind.)

A second major category of proposed goals was characterized as "RENEWAL." To that end, plans were drawn up to improve what was referred to as school culture. The emphasis was on energizing highly qualified teachers who would introduce high standards for teaching and learning. Renewal also aimed at developing a strong partnership with parents and other members of the community, and it included making the campus a safe place for all.

Finally, "RESULTS" were anticipated in terms of developing a leadership unified in support of a coherent assessment of clearly identified goals.

In sum, a mantra was created that emphasized three new R's: READING, RENEWAL, and RESULTS. It is notable that the required "results" promised for Fremont did not mention the upgrading of academies as such, but instead specified an intent to develop what were described as "small, personalized learning communities." Based on that semantic twist it was possible in planning sessions to talk overtly about "career academies" while strategizing covertly for the creation of "new small autonomous interconnected high schools" to which the district, including the new principal, was dedicated. They navigated the double bind by playing word games as the terminology morphed from old-fashioned into newly acceptable.

## Prepare to be Shocked

Developing the II/USP school policy document for the state turned out to be easier by far than what we had just endured while writing new small school policy statements for the district, because the district protocols were entirely without local precedent and required extensive second guessing and improvisation. In contrast, a small industry had grown up around the requirement to develop school policies to meet requirements of the state II/USP program. Principal McKibben worked with a private firm of so-called "external evaluators" who were approved by the state to guide schools through the process. The firm provided experienced, politically savvy consultants to guide discussions of a possible action plan, which in broad outline was dictated by specifics in the legislation. At each meeting we debated the details. Between meetings, McKibben and Dr. John Browne, the consultant, re-wrote and fine-tuned what had been recommended by us as the so-called committee. Their summaries were distributed for approval or emendation.

Problems did arise, but they were manageable. At the second meeting on June 4, Browne told us that in the state as a whole, 430 schools had been funded for II/USP programs that year. Fremont was the only one that had not yet completed the process because the new permanent principal did not assume his duties until February. The following discussion is quoted from my videotape of the meeting.

*Browne*: For that reason we were told that we have until the end of July.

*Unidentified Voice*: Is Fremont the only one not ready to go?

*Browne*: Yes. The others' plans have already been submitted.

*McKibben*: But last week that changed. We were told we have to turn it in by July 2. No extension. So tonight we have to build budget and build the master program. We'll do nuts and bolts next week.

*Browne*: We can do it. We can meet the new deadline even though we just got it.

*Unidentified Voice*: I'm uncomfortable with it.

*Second Voice*: Parents aren't involved.

*Third Voice*: Who's 'we'?

*Browne*: We will form a formal committee later. We had three parents and ten staff last time [plus seven students and two adults from the (Mills) community], but we want more to be involved. By state law 50 percent plus one must be non-staff; 20 percent must be parents on the application we submit. The school decides who they should be.

At the third meeting on June 6, in spite of considerable effort to encourage parents to participate, it became clear that the official committee would have to be small.

*McKibben*: We have not been that successful in getting parents here. We had three parents at the first meeting, only two at the second, and tonight we have five (out of a student population of more than two thousand). . . . Because we have only five parents here tonight we cannot have more than twenty-five members on the committee, and thirteen have to be non-staff.

*Browne*: The state wants the committee to represent all groups.

In short, McKibben had his back against the wall, but in collaboration with experienced consultants, and because what needed to be planned was rigorously specified by state directives, he was able to come in under the wire on July 6, almost a month earlier than expected when we convened for the first meeting on May 29.

To this point I have described the process of developing a state sanctioned plan for Fremont High with an emphasis on how it was imposed. Now I want to acknowledge that under McKibben's leadership (with Browne as convenor) the "committee" meetings brought faculty leaders together in a way that encouraged valuable, open conversations about a number of problems in need of solutions. One such problem was that of coping with large enrollments on a small campus.

*Browne*: Which topic is next?

*McKibben*: Enrollment. The only point made last Tuesday was that the size has been brought down from 2300 to 2200. . . . We only graduate about half of the entering class. We get around 700-800 in the ninth grade, but graduate only 300 or so. . . .

*Jackson*: "The campus is too small. We need to expand the plant or reduce the number of students.

*McKibben*: If the campus were built today it would only be legal for 600. The campus is 4 ½ acres. It should be 42 acres.

*Unidentified Voice*: What can we do?

*McKibben*: We must hold the superintendent to his cap [on enrollment] as a first step. Get it to 1750, a drop of 500.

*The Same Voice*: "Enrollment" is code for "too crowded."

*Second Voice*: We are moving out a small school [Life Academy] next year. That will reduce size. [After Life won out over Media to become the first small autonomous school we learned that they would move two miles away to a district building no longer in use for adult education.]

At this point Jackson complained that sophomores were being enrolled in academies for which they were not prepared and to which they were not committed.

*Jackson*: An Academy only houses them.

*Browne*: What do you suggest? Your sophomore data are worse than Freshmen. The 9th grade is most at risk [of dropping out, their numbers] plummet, especially with academic rigor instead of social promotion. The 10th grade is even worse.

*Unidentified Teacher:* We don't have staff to teach 75 ninth graders who didn't apply to academies. They're going to be dumped. A lot of academies are state funded. In academies we track on them. But we will have non-academy students whom we won't track on and they will be unmotivated. They are the ones with the lowest test scores.

(In the back of the room an agitated academy co-director vented to several of us who alone were within earshot.) "McKibben is going to destroy us. I'm going to speak out against him. He's a nice guy, but wrong! His whole interest is in sophomores. He'll destroy the academies. He'll have 50 students in a class (pause) with an inexperienced teacher. He'll destroy the academies and the small school concept (Pause). If necessary we'll apply to be a charter school."

*Postscript:* that quiet outburst demonstrated emotional volatility rather than firm intention. It was ephemeral, not taken seriously even by the speaker, and soon forgotten by all within earshot. Meanwhile, facing us as we sat on benches at cafeteria tables, Browne continued the committee discussion.

*Browne:* There are equity issues around how academies are being run. Ever since you took 9th graders you've not dealt with them. Academies have been a bit elitist! Schools within schools got set up and older students got set up for failure. You need to address this.

*First Teacher:* It is not a solution to put all low achievers in one group [as was currently true of the Electronics Academy].

*Second Teacher:* If you double the number of students without doubling the number of teachers, that's what is going to happen next year.

*Third Teacher*: Certain kids are selected [because they are good students]. We do that.

*Unidentified Parent*: Is every student in an academy after 9th grade?

*Unidentified Voice*: All except non-English and some special ed.

*Browne, scanning the audience*: Our goal in the first half of the meeting tonight is to get issues on the table. We are going to be held accountable for every student."

*McKibben*: We have to plan for three groups of students: (1) Kids who don't come. Solution: Put them on inactive status. (2) Kids not making it. Solution: Roll them into the academies, asking academies to come up with interventions. (3) A middle group. Solution: create an opportunity program analogous to what retained 8th graders get [in middle school].

So, the above illustrates how dialogue was encouraged and decisions made. In this, the second of five meetings, we divided into three subgroups during the second half of the evening, each to discuss one of the three themes that had been agreed upon in the first meeting: reading, renewal, results. The third meeting on June 6 began with an acknowledgment that four or five of those present were participating for the first time, so the meeting began with a review of what had been done so far. After that, McKibben handed out photocopies of the draft in its newest revision.

"We will meet in six small groups [of 6 or 7 per group] tonight to talk over dinner," McKibben announced. "Most of the meeting will be in [these] groups for questions [and dialogue]. Next Monday [June 11] we will have a revised draft [to hand out] based on your input today, plus a budget breakdown [of how we plan to use the $400,000]. . . . Tonight we have 7 students and 5 parents. We cannot officially have more than 25 on the committee, but we invite everyone to participate.

"We chose to begin this proposal with safety in the school. That was a big issue at our first meeting. Until you have a safe and secure environment it is hard to do anything else. . . . Part of school climate [code word for safety] is crowding. My first priority is to have an individual classroom for every teacher. After that, a space for a "career center" [which can be used] for conflict resolution, where parents can meet, where students can come to fill out college applications – we will have college catalogs. We will have more space when some [i.e., the Life Academy people] leave. I wish there were a nice dry place [the large auditorium the district couldn't afford to build in 1978] where I could bring the entire student body together."

By the last meeting on June 13 a wide range of issues of importance had been discussed in frank and open exchanges with resultant recommendations built into the proposal. In that final meeting, Browne explained, "The job of my firm is to make sure that you get funded by doing all that the state says you must do, and we know how they will look at these plans. They will look for consistency from one part to the next. They will look:

- At data and analyses of where the school is today
- At the barriers to see if we did what we were supposed to do
- To see what we propose to do
- To see how we propose to spend our money."

I was asked later to come by the principal's office to sign off on the school-wide small school proposal. That's when I discovered that I was an official member of the committee (one of the 50 percent plus one not on staff). I was not present later in the summer when the verdict came down, but the news was good, the proposal was approved, and the funding was authorized.

## Impact of the Federal No Child Left Behind Act

In May, 2001, the Fremont High community learned that failure to meet the State of California Annual Performance Index (API) requirements stigmatized them as an underperforming school and would require them to initiate, as they did, prescribed reforms under the state II/USP program. Earlier, in January, 2001, the United States Congress had already voted the No Child Left Behind (NCLB) Act into law. With that, a federal mandate authorized its own requirement to demonstrate what was termed Adequate Yearly Progress (AYP) on standardized test scores.

On the federal as on the state level, failure to improve subjected a school or district to rigorous sanctions. A school that did not improve its AYP scores for two years in a row for the school as a whole, as well as for every ethnic and special needs subgroup, would be labeled as needing improvement. The failure of just one or two special needs students, or a couple in a small ethnic subgroup, could put the standing of the school as a whole in jeopardy. It would be required to design a two-year improvement plan under the supervision of non-district technicians. Under the same guidelines, if the school failed to meet AYP goals for three years, it could be subject to takeover and could be forced to pay for students to study in other schools, if such could be found.

The NCLB act was criticized for imposing federal control over city and state matters, for making ill-advised demands on schools, for not providing funds to cover the added cost of compliance, and above all for relying excessively on standardized testing (Robelen 2004). Although failure to meet AYP requirements would not impact Fremont High for at least another two years, NCLB had the effect of reinforcing the tendency under the state API requirement to "teach to the test" by emphasizing math and reading at the expense of broader and deeper kinds of learning. Jaime O'Neill, a former English teacher, was among those who decried this targeting of the educational cost of "drill and kill." It turns teaching and learning "into mere exercise in prepping students to test well," rewarding them for being passive and compliant. In so doing, what gets killed are, as O'Neill put it, "a great many other educational goals, like fostering curiosity, unfettering imaginations, developing individuality and encouraging creativity" (2006: E5). Student-centered inquiry-based teaching would go down the tubes.

"In our effort to close achievement gaps in literacy and math," according to Bartlett and von Zastrow, "we have substituted one form of educational inequity for another, denying our most vulnerable students the kind of [liberal arts] curriculum available routinely to the wealthy" (2004: 38). As game theory would have predicted, standardized testing denies opportunities for our most promising students, because they can be expected to pass standardized tests with a minimum of teacher investment. "We'll be in big trouble if NCLB succeeds," in the words of Alan November, "because it concentrates attention on lower-performing students at the expense of providing educational opportunities for those who achieve at a higher level." But, as game theory would also predict, the very lowest performing students with the least chance of passing standardized tests will also suffer neglect, because teachers will be tempted to invest their efforts in underperforming students with the greatest likelihood of being able to improve enough to win passing scores. It is classroom realities such as these that led November to conclude, "We have a national fetish with driving toward mediocrity" (cited in Pascopella 2005: 32).

## Impact of the New State Exit Examination

Critics sometimes speak derisively of a "No Child Left Untested" mentality in contemporary public education. I do not mean to offer that pun, an expression of more is better, as a scholarly assessment, but it does draw attention to an extraordinary proliferation of test demands, of implementing a more is better policy that was imposed on California students between 1998 and 2001. Theodore Sizer questions the wisdom of what he sees as a nation-wide tendency to avoid the need to introduce fundamental changes in how high schools function. "They can let yet another testing scheme be inflicted on their students, one that they can mindlessly prep their students to manipulate and that will prove once again that poor kids score poorly and richer kids score better" (1997: xii).

One of the potentially most frightening tests for Fremont students is the California High School Exit Examination (CAHSEE) that replaced local requirements for high school graduation as a new statute of the Education Code (Section 60850) early in 2000. The exit examination, which set proficiency standards in English-language and mathematics, was required of all 10th grade students beginning in the spring of 2001. Those who did not pass both parts had to retest, which they could be required to do as many as five times over the following two years. There were to be no consequences for failure, however, until the time arrived for the class of 2006 to graduate. Students in that class who failed the test, and all students thereafter, would be doomed to leave school without diplomas. By then the exit exam would also have consequences for Fremont as such, because results would be calculated into the Academic performance Index (API) for state accountability. Taking the CAHSEE test was worrisome for Fremont teachers and administrators from the year 2000, but merely troublesome for students until February, 2004, when members of the class of 2006 sat for the test for the first time.

Yet another standardized test was imposed on high school students in that four-year climax of reformist zeal. California State Proposition 227 was voted into law in 1998. With limited exceptions, it required that bilingual programs for immigrant children be replaced by an English immersion approach in which classroom instruction had to take place overwhelmingly in English. As a key requirement of the law, students classified as English learners would eventually have to pass the California English Language Development Test (CELDT) to document reading and writing skills. Until they successfully transition out of their English Language Deficient (ELD) status they are limited to taking subject courses that do not prepare them adequately for college. Also, they were not eligible to take advanced placement (AP) courses that offer college credit to high school students.

It appears that students do as well in English immersion programs as in bilingual. However, at Fremont High as in the state as a whole, many students who have succeeded in learning English fail to move into the mainstream English-speaking program. Students themselves often prefer to remain in classes with other recent immigrants, and their parents assume that in so doing they are progressing nicely. In addition, the school receives extra funding as long as they are enrolled in English immersion programs. Overburdened counselors, with no pressure on them to do otherwise, tend to let reclassification slide. What students and their families usually do not realize is that subjects mastered in courses for non-English speaking matriculants do not qualify them for later post-secondary schooling (Torrance, 2006).

## The End of Year One

It was a difficult year of emotional ups and downs for teachers, staff, and administrators. Goal achievements stalled in large part because the district attempted to create new small high schools by means of a proposal process that incorporated double binds originating in the power of the superintendent to impose rules rather than to put a constructivist process in place based on reciprocal discussions and the uninhibited exchange of information. One unfortunate consequence was that some teachers, feeling powerless, substituted cynicism for personal commitment (Block 1996: 221).

From a cultural perspective, however, it was also a troublesome year because of a failure to adhere to well-defined clear-cut educational goals. As one demand in a double bind, strong support was evident for developing a program in support of a broad, liberal arts curriculum that would build on the diverse talents and interests of Fremont young people. Every student should and could be helped to realize a unique personal potential. Accountability would be based on student-initiated projects and cumulative portfolios. As a contradictory demand, elementary and middle schools were failing to bring all students up to grade level in literacy and math before being promoted to the 9th grade. Administrators and teachers tended to think that it was unrealistic to attempt to provide opportunities for intellectual growth for entering high school students before they had caught up, above all, in reading and writing ability. Yet, it has been demonstrated that skill deficits "are not intellectual deficits, and students *should not be denied* the opportunity to think about intellectually interesting and challenging problems because they lack certain skills." On the contrary, "research shows us that students who regularly engage in authentic intellectual work – regardless of their current skill levels – show greater improvement in standardized test scores" (Small Schools Project, 2003, italics in the original).

In looking forward to the second implementation year, the double bind contradiction of needs versus goals loomed as an enormous long-term threat to success given that reliance on standardized testing as the single most important measure of achievement was mandated by district, state, and federal laws. Because requirements to pass tests were non-negotiable they had the potential to impede teachers from providing learning environments that could maximize opportunities for young people to grow into wise, knowledgeable, skillful, civic-minded adults.

# Chapter Five

## The Struggle: Matrix Year Two

### Cultures of Conversation

*Conversation, as we know, requires listening as well as talking. One of the first rules . . . is that each participant listens to and respects the experiences and opinions of others.*

Jennifer Schirmer
Anthropology News
November, 2007, page 9

### Conversations Across a Complexity of Cultures

One way to think analytically about the second implementation year is to highlight the process as one of confronting the labyrinth of cultural complexity. The culture of a large high school was challenged by a nation-wide culture of reform that in important ways had its inception in the Coalition of Essential Schools. Other cultures that impacted the process included the culture of the school district, which itself was embedded in city, state, and national political cultures, each with their own educational agendas. Often neglected and yet critically important were the cultures of families, teenagers, teachers, and college professors (which is where I fit in).

Complexity was further compounded by a pervasive reality, which is that cultures as such constituted scattered and unruly aggregations of individual spin-offs, of individuals caught up in subcultures, and of borrowings across permeable boundaries among cultures.

The analytical challenge is to describe and make sense of how participants engaged one another in this context of multiple morphing cultures. The challenge is to document how individuals struggled with and against one another to cook up a wizard's brew of educational innovations. The goal is to understand this process in terms of "agency" and of individual "subjectivities" (see Ortner, 2006: 130-131).

Please forgive that last bit of jargon. My professional culture requires that I speak the postmodernist language of anthropology and sociology from time to time. All it means is that I propose to discuss this magnificent effort in terms of real human beings like you and me who struggle to do what is right and good, who screw things up sometimes, but at other times succeed reasonably well. Roy Rappaport, as president of the American Anthropological Association, urged us to give voice to those real human beings who normally are not heard, to involve ourselves in "the anthropology of trouble" (1993: 301; Walsh, 2005: 656). With that as my goal I found it useful to focus my interpretation of Matrix Year Two on how people talked with one another, of how their conversations were shaped by social conventions, and of how performances backstage were as important as those under floodlights. In short, of how we all muddled through, which is the most one can hope for, by having many conversations across cultures, nearly all of them difficult and incompletely satisfying, yet all of them meaningful.

# A Culture of Conversation: Writing Proposals

Let me begin by noting that students returned for the new school year to be greeted by teachers wearing green tee shirts emblazoned with tigers and bright yellow lettering:

> **Fremont High School**
> **2001-2002**
> **Renewal, Reading and Results**

Actually, many were provided with a Spanish version of the shirt, sacrificing the power of alliteration to announce that they cared about their Latino students. For the Media Academy it also resonated with a newly agreed upon goal that every student would become bilingual in Spanish and English.

> **Escuela Preparatoria de Fremont**
> **2001-2002**
> **Renovacion, Lectura, Resultados**

Introduction of the new policy in the second implementation year was carried out in an organized manner as authorized by the superintendent in collaboration with the principal. Actually, it was a learning process for all concerned. It seems to me that one important lesson was that the policy guidelines imposed too many constraints and trusted too little in the ability of participants "to invent something that can be exciting" (Ancess, 2003). As Meyer and Rowan pointed out, writing in the sociological jargon of their era, "conformity to institutionalized rules often conflicts sharply with efficiency criteria" (1977: 340-341). Those authors could have been anticipating the unintended consequences of attempting to create new small schools in the 21st century by requiring design teams to spend months and months in attempts to write and rewrite winning proposals.

The process was still not fully up to speed during this second year. It was organized by scheduling weekly, sometimes daily, meetings of various kinds – many, many meetings - in which participants were provided with guidelines and opportunities to ask questions and express opinions. The formatting of most of those meetings was based on time-honored conventions of conversation. That helped, but at considerable cost in terms of interpersonal stress and the culture shock of implementing a massive change under time pressure.

For the Media Academy, restarting the process began that fall as a struggle to revise the proposal that had failed under the matrix-bound proposal-writing conventions of the previous year. One major constraint was the paradoxical requirement that the academy had to be described as a successful small-school-within-the-school while at the same time was also required to explain how it needed to be totally transformed, if approved and funded, if it was to become a successful new small autonomous school, a new kind of institutional structure, a change in culture. It was a double bind.

The first page of instructions began with that issue, and the Media team response illustrated how making a sales pitch subdued realities as collaborating authors wrote statements they thought evaluators would like to read. The first question asked, "What serves as the impetus for you and your team to seek to create a school at this time?"

Remember from a year earlier, when the Media leadership first began to reflect on how they might qualify to be reconstituted under the new small school policy it seemed obvious to all concerned that the need was straight-forwardly to improve what they had. The design team was convinced they would succeed if only they were given more funding and more autonomy, especially over the selection of teachers. (Don't ever forget what Steve told me, "I would throw away the money if I could just pick staff.") Contrast that firm conviction with how the answer read in the December revision of the proposal. (Note that the italics and capital letters were in the original.)

"First: *We are not just moving the Media Academy, which has existed as a California State Partnership Academy for 17 years. . . . We will build something very different from [sic] the foundation of something very solid. . . .*"

"Second: *a program is not a school.* Despite our successes, we know that we can accomplish much more through the formation of a small school, grades 9-12. We have never reached our potential because of the competing priorities of a large high school. . . ."

"Three: While partially successful at different schools, *the academy model is incomplete.* AN ACADEMY IS NOT A SCHOOL. Students have other classes outside of the four-course academy structure."

The formal proposal catered pitifully to what the design team believed, perhaps falsely, that those with the power to approve or deny wanted to be told. In a keyboard moment of capitulation, they deleted their dream of building on their small-schools-within-a-big-school model. It was a grueling and disheartening process.

Remember, in contrast, how the informal way in which the Media Academy was implemented in 1986 worked well and was better for morale. As Steve recalled, it was a simple process based on trust between teachers and the principal. "[Donald Holmstedt] gave me time off the semester before to plan it. . . . I attended some meetings. The District helped set up an advisory board. . . ."

## A Culture of Conversation: School-Wide Meetings

Teachers in school-wide faculty meetings usually sat in rows in the school auditorium and listened quietly, in part because most announcements from the platform were about routine administrative matters. That custom failed to suppress individual criticism and complaints when the small school movement appeared on the agenda. On January 16, Dr. Betty Daspenza-Green, who had been successful as a principal in the transformation of a high school in Chicago, flew to Oakland as a paid consultant to review the documentation of our progress in private meetings with McKibben, and to share her experience with the faculty and staff as a whole. In a speech from the stage, she spoke with evangelical fervor.

The question and answer period was lively and revealed in no uncertain terms, in spite of Daspenza-Green's inspiring success story, that many teachers remained opposed to the small school policy. The head coach was especially outspoken. Coaches and art teachers - potential carryovers if the comprehensive school as such survived to provide shared-services - spoke of being worried about how they would fit in. One teacher expressed outrage at the implication that at present they were not doing their job. An English teacher complained that the burden of writing proposals made her angry.

## A Culture of Conversation: Backstage Chatter

It is important not to underestimate "the ebb and flow of groups of faculty in the shaping of a school's important cultures" (Sizer 1997: ix). When school reconvened in January after the winter vacation I found myself in a couple of friendly conversations as we waited for a meeting of Media personnel scheduled for later in the day. In an empty classroom one teacher said to another that he didn't want to get into specifics in the upcoming meeting because [deleted] would be there from [deleted] academy. "He'll steal our ideas. He's probably a good teacher, but he's a snake in the grass."

Media, of course, had lost out the previous spring in a two-way competition to win approval, so that competitive fear was grounded in a disappointing experience. On the whole, however, a sharing of ideas was the recommended way to go, as in 1987 when the Wehlage research team flew Steve and Mike to Wisconsin where they "stole all kinds of stuff" from other career academy teachers as acceptable and beneficial for all concerned.

Later, over lunch in the cafeteria staff room, I had a conversation with another teacher. From my journal: "She told me she is unenthusiastic about the small school initiative. 'What we need,' she said, 'is to be able to get rid of students who do not belong. Students who are seventeen and who have only a few credits, so they will never graduate.'"

That, of course, would be contrary to the goal, which was to salvage failing students by creating a school in which every student would profit from personal attention and would continue on to college. In informal settings individuals often combined paranoia with petulance. Venting negative feelings is a predictable part of the process. It can be helpful as people talk out their concerns and reconcile their differences, but it can also be hurtful.

## A Culture of Conversation: Groups Backstage

*January 9, 2002*: The scheduled meeting of eight Media faculty plus the counselor (and me) was fluid and informal. It illustrated how faculty politics get worked out in daily practice. The purpose of the meeting was to resolve some current issues as we anticipated the distribution of new instructions and conditions for resubmitting the proposal. A few extracts will give the flavor of the conversation in which constraints were resented and opportunities appreciated, in which cynicism alternated with optimism in an atmosphere permeated with uncertainty. I quote here from my video record.

*Michael Jackson*: "It amazes me we aren't even supposed to see this [revision of proposal instructions specific to Fremont] until Friday."

*Greg Gordon, Teacher and Union Representative:* "I spoke with [BayCES Executive Director] Steve Jubb. He said the District makes decisions on the time line."

*Steve O'Donoghue*: "It's not just BayCES. Probably OCO is the most powerful. They started this and they saw size [of the school] as key. The first possible roadblock is if the whole school doesn't agree."

*Jackson*: "If we don't push it somebody else might come in and take our [classroom] space, or some of our space."

*O'Donoghue*: "It's a new school. We can select faculty and the union can't object [which turned out to be a false expectation]. There will be a site principal." (Later in the discussion), "Two people want to be principal, Schmookler [who eventually got the appointment] and [deleted]."

*Jackson*: "We have an opportunity to shape the lives of 250 to 400 kids." He then spoke optimistically about the main classes they would offer and how they would handle the 9th and 10th grades along with juniors and seniors. "It will be our dream school, clustering 9 and 10, 11 and 12, as building blocks. It can be 2 plus 2, with 9th and 10th getting ready for 11th and 12th."

*Dan Hurst, Teacher [and eventual principal of the Architecture School]*: "Specific guidelines limit this dream, so don't waste time dreaming dreams we can't achieve."

*O'Donoghue*: "Mike wants to deal with nuts and bolts. We can't worry about that. We need to dream. We have to look at the long view, our experiences at Media. We built [the Media Academy] over years, bit by bit. We had the luxury of building it grade by grade [instead of beginning the new autonomous school with all four grades in place, as we were told we would have to do for the new small school]. . . ."

*Gordon*: "I like to be unrealistic at first. For example, can we plan for team teaching? (Pause) To what extent are we working within last year's proposal?"

*Hurst*: "We aren't starting from scratch. What are the givens?"

*Jackson*: "We have the academy structure."

*Hurst*: "It has to be limited by that?"

*Jackson*: "Yes, we build on that."

*Gordon*: "So we waste our time if we dream of what is not permitted. . . ."

*Hurst*: "How much does last year's proposal limit us?"

Jackson: "We build on our proposal in its present form."

*O'Donoghue*: "That's why we're further along. If it's not evolutionary it dies."

*Hurst*: "I'm on board. So let's see what we are dealing with. . . ."

*O'Donoghue*: "About the retreat, Brian said, if you aren't there and you don't like [the small autonomous school plan], you're out [that is, you will be transferred to teach in some other school]."

*A Math Teacher*: "[Planning] interferes with teaching."

*A Spanish Teacher*: (emphatically) "Yes!"

From early on, a major concern of many teachers was whether they would still have jobs at Fremont High after the breakup into small schools. Design team leaders had reason to be very worried about how teachers would be assigned. Success would depend on creating a small faculty of highly committed excellent teachers. Success would be sabotaged if inappropriate or inadequate teachers claimed appointments based on seniority. That came up in our Wednesday afternoon Academy meeting of January 23.

*Styles Price, Teacher*: "Teachers [by contract] should follow students [if they are moved to a different school]."

*Gordon*: "This morning Sheila Quintana [president of the union] said it is a violation of the union contract [if a teacher is subjected to an involuntary transfer to another school]."

*Schmookler, Convener of the Meeting*: "Teachers work in the district, not in a school, so they can be moved."

*Gordon*: "We have specific language in the [union] contract. If a new school is created, then the teachers follow the students. . . . Many teachers worry about this issue."

*O'Donoghue*: "There's no point getting into it at this phase. We don't control everything."

*Jackson*: "Focus on what's best for students, not on who will have a job."

*Schmookler*: "Everybody won't have a job on his site."

*O'Donoghue*: "If you are integral to the plan you make yourself more valuable."

These conversations were disjointed and unfocused, but participants worked their way through a number of highly relevant issues. They included attempts to identify constraints that limited their freedom to make plans and the extent to which opportunities for innovation (for "dreams") might be permitted. In these two rather characteristic meetings the question of constraints versus opportunities included how free they were to be innovative in teaching strategies, the extent to which they would be autonomous in selecting good teachers, and how teaching strategies might benefit students. In other meetings other aspects of the proposed change to small schools were also discussed.

Implicit in most meetings, often more a matter of tone than of outright declaration, was the feeling that the process was wasting people's time ("[planning] interferes with teaching"). This came out directly in a conversation on March 20.

From my daily notes, "Ben Schmookler said we will not meet at his house on Saturday to work on the RFP. Instead, we have to attend the incubation meeting in downtown Oakland. Michael Jackson said he could sit in the back [with his laptop] and work on the proposal. Ben said, 'No, we have to go along with the game plan.' Mike and I agree it is a waste of time, just as yesterday's evening incubator was."

## Cultures of Conversation in Context

To get a feeling for how conversations evolved cumulatively in the evolution of policy proposals you have to interpret any one meeting in the context of many others, some intense and some casual. To convey a sense of how that was, I excerpt here from my journal and field notes for 14 days during the second half of February, 2002.

**Monday, February 11, 2002**
**• 8:30 a.m. to 4:00 p.m., an all day Media retreat at Mills.**

For the two weeks that led up to this retreat several so-called incubators were held off-campus. An incubator was a meeting led by a trained BayCES staff member. It might include a consultant as well. It was part of the effort to organize conversations in ways that would make them more productive. To follow up on an incubator at the Marriott Hotel in Oakland, I hosted 16 members of the Media design team at Mills to spend a day working on the proposal to become a new small school in the following August. From my journal, "I described and handed out the proposal I wrote during the weekend, but instead of taking that as a starting point they followed an agenda printed out by Mike Jackson. So we spent the day discussing the bell schedule and other work-a-day issues. I was disappointed but not surprised."

**Tuesday, February 12, 2002**
**• 7:30 a.m. to 8:15 a.m. at Fremont, the weekly meeting of leadership teams.**

From my journal, "Discussing how to plan a proposal for a small school. I gave copies of my Media proposal to Brian McKibben, [Michael] Moore, and Maureen [Benson]. Back to Mills to write up minutes of the meeting."

As cited in my official minutes, *McKibben made a mind-boggling confession*, "You are working on design plans while I am working on the RFP that establishes the guidelines for those plans. Unfortunately, because of time constraints, there is no other way to do it." That struck me as a very strange way to proceed, but obviously McKibben felt he had no alternative.

**• 11:00 a.m. to 12:30 p.m. Weekly meeting of the Faculty Council (a school site branch of the teachers' union).**

From my journal, "They are offended by [deleted] who, in the leadership meeting [this morning], said that the Faculty Council [representing the union] is working against the change to small schools." According to another member of the Media faculty who spoke privately with me, "the hidden but known agenda is to get rid of deadbeat teachers." The convener of the Council, Craig Gordon, became very defensive. He clearly feels threatened, since teachers not supporting the change to small schools will get involuntary transfers [which is contrary to the union contract]. He said he didn't want to be an obstacle and would be willing to step down as the union rep. The principal was present for this meeting."

"While this meeting was going on, Theresa McKinney, one of my Mills students, used one of my cameras to vidotape the Mardi Gras dancing and singing on the plaza. Later, I spent time with [Mills student] Caroline Korpi and Fremont Business Academy students as they were boarding a chartered bus to go to a bowling alley as a business project."

**• 5:45 p.m. to 9:15 p.m. at Mills.**

"Back at Mills – so much work – teach this evening 6:00 to 8:30."

**Wednesday, February 13, 2002**
**• 1:00 to 2:00 at Fremont for a meeting of the student services committee.**

The meeting of voluntary associations that come to the campus regularly to organize programs for students was cancelled. I used the time to put copies of my minutes for the Faculty Council meeting in teachers' mailboxes and observed a Mills student assisting in a class.

• **2:00 to 3:30 p.m. for a meeting of the Media team.**

From my journal, "This was a strange, strange day, indeed, in the move to change Fremont High into a cluster of small schools. The strangeness of the early afternoon continued with the after school meeting of the [Media] Academy. Ben Schmookler on Monday said we should start at 1:30 instead of 2:00 because he had other appointments, and Steve O'D announced that. I arrived at 1:30 only to be told that it was 2:00, the usual meeting time, scheduled to end at 3:30. They always start late, just like meetings at Mills, but they are also always sure to adjourn promptly at 3:30, unlike at Mills, where my colleagues tend to talk on and on.

"Ben, automatically the convener, not because he is an assistant principal but because he is the principal-designate of our new school, an appointment as mysterious as it was sudden, an announcement rather than an election. Ben hates meetings and keeps them as short and focused as possible when he is in charge. [I appreciate him for that. I wish he could chair meetings in my department at Mills.] It was quite in character that he began this meeting by suggesting that we not meet, it being pointless, he explained, until we have the RFP specific to Fremont High School that the principal is working on.

"Ben said he didn't know much about it. It's being created by Brian [McKibben] and [Assistant Principal] Michael Moore. 'I'm not involved,' Ben told us, 'because being on the Media design team, it would seem unfair if I had inside knowledge'." [Note how, in spite of good intentions, openness succumbs insidiously to old habits of bureaucratic reliance on insider decisions and handed down pronouncements. Note, too, that while we on the design teams were struggling to write to seemingly set-in-stone demands, in the central office they were still trying to choose which among several implementation schemes was worthy of support.]

"Then [Ben] suggested that he did know that they were considering some severe limitations: possibly that only 9th grade small schools would be permitted. Or, only 2-year, not 4-year, schools. 'So, why waste our time until we get the RFD [Request for Proposals].'" (This after we had struggled in the first year and last fall to meet a four year requirement in the first version of the RFD!)

"Mike Jackson, in his customary overpowering way, tried to counter Ben, wanting us to discuss teaching. In a surprise response that hints at interpersonal conflicts down the line, Ben abruptly, since he is a man of few words and rare smiles, ordered Mike to 'calm down and be quiet'." (Ben, from a meeting two days later, "'You know, Mike, sometimes you piss me off because you want to argue about stupid stuff.' Craig Gordon [the union representative] interjected, 'We need to go over our ground rules on how we dialogue.'")

But to continue from the meeting of February 13, "Rather than argue, Mike merely continued, and Ben eased off, but the decision was still unresolved. Should we just get up to go?

"Mike prevailed. He pulled out a version of *Habits of Mind* that the Coalition of Essential Schools recommends as a learning goal for all children. They were developed by Deborah Meier and her teachers as they made Central Park East Secondary School in New York the first influential small learning community beginning in 1985. Habits of Mind are advocated by Ted Sizer as part of the program of the Coalition of Essential Schools (CES) and thus of BayCES to help children learn how to think logically, effectively, and critically. Without saying a word, Steve agreeably went to his computer to print off a big sign with the keyword to the first habit of mind, PERSEVERE, while Mike, in his intense style, asked each teacher to talk about how that word could be worked into a lesson on an agreed upon day so that the whole small school would propagate the theme."

What Mike was getting at here is a key proposed methodology of the small school movement known as "teaching across the curriculum." When it works it can be very effective. For example, the following

September, when students in the academy were reading *Fast Food Nation: The Dark Side of the All-American Meal* (Schlosser, 2002), those teaching English, social studies, journalism, video production, chemistry, and math were each asked to find a way in which their subject could be made relevant to what students were learning about the American culture of fast food outlets."

**• 3:45 to 4:00 at Mills – A "sexy encounter."**

"Back at Mills I found out that Edna in her office had not eaten lunch, so I walked to the college Tea Shop to get her a café-au-lait and snack. Near a table I heard a student call out, 'Oh, Dr. Bob,' so I stopped to accept a green condom, lubricant, and candy from two young women. Just then the Director of Student Activities came up and said, 'You'd better give him a packet of Viagra as well.' I agreed, laughing, and added, 'Better make it two.' What a strange world we now live in."

**• 4:30 to 5:30 at the OUSD headquarters in downtown Oakland.**

"The strangeness of the day continued. [At Fremont] we had been told that at least two of us needed to attend a BayCES meeting later in the day at 4:30. Everyone else was tied up or unwilling, so Craig Gordon and I agreed to represent our design team out of fear that if we didn't the higher-ups might not take Media seriously in the future. I returned to Mills for an hour and then drove to the Harper Building, Huerta Hall, [about 6 miles away].

"The evening was announced as an 'RFP Exploratory Meeting,' with this added note, "It is urgent that your design team be represented . . . if you are intending to submit a response to this round of the RFP.' However, when I got there I was told it was only for those who were planning SLCs [small learning communities], not NSASs [new small autonomous schools at an existing high school], so it would not be helpful to us. Craig arrived and was annoyed. Several others were there from other Fremont academies.

• **5:45 to 9:15 p.m. at Mills.**

I stayed at Fremont long enough to videotape [Superintendent] Chaconas give his pep talk and left, because I had to teach a class at Mills from 6:00 to 8:30 p.m.

**Thursday, February 14, 2002**
• **11:30 to 1:00 at Fremont.**

I met with some Fremont teachers at lunch (Backstage chatter) and observed a Mills student assisting in a classroom.

• **1:15 to 5:30 at Mills working in my office.**

• **5:30 to 7:00 at Fremont for a meeting of immigrant parents.**

"I arrived at 5:30 and went to the staff room where my meeting was to start at 6:00, and arrived in time for the end of a youth meeting: AYPAL (Asian and Pacific Islander Youth Promoting Advocacy and Leadership). About 15 kids (Filipino, Vietnamese, Tongan, Mexican), not all from Fremont. Usually they meet in Mrs. Hale's room, [Portable] B-4, but because carpeting there is being replaced they met in this part of the cafeteria from 3:30 to 6:00. They have just gotten a $5,000 grant. . . . Kawal, site coordinator from FAA (Filipinos for Affirmative Action) borrowed my camera and interviewed kids about what they had done today."

I was there to take part in a regularly scheduled meeting of parents, *Reunión de Padres*. Every school with at least 21 students who are learning English is required by the California Department of Education to organize an English Learner Advisory Committee (ELAC). Since most (but not all) of these families are Latino, meetings are conducted in Spanish, with quiet side-translations provided for a scattering of other, mostly Asian parents.

My journal reads as follows: "I walked around the campus, waiting, and when heading back to the cafeteria encountered Brian McKibben, Principal. He behaved in a way that is distancing – [evidently] not happy to see me the way he was last September. Michael Moore was there too, and they went into the office, turning their backs on me."

"Not long after, they arrived at the faculty room of the cafeteria where the meeting was to take place. The set up of tables was counterproductive [in terms of power politics]: Two rows of tables facing each other at a distance across the center open space of the room. McKibben and Michael Moor sat alone [at one row of tables] with their backs to the wall, eating and chatting with one another." [Eventually, parents and a few children sat facing them 15 feet away at the other row.]

"The room was just filling when I arrived. [Parents, guests and children] picked up sandwiches, salad, and sodas and stood around chatting as they ate their dinners in a far corner of the room distant from McKibben and Moore. Meanwhile, I took a seat [at the parents' table] and [out of earshot of parents] spoke across the divide to brief McKibben and Moore on what they can expect in the morning (Friday at 7:30 a.m.), which was mainly that teachers are frustrated in trying to write proposals without the FHS-specific RFP. They were reluctant to converse, but did. "I should have been more considerate of how distracted they were that evening, but at the time I felt I was being a good collaborator."

"I told them a major issue would be to insist that they be told if they can plan a 4-year school. McKibben said yes, if it included 2 + 2. I spoke of their plans to loop 9-10 and 11-12 with the 11th grade offering an introduction to journalism. McKibben jumped on me, 'That's the old model,' [and for that reason not acceptable]. I was taken aback. I thought it was the new model, since they currently introduce journalism in the 10th.

"He then spoke of how students need to be free to change academies when they move to 11-12 [which struck me as fitting well with introducing journalism in the 11th instead of the 10th, and of fitting with the wall-to-wall academy model but not with the new small schools model, but I held my tongue]. So I compared it to changing majors in college, and they agreed. BUT WHAT STRUCK ME IS THE INSISTANCE ON EVERYTHING NEEDING TO BE NEW, AS THOUGH NOTHING NOW WORKING HAS VALUE OR POTENTIAL" (emphasis in the original).

"I asked if we would have the FHS-specific RFD by Wednesday, to which McKibben responded sharply, 'I'm still working on it.' Contrary to rhetoric about parent, student, staff involvement, this is a secret chamber process of just McKibben and Moore. [In fairness to the principal, who is usually very pleasant in demeanor, that was a time when he was struggling night and day to mediate between the office of the superintendent, the BayCES leadership, and teachers at the school. He also knew in advance, as I did not, that he was going to be attacked by parents in the meeting that was soon to begin.]

"I felt put down when I asked Moore if he would like me to take notes and write minutes [as I had been doing routinely all year for faculty meetings of various kinds]. 'No [he replied]. We have someone to do that.' Of course I took notes anyway [for my own use], but what I conclude [perhaps in error] is that they are not pleased that I write detailed summaries, including faculty and staff complaints, and distribute them to participants, documenting for all to see. . . . But if so, they have not talked with me about it."

I then shifted the conversation to discuss campus-wide services for the small schools, beginning with physical education. "Each small school could schedule PE on its own schedule, so PE would be offered all day long, but separated by academies, so that each academy would have that PE time for staff development." Here in my journal I interjected a comment on their use of the term academy, "a designation that will be dropped." As time passed, the bell schedule issue became increasingly contentious. Autonomy was supposed to ensure each small school the right to schedule classes as best fit their needs. Yet, because they had to share campus facilities, that autonomy would have to be compromised.

"McKibben told me they are frustrated by the BayCES failure to provide coaches for the design teams, so they have hired [consultants], not cheap I'm sure. Admirable resiliency, but [I question how effective they have been]. . . . And what a failure this evening with Latino parents [has been]! I did not videotape. It just would not have been appropriate because parents were very angry and vociferous. I was astonished, because the last time I attended this kind of a meeting I was impressed by the neighborly *bon amie.*

"It became a verbal fight [from the moment it got started]. The white-haired secretary and father of an 11th grader, Sr. García [not his real name], said they did not have a quorum (only 11 present), so they could not officially meet." (The clear implication came out later. He blamed the principal for not getting announcements to parents in a timely fashion as is required by statute.) All but two were women, and some were outraged and shouting at García, but also at McKibben and Moore, who sat alone and in stoney silence at the table against the wall. . . . Basically they accused the school office of not meeting their needs. They were angry that the II/USP was not translated. (McKibben blamed the district.) 'What are the rights of parents?' 'The money is not being used for our students.' 'We want to know about the education of our students.' 'Other parents are not attending parent meetings.' 'There's no communication between parents and community.' ' The school office is not responsive, nor is McKibben.'

"Sitting among the parents, a representative from OCO spoke. Later she was criticized. Someone said, 'OCO represents 40 churches but not the community.' She left early, outraged [at that unjust accusation].

"Moore attempted to explain the budget (in English) but got no response and gave up.

"Voice: 'We need to discuss the many problems of our students.'

"(After a long silence when he and MM just listened without responding to the attacks) McKibben argued [in Spanish, which he speaks fluently] that the school is much better." (One of the first things he did was to humanize the front office!) "He reminded them that parents, students, and community are members of the school site council [which is true, although meetings are rare and sparsely attended]. The school is safer [also true]. But we still have problems [which was forthright]." McKibben suffered a lot of verbal abuse that was unfair in that meeting. It should be noted that García has held a grudge against the school ever since they turned down his wife when she applied for an office position a year or so earlier. He used his position as [parent] convener this evening to take out his anger on the principal and vice principal in ways that struck me as unfair, uncalled for, and unproductive.

"7:00 p.m., after only one hour, the meeting ended abruptly. People gave up trying to accomplish anything. McKibben and Moore turned their backs on the rest of us without socializing, and walked off through the cafeteria to their offices. Parents picked up leftover sandwiches, cookies, and sodas to take with them. Me too. I hadn't eaten when food was served, so I grabbed two sandwiches that Edna and I ate for dinner at home."

**Friday, February 15, 2002**
**• 7:30 a.m. to 8:15 a.m. at Fremont for a meeting of design team leaders.**

"We were introduced to Bob Haywood, a consultant who will advise us. He was described as a businessman from a Fortune 400 corporation and his card indicates he is a professional engineer. McKibben had all three of his vice principals there plus Maureen Benson." Maureen was an English teacher last year, but at the beginning of this school year she was appointed as a special assistant to the principal in charge of coordinating the change to small schools." [Eventually she became the founding principal of YES, a new small school on the Fremont High campus.]

**Tuesday, February 19, 2002**
• **7:30 a.m. to 8:15 a.m., at Fremont for the weekly meeting of leadership teams.**

• **9:00 to 10:30, at Mills working in my office.**

• **11:00 to 1:00, at Fremont for a meeting of the Faculty Council (union).**

• **1:00 to 2:30, at Mills preparing for my 2 ½ hour evening class.**

• **3:00 to 4:30, at Fremont for a school-wide faculty and staff meeting.**

"McKibben is sick so Michael Moore presided. I understood that Betty Daspenza-Green would be there, but that is tomorrow for consultations. We were supposed to discuss small schools, but that didn't happen. Instead it was routine stuff and boring. . . . The auditorium is dismal, with no lights except dimly on stage against a backdrop of curtains that sag in rotting ceiling-to-floor lacerations. The podium is to one side of the stage where it is dark. The only other lights are just inside the entrance door at the rear."

• **5:45 p.m. to 9:15 p.m., at Mills.**

"Taught my class on medical anthropology."

**Wednesday, February 20, 2002**
• **7:30 a.m. to 8:15 a.m. at Fremont for a meeting of leadership teams with Betty Daspenza-Green as consultant.**

*Dan Hurst*: "As a priority we need to make decisions about how we are to deal with developing a compatible bell schedule, the timing of a common lunch, and the modular schedule [tricky issues for sharing the big school campus in mutually supportive ways].

*McKibben*: "That is a profound problem. We cannot have different bell schedules for different buildings."

After half an hour devoted to talking about the bell schedule the conversation took a dramatic turn.

*O'Donoghue*: "What has been skipped over for years is that the academies are founded by the state as 'at risk' programs, specifically for retention. Mike and I have found that in the years when we had a team of at least four teachers who worked closely together we lost very few sophomores (which was the entering class in those years.) The most important issue of autonomy is to control the appointment of teachers. The rest can be negotiated. We have to start with that. The incubator meetings last year were not helpful. What is important is autonomy, so you can do what you want. You must have a team of teachers who agree."

*Daspenza-Green*: "Right. Forget bell schedules. Don't let it dictate your program [but ultimately it did complicate small school programs enormously.] Bell schedules just help you get it done. Mr. O'Donoghue said it: The key is a team of teachers with the same kids who develop strong relationships with their teachers."

*Ellen Salazar*: "Small is the point. . . . But we are fuzzy on the meaning of autonomy relating to issues such as hiring, seniority, preps [i.e., the number of different class presentations per day, which the union contract limits to two].

*Hurst*: "The Media Academy is ready for autonomy. Several of us philosophically are ready . . . to put strategies in place. We are frustrated trying to get there."

**Thursday, February 21, 2002**
**• 7:30 a.m. to 8:15 a.m. at Fremont. Special meeting of leadership teams. Excerpts from my official minutes:**

*McKibben*: "On identifying one or two groups as prototypes, as teams who will be given a go-ahead in applying for 2002, I will discuss this strategy with Chaconas. The concept is that they will be designated to go ahead [2002-2003] and everybody else will buy time . . . [and] mainly focus on the transition year. We will have 1700 kids next year and not all will be in SLCs [small learning communities]. . . ."

*Robin Glover, Team Leader for the proposed Mandela small school*: "It's unfair. It should be equitable for all teams, so we need criteria in writing. There are three steps, ours, that of the school administration, and that of the downtown office. I want criteria at each level."

*McKibben*: "The six autonomies can be taken as criteria, but it is like judging ice-skating." [*The six autonomies* had just been distributed to us that morning as a new organizational structure *that would require further revisions of our proposals.*]

**• 8:30 a.m. to 11:15 at Mills College working in my office**

**• 11:30 to 2:30 at Fremont for lunch with a teacher and to observe three Mills students assisting in classrooms.**

"I returned to Fremont at noon, bought a sandwich, and ended up in Steve's room sitting with Mike Jackson, who seemed to feel like talking. He talked about the proposal for the Media Academy. . . . Mike's two main comments: He told me he wants me to go through his pages from the failed proposal of last year, now needing to be arbitrarily crammed into the promethean bed of six autonomies, and insert some of the 'beautiful sentences' he has written.

"Our latest instructions were to beef up our discussion of how we would use the power of decision-making (*autonomies*) relating to:

(1) hiring staff
(2) allocation of budget
(3) design of curriculum and assessment
(4) school governance and policies
(5) school calendar and schedule
6) use of space

Additionally, he wants to elaborate how teaching will build on the *Habits of Mind* that came up in our academy meeting of February 13."

"Mike is now sold on using my [rewrite of the] proposal, which is a big change from ten days ago at Mills when he seemed to be annoyed that I brought it to our retreat."

• **3:00 to 6:00 p.m. at Mills**

"Back at Mills I went for a walk and ended up having a long chat about developments at Fremont with Krishan Laesch in his office as Executive Secretary of the Oakland Education Cabinet. So I spent more time on Fremont issues instead of working on a lecture. He told me how [the principal before McKibben] was fired."

**Friday, February 22, 2002**
• **1:30 to 2:30 p.m. at Fremont for a meeting of the Student Services Coordinating Committee.**

The eight to ten student services include Youth Together (for social justice) Teens on Target (for violence prevention), and the Youth Clinic located in the gymnasium. "I took notes and wrote the minutes. . . . Very few present. No follow through (e.g., on the February 1st meeting decision to have more DJ music [on the plaza at lunch time] with tables advertising different student services. It didn't happen)."

**Sunday, February 24, 2002**
**• 11:00 a.m. to 1:00 p.m. in a West Oakland church.**

Michael Moore was the gifted number two to Brian McKibben. His administrative achievements, which are many, included discovering many thousands of dollars that became available to the school the previous year when he took up the task of sorting out accountancy errors. When I learned that he was an ordained evangelical minister, and co-pastor with his wife of a small African American church, I took advantage of a Sunday when Edna was in Boston, because she and I are not church-goers, to attend the Joshua Christian Church. I wanted to get to know more about this remarkable man, and I was not disappointed. I grew up in evangelical churches, but I never attended one in which scholarly outlines of the sermon were handed out along with internet commentaries.

In my journal: "From the pulpit he acknowledged the visit of 'Bob' from Fremont. Later, preaching on David and Goliath and the theme, don't let others diminish your sense of purpose, he said, 'At Fremont it seems a Goliath is challenging change at that school.' He commented on how Bob and he have noted in our meetings how impossible it seems and that he prays every morning that God will bring about a change, a miracle, and he believes it will happen."

**Monday, February 25, 2002**
**• 12:00 to 2:00 p.m. at Fremont for lunch with teachers and to observe two Mills students assisting in classes.**

"I had lunch in the staff cafeteria. The food is terrible. On Mondays it is meat balls and macaroni slathered in unpalatable sauce. But the conversation with four teachers from the Mandela small school project was worth it: Isabel Lopez, Debbie Juarez, Ellen Salazar, and Patricia Arabia (a law school graduate with a J.D. degree who earned her teaching credential at Mills). They designate themselves as Mandela High School in their attempt to design a school built around language.

"When I told them how I was justifying the bilingual program in the Media proposal they asked where we got the idea for bilingual. They assumed it was taken from Mandela." Borrowing in that way clearly struck them as bordering on unfair competition. It reminded me of when a Media teacher worried that [deleted] from another academy might 'steal' Media ideas. Since I advocate complete openness and sharing as opposed to guarding a competitive silence, I told them that I personally had advocated two languages as a way to teach English as well as Spanish grammar [to students from Spanish speaking families]. They agreed it would work. . . .

"I brought up the subject of maintaining aspects of the comprehensive high school, to which I attach major importance. Ellen especially said, 'No, you can't work together. It always breaks down.' I tried to explain my thoughts on open communication, based on what anthropologists know of health care (e.g., the Navajo-Cornell University project on preventative medicine), but they didn't listen or let me explain.

"They said, 'Why are you working with Media? Haven't you noticed they are a white academy?' [Disclosure: I am white myself.] They want me to work with them. I told them I would be happy to share the proposal I have written, so I will get copies to them, but not until I clear it with Steve.

"The next day I told Steve O'D that Mandela said the Media team is all white. Steve, 'No, we have a black principal [Ben Schmookler], as well as [some teachers of color].' I told him they said Media stole the idea of bilingual. He said, 'No, Mike came up with the idea a year ago, before Mandela existed. I said I was going to share my proposal with Mandela. He said, OK, but since Ben is principal [designate] it would be a good idea to pass it by him. I said OK, and later he also agreed it was OK.

"I then went to the main office to put my minutes for the coordination meeting of last Friday in some of the staff mail boxes. I looked to see if Michael Moore was in his office. He was and he waved me in. He was so pleased that I had attended his church; called me a new member. . . . I then told him that I woke up at 2:00 a.m. and realized that the African American church offered a way to get parents involved. He agreed completely, and told me he was meeting his pastor, [Rev.] Bob Jackson of Shilloh [a church with a large congregation], to discuss having local churches encourage parents to send their children to the small schools; that they were not just another passing fashion, but really would make a difference. We agreed that the church could be used for Hispanic, Tongan, and Asian as well. I told him I was going to write that into the grant proposal [and I did, but nothing came of it].

"I had hoped to make emendations to the proposal over the weekend, but didn't have time, and I will probably not have time today either. I'm supposed to pick Edna up at SFO, arriving from Boston at 8:30 this evening."

*To sum up*, these two weeks of meetings took place as the context for many conversations extending from private, brief, and chatty to a formal two-day retreat. As days went by, everyone concerned was exposed to issues under debate, ranging from what a new small autonomous school should look like, what autonomy meant for a school, which teams would get final approval, who would belong to which schools, how teams compete with one another, ways in which issues of race factor in, how teaching would be carried out, what would be taught, how parents might get involved in governance, what churches might contribute, and how the proposal process looks to consultants. The larger context drove some participants apart from one another and drew others together. It moved simultaneously toward both consensus and divisiveness. It was complex. It was invisible. It was powerful. It was debilitating. It was a labyrinth.

## The Culture of Troubled Conversations

It has always been difficult for ethnographers in the field to keep from getting caught up in community politics and, as is already evident, I did not escape that inevitability. The principal, who advocated complete openness by all participants, for a time, because it only lasted a short while, evidently came to feel he needed to exclude me from the inner workings of his office. The first time it became obvious was at the meeting with Latino parents on February 14. It was no better twelve days later.

**Tuesday, February 26, 2002.**
**• 7:30 to 8:15 at Fremont for the weekly meeting of the leadership teams.**

" I took notes for the minutes, but did not videotape this time. . . . As I was walking to the meeting Brian drove past me to park. He walked away from his car, ignoring my presence. The distancing symbolism was unmistakable.

"Yesterday I wrote draft # 2 of my version of the proposal. I gave him a copy and asked him for feedback. His response was hostile: 'It has to come from the team.' He has not acknowledged draft #1, my videotape of Mills students at Fremont, or any of the minutes I put in his box. Nothing.

"Michael Moore, on the other hand, is very receptive. I handed him draft #2 and asked him to give me feedback on pages 8-9, where I incorporated the idea of getting parent involvement through churches. He was pleased. Later Maureen Benson also thanked me. It's just Brian, which really makes me feel bad, especially since consultant Bob

Haywood is lauded by him. Today he asked Haywood to say a few words at the leader-ship meeting. Haywood said he didn't have any experience with this kind of educational project but his basic advice was to go at it piece by piece – exactly what I have been saying and doing with the proposal. After, I gave him a copy and asked for feedback. He seemed well disposed to it."

**Thursday, March 14, 2002**
**• 3:15 to 5:30 p.m. at Fremont for a school-wide faculty and staff meeting.**

"I had a long talk with Allie Whitehurst, who is the OUSD Director for Academies. She arrived late and sat next to me. I walked over to a table and got her a copy of the Request for Proposals because I thought she might be a parent or a teacher. She was unsmiling and seemed like an angry black woman. However, after all of the others were gone and we could talk I found that yes, she was angry, but it was not diffuse anger, and it was not racial. It was focused on the change process. She and I had a cordial talk, agreeing that in designing a small school we need to build on the Media Academy to perfect what we have, to evolve rather than invoke total structural change. I pointed out that, in fact, in today's new RFP there's a new paragraph that adds that we should discuss how the academy was successful and where it could be improved! A subtle but major shift from Brian's insistence that everything has to be different. So she is not there, like José, to push the superintendent's agenda, but to try to moderate it. She is an ally, not an enforcer."

**• 6:00 to 8:30 p.m. at Fremont for a meeting of immigrant parents.**

"I had to rush immediately to the cafeteria for the meeting of *Los Padres*. Brian was not there, so [Spanish teacher] Isabel Lopez stood in for him. The meeting was convened as last time by García. . . . He is nasty, with a personal agenda. Just as he did a month ago, he convened the meeting only to announce that there was no quorum and cancel it. He then proceeded to lambast McKibben. . . ."

"Isabel Lopez was wonderful. When García said the school disdained parents she dramatically repeated three times, 'We love parents.' She struggled to keep García from silencing her, but always in a cheerful, smiling way. What a pity. The parents who came last month seem not to have come again, and those tonight will probably also drop out."

"I left at 7:30 and Isabel followed. We went across the plaza to Robin Glover's room for a parent meeting of Mandela, which was a total contrast!"

## Modifying Conversational Culture at a Formal Retreat (With the Cecil B. DeMille of Fremont High Filming)

The second half of the school year began with a January 11-12 weekend retreat at the Marriott Hotel in downtown Oakland. My journal reads, in part, that on the evening of January 11, "I drove to 14th and Broadway. [Stan and I as boys during the Great Depression used to walk there from 52ed Avenue on East 14th Street (now International Boulevard) selling magazines or shining shoes.] I was able to park on the street, which was much quicker, easier, and cheaper than valet parking.

"Dinner meeting from 6:00 to 9:00 p.m. At the bar around 5:30 I had a glass of wine and bought a beer for Edmund Abrams, the physics/chemistry teacher. We were soon joined by Charles Hoffman, who teaches biology and chemistry." Visiting at the bar belonged to the familiar genre of ordinary conversation [backstage chatter] that endlessly fed into the change process.

"After we were seated for the formal dinner meeting, Brian Mckibben in introductory remarks asked me to say a few words, '*speaking as the Cecil B. DeMille of Fremont High.*' That offered a welcome opportunity to explain to any who might wonder that I was making a record of the process of momentous change at Fremont in part by videotaping all meetings and activities (hence, McKibben's joking reference to Cecil B. de Mille). By then I had already set up my older Digital camcorder on a tripod at the front (terrible lighting, but good mike-sound) and was using my small hand-held camcorder for roaming."

While we ate dinner the culture of conversation was familiar, still in the mode of chatting at the bar. That changed, however, when we were asked to participate in a style of conversing that freed us somewhat from older cultural conventions. Maureen Benson, the teacher on special assignment to assist in the creation of new small schools, got us started with an ice-breaker. Each of us was asked to leave our seats and to wander through the crowd asking for someone who was born in the same month. The game forced us to meet people we didn't know. It was effective in creating a lighthearted sense of community.

After establishing a convivial mood in that way we were asked to join one of seven tables for discussion, each identified as a possible new theme high school: four that eventually were authorized (Media, Arts, Architecture, and Mandela) and three that dropped out of sight (Physical Education, Ninth Grade, and Business). Two that eventually gained approval were not even thought of at that time (Fremont in Transition and Youth Empowerment School (YES).

Open-ended table discussions of how to make small schools work ended with one person selected at each table to report in the full meeting on the tenor of each group conversation. That was followed by responses from representatives of BayCES, OCO, OUSD, and the facilitator from the II/USP meetings of last summer, Dr. Browne.

In that way, the whole school was able to have a serious conversation about issues of concern. It was liberating and unifying. Although I wasn't aware of it at the time, the process was a harbinger of how the culture of communication would be even more completely restructured during the third year of implementation. But that was still in the future, and for the most part, the second year was a time of conventional dialoguing, including our meeting the following day.

On the second day of the retreat we met as potential new schools. For the first time, Vice Principal Ben Schmookler was formally identified as the design team leader and future principal of the Robert C. Maynard Media Academy High School. As our deliberations progressed, every team member was assigned to two or three of eleven subcommittees, each tasked with researching and contributing written text for a part of what had to be addressed in the final proposal. For example, two were assigned to special education (along with a special education consultant), one to parental involvement, one to coordination of community partnerships (assisted by three representatives of the OCO), two to technology, three to curriculum, and so on. Along with an outside provider I was appointed to the committee on campus-wide student services [that dealt with the clinic along with after school and weekend activities].

In addition I agreed to serve as lead writer of the entire revised Media proposal. As lead writer on the proposal committee, immersion anthropology was beginning to feel more like submersion and near drowning. But it wasn't that big a deal. I merely had to make the proposal read well based on what the design team decided. A lot of it was about what O'Donoghue earlier referred to as "nuts and bolts."

## Modifying Conversational Culture in "Focus Groups"

Drawing on a sociological technique that is much used in marketing research, but structuring it differently, in March, 2002, Maureen Benson, as change coordinator, conducted four "focus groups for teacher input on the site plan for small schools." The key to a focus group conversation usually is for the facilitator to take a completely neutral position on issues under discussion, to encourage every one of the six or so participants to speak frankly of experiences and recommendations, and to stimulate cross-table talk.

Maureen organized her conversational groups in the very different way developed by BayCES, as the agenda demonstrates. She explained, "We are meeting because we have a huge concern. We don't want outside people to come and say, 'this is the plan' . . . My job is to make sure that your voices are heard." She posted a large sheet of paper on the wall for all of us to read.

## Agenda

I. Getting food, Welcome, Reading Handouts, and Norm Setting (5 minutes)

II. Dyad guidelines (2 minutes)

- Get into pairs with someone you don't work with often
- Each person is given equal time to talk
- The listener does not interpret, paraphrase, analyze, give advice or break in with a personal story
- Confidentiality is maintained
- The talker does not criticize or complain about the listener or about mutual colleagues during their time to talk

III. Dyad prompt (5 minutes: each person speaks)

## Focus Group Norms

- Assume the best intentions of others
- Value whatever someone brings to the table, regardless of their position or length of time at the school
- Check and clarify our assumptions
- Allow differing ideas to exist – creative tension is normal
- Be mindful of patterns of participation

Benson did her best to recruit teachers to take part, writing in her invitational announcement, "I know this is a small consolation, but you get a free lunch in our beautiful library." She wanted participating teachers and others, including me as participant note-taker, to discuss a range of issues, one of which was externally provided student services, since they were seriously threatened by the changeover. She needed teacher and staff input on, "How will youth services, school wide resources and athletic teams be shared across the school?" This was a critical area of discussion to the extent that the new small schools expected to continue to function analogously to the wall-to-wall academies in claiming the benefits of small learning communities without giving up the advantages of being part of a large comprehensive high school. It would continue for me as a major focus of concern for years yet to come.

## Failure Again after 2 Years of Exhausting Work by Teachers and Administrators

The design team met the May 1 deadline to turn in a final draft of the "Proposal for the Robert C. Maynard High School," fully confident that we had overcome all potential objections and would surely be approved to begin the coming school year as a new small autonomous school. Three weeks later eight of us defended the proposal in a formal interview at district headquarters. Other applicant schools had representatives there for the same purpose. We thought we made a good impression. I e-mailed the others on May 22 to say, "I felt it went extremely well. Ben did a splendid job, especially on difficult technical issues. Yurai [a student] only spoke a couple of times, but said exactly the right things and sounded very wise for a young woman. Tanya Dumas-Land and Venus Mesui [parents] were also excellent and demonstrated involvement in ways that seemed to speak for all parents, making it come alive with references to their own children. Susheela Moonsamy [counselor] did not say a lot, but what she said had impact."

We felt totally demolished on June 6 when we found out we had failed again to qualify as an autonomous school. In a few days we were to be notified officially that that our proposal needed additional revising and for that reason we would be advanced to Stage 3A of the approval process.

What in the world did that mean? It angered Ben that stages 3A and 3B had never been discussed. Someone else interjected, "Right, how many stages are there? What's 3C? 3D? 3E?" We had not expected the result to be anything other that approval or denial, as it had been when Media and Biology submitted their proposals at the end of the first implementation year. What we didn't realize was that BayCES quietly decided this year to retool approval, Stage 3, into two phases, 3A and 3B. It was only after we learned we were 3A that we received the following explanation by e-mail from the superintendent's office:

"Advancing to Stage 3A is *not* approval to open [emphasis in the original]. Advancing to Stage 3A means that proposals have met the criteria laid out in the RFP. During Stage 3A [which will take place during the 2002-2003 school year] design teams will be responsible for three primary areas of work:

(1) Developing a plan to make the changes, improvements and corrections suggested by the readers or required by the district.
(2) Developing an implementation plan that outlines the concrete steps that will be taken.
(3) To identify and negotiate with the district (and, in the case of Fremont, the site) around the 6 autonomies and develop agreements and MOUs [memos of understandings] on these and other issues such as facilities, date of opening, etc.

"On the conclusion of satisfactorily completing this work, the Superintendent will then make a decision about schools that he will recommend, and the Board will be asked to give approval to the opening of a new school." [Grammatical error in the original.]

This was beyond belief. Teachers were angry, bitter, and disillusioned. In protest, O'Donoghue showed us the draft of a letter he wanted to send to Superintendent Chaconas, but didn't. It read, in part, "There is a growing impression at Fremont that there are no serious plans to open small learning communities at Fremont in the near future. . . . The feeling of many staff here is we are being set up to fail. . . . We would appreciate knowing today: (1) Will small schools open at Fremont in the Fall of 2002? (2) Will small schools open at Fremont in the fall of 2003?" Steve proposed that this be signed, "Design Team," without names.

When we talked about the letter, Ben said that once again the goal posts had been moved. None of us were told that after approval there was yet another stage. As we speculated specifically about the question of postponement until 2003 Ben Schmookler stomped out of the room, commenting to anyone within earshot, "Forget about 2003! I don't care, I won't be here!" (He had the credentials and experience he needed for promotion to a position as principal and could undoubtedly escape to find a good placement in another school.)

In an e-mail that Steve did in fact send out, he announced the news to Media people in his own way. "We passed the first test and are now rated 3A. (Don't ask what it means or how many more levels there are, we don't know.)" From my journal, "I spoke with Mike Jackson. He is furious. . . . He said, 'They wasted our time this year and now they want to continue wasting our time next year.' I said, 'evenings and weekends,' and he added, 'without pay.'" And that's what happened, except that Ben cooled down and stayed on for another year as principal designate.

# Chapter Six

## The Struggle: Matrix Year Three

### Cultures of Conversation

*At the outset it must be noted that conflict or confrontative behaviors and harmony or reconciliation techniques are not antithetical. Any theory of cultural control would merge conflict and harmony as part of the same control system, albeit at different ends of a continuum.*

Laura Nader
Anthropology News, 48 (6)
September, 2007, page 114

### Pick Yourself Up and Have a Conversation

The next school year started before the current year had fully run its course. Principal McKibben invited the six design teams to attend a special meeting on June 11 for "a formal announcement" that would, he wrote, become "a significant part of [the] history . . . of growth and change" at Fremont High. "We all know," he added, referring to the decision not to authorize any new school to start up in the fall, "how challenging the last few days have been. Things are now moving ahead.

Information will be forthcoming. It will be clear. It will be challenging. To all of you who have worked on design teams, I offer my appreciation and admiration."

Each team was invited to a have a conversation with the decision makers. Steve Jubb of BayCES presided, with McKibben and Moore from Fremont to back him up along with two representatives each from the district office and Oakland Community Organizations. The first conversation was scheduled with Media for 1:00 p.m. The ceremonial meeting for the ensemble of teams was to start at 4:00 p.m.

As we made our way to the one o'clock conference a smiling Steve O'Donoghue muttered in a soft voice, "It's going to be pretty good news." I didn't know what he hoped for, but within minutes we were confronted with a depressing reality. The team would have to spend yet one more dreary year of work on proposal writing, and the first new deadline was only weeks away.

Approval, we were told, was called Stage 3B, and we weren't there yet. As we stood around, dumbfounded, Jubb said in an avuncular voice, "I understand your frustration." His colleague from BayCES explained what she thought was good news, which was that we were invited to apply for a bridge grant of $30,000 for the coming year. "It is probably the most unrestricted grant you will ever get. . . . Today you will get $10,000 from the grant that is already here." However, the overriding downside was that fully autonomous schools would not open for another year, if then.

Not the least intimidated by the row of higher-ups who listened across from him in stony silence, Ben, very tall with the body of an athlete, spoke quietly but with emotional strength, looking Judd directly in the eye. "It was always explained that at least two schools would open by the fall of 2002. It was never explained any different than that right up until we got the letter. We were supposed to hear on June first. That did not occur. Then we were supposed to hear later that week. That did not occur. Then we were told, 'some time in the future.' This is the future.

"What you gave us is basically unprofessional. I don't know who is responsible for it, but the fact is, you took the time of many valuable people who spent their time, their weekends, their Saturdays, their Sundays, their holidays, in order to create a school. The Media Academy - the Maynard School - is better [prepared to start] than any other school here right now, and it is probably better . . . than many schools that are already [autonomous] in the district. Clearly, we have the capability of opening a small school. . . . The fact is, the district . . . is not playing in a fair way. For that reason, I'm taking myself out of this process."

As one design team after the other exited from their half-hour conferences a campus-wide plan came into focus. It seemed that Media and Architecture were scheduled to work another year with the expectation that they would become autonomous in the following year (beginning in the fall of 2003). The others should aim for the year after that (beginning in the fall of 2004). Of those, Mandela seemed to have the best prospects for succeeding within that time frame. Physical Education and Business were stalled, not having made any discernable progress during the last year. Youth Empowerment School (YES) was a totally new potential school with no track record at all, but looked promising nonetheless, if only because the prospective principal was Maureen Benson.

As we chatted in our discontent, Ben added a seeming non-sequitur, "I can't believe they have removed the 9th grade." He was re-reading the written instructions handed to us in the meeting we just left. The readers who reviewed the Media proposal and moved us to Stage 3A stipulated that in the coming year Media would be classified as a "pilot program" that "should not include implementation at the 9th grade, but should significantly impact the 10th grade."

This made no sense, since we had been told in several versions of earlier instructions that we had to plan for a "2 plus 2" program that would loop the 9th and 10th grades as well as the 11th and 12th. Also, the concept of a "pilot program" was new and void of meaning for us, except that it seemed to be a synonym for "Stage 3A."

Not the least, these new demands would co-opt the normal summer freedom teachers depend on for rejuvenation, self-improvement, and often, for temporary jobs to supplement inadequate salaries. "Pilot plans," we were informed, "must be approved by both the Principal and the Superintendent prior to implementation in Fall 2002," which was just two months down the road. To earn that approval the design team would have to write still one more major revision of the proposal, with a deadline of July 15, only one month away.

As an irony, we also learned from the written memo that the delay of the last two years was not merely because evaluators detected flaws in our proposed plans, as we had guilelessly assumed. A deeper cause of the delay appeared to be that the bureaucracy had not figured out how to accommodate six new schools on a single campus. In their words, "The conditions of advancement for the Maynard/Media design team are related to the unique circumstances of New Small Autonomous Interconnected Schools that require that the new schools are developed within a cohesive plan for the whole school transition." The shift in terminology that for the first time added "interconnected" signaled a new way of conceptualizing the implementation policy. Ben had complained that they kept moving the goal posts. Now we knew why. They had not yet figured out what to do with the comprehensive component of Fremont High.

For the first time we were told that Media and Architecture had to wait until the other schools caught up with them. Gone, the quick and easy independence granted to Health and Bioscience (which became Life Preparatory High School) at the end of the first implementation year. Gone, the promise of advancing individual schools as soon as they met published criteria. A new and unexpected requirement had been added. "This plan and the design team proposals," they now told us, "should satisfactorily address critical issues for the success of all the schools sharing the campus. . . ." More than a year later we would in fact learn that sharing the campus – preserving what would survive of the comprehensive school – would persist as a formidable stumbling block to success.

Rebellion grew as we clustered numbly in the hallway, waiting for the formal ceremonial meeting that was about to begin. In growing consternation, Mike, Steve, and Ben came to a decision. "We're going to boycott the meeting, Bob. Videotape it for us, and if they ask where we are, tell 'em we've gone off to review our options." Mike's frustration led him to add his own personal footnote, "We need to get out of Fremont and sink or swim on our own. Life did that [when they moved to their own building downtown] and they're doing fine."

As the sole representative of the Media team still present, and not a teacher but only a loyal and peripheral supporter, I walked with Dan Hurst as he entered the library for the ceremony. Not unexpectedly, as teacher alliances shifted against uncertainties, Dan had recently quit the Media team to become principal designate of the architecture school. When I told him that Steve, Mike, and Ben, as a form of protest, had gone off to quaff brews at a bar in Jack London Square, he said, "I needed to know that." I soon understood what he meant. It steeled his resolve to act out his own boycott on behalf of Architecture.

The ritual highpoint of the meeting was for the principal to hand over a $10,000 check to each team together with some books for the new school libraries, including one written, according to the title, . . . *for Dummies*. The word "*dummies*" was very unfortunate for the occasion, since Architecture and Media felt they had been dummies to believe that their two-year investment in writing proposals would pay off with autonomy.

As the formalities unfolded the moment came when Brian asked for the representative of Architecture to come forward. Dan, unsmiling, walked laggardly to the front, accepted the check without saying a word, briskly turned his back on the principal, and headed for the door. Brian called after him, "Wait, take the books, too," but Dan, in obvious disdain, continued out the door.

As he prepared to make his next presentation, Brian searched the room for Steve, Mike, or Ben. In their absence he directed his gaze at me and asked if I was there to accept the check, or if he should wait. I said, "You should wait." What none of us in the room could know at that moment was that, in discussing their options over drinks at Jack London Square, the Media leaders decided they should take the $10,000 and work with it.

Dan and his people along with leaders of the other design teams eventually decided to do the same, but not without a coda to the "historic" ritual. As soon as the meeting was formally adjourned Dan marched back into the room, made his way directly to Brian, and returned the check. He told me afterward he didn't feel right about accepting it without consulting the others. He also said he was offended by the proffered gift of a book written "*for dummies.*"

## Dust Yourself Off for More Conversations

Graduation ended the school year on June 12. Five days later the design teams met in the school library with the principal. The power dynamics were very different from that previous meeting, when the convener was the Executive Director of BayCES, and McKibben sat as just one among half a dozen representatives on the power and control side of the table. At this meeting McKibben presided, but in his role as mediator and problem solver, subordinating his principal's right to announce decisions and give orders to his need to inspire collaboration. Except for one momentary but unfortunate slip-up, he succeeded.

In a sport shirt and sunglasses he looked relaxed, casual, and in good humor. He told us that Betty Daspenza-Green had flown in from Chicago and would join us later, "mostly just to listen, but you may have some questions from her." The most important thing he hoped to accomplish that afternoon was "just to take the pulse," he said, adding, "as I was saying to Steve Judd this morning, this had to be the agony and the ecstasy, with good stuff and bad stuff, and I just wanted to get a sense of where you are."

He went on to explain how he was sure that the meeting was "going to be a conversation . . . about how your programming is not only OK but is blossoming." Then, without pause, he moved on. "For starters I'd like to have a status report of where you are and how you are in terms of absorbing the news from last week."

The ensuing conversation provided an opportunity for team spokespeople to vent their frustration, but also to acknowledge a willingness to persevere. We heard this in the remarks of Ben Schmookler, who spoke for the Media team. Unlike the last meeting when he wore a formal jacket and tie, that afternoon he dressed casually in a red polo shirt and was stylishly unshaven. In abbreviated form, the conversation went on as follows, based on my videotaped record.

"Over the weekend I thought about it a while, and I feel we haven't been given enough instructions. . . . I feel that until we get something in writing from the District, or whoever those powers may be, as to what exactly a successful pilot program is specifically for each and every design team, then we will not do any further planning. If they want to continue making it up as they go along, I'm fine with remaining in the candidate model for another year, working on our RFP. . . . " Referring to the check for $10,000 and the promise of $30,000 as a way, it seemed to him, to encourage the teams to "keep playing the game," he concluded by saying, "I'm not going to play that game. I need to have something in writing."

Without a word while shifting his gaze, McKibben turned away from Ben and in a soft, low-keyed voice said, "OK, Dan?" Dan Hurst, in shirtsleeves and khaki trousers, spoke for the Architecture team. "Yeah, I concur with everything Ben said. I would add that the response that we got was that the proposal was acceptable. It met the criteria. . . . Now they're insisting something other than that remains that we are held accountable for, well, I don't have a plan for that. . . . All right, I'll run the academy model, I'll move it further, but it's just the academy model. We'll do that while we answer questions and work on the paperwork. OK, that's not my first choice, but all right . . . Specifically, I want to know what are their instructions."

Hurst was followed by Ellen Salazar, Robin Glover, and Debby Juarez on behalf of the Mandela team. Salazar began by saying, " Well, we're at the point of trying to determine what is reasonable for us to do next year because we understand that next year is to be a pilot of our methods. . . . Glover added, "I personally agree with what they [Schmookler and Hurst] are saying. . . We can't say what we will do in our academy. We don't have an academy, so. . ." She was interrupted by Debby Juarez who interjected, "We already knew ahead of time that we were going to do piloting this year. . , we were going to have to, because we have no program."

This is where McKibben inadvertently riled tempers. "One of the things, and not just at this school, but everywhere I've ever been, teachers and site people complain about top-down management, and now in its absence you are confused."

Oh, oh, that upset everybody in the room, with cries of "no," "no." Craig Gordon of Mandela overwhelmed other voices to correct the principal. "They say, well, we'll see how you do this coming year. . . . It's still completely top-down. What we would like is for you to give us support and give us some parameters, and give it to us in writing, and that hasn't happened."

Maureen Benson, speaking for YES, added, "Something that's really alarming to me is, I'm hearing everybody saying that there are programs to be evaluated. That's the first I'm hearing about it. . . ."

Finally, McKibben retreated and recouped. "Well, the inference I draw, looking at the letters that the 3A people received, was that the 3A status people have a concept . . . the pilot should be a microcosm of what the new school is going to look like, and, looking at what Maureen and Ben are saying, I can certainly understand what they are saying. To me it's a given that the success that the 3A team has this coming year is going to play a major role as to whether they will be a school thereafter."

I have only provided snippets of that prolonged conversation, which continued for another hour to alternate angry voices with acquiescence and even occasional outbursts of laughter. As the clock approached 11:00, signaling the end of the session, McKibben turned to Daspenza-Green, who had quietly found a chair at the large square table. "Betty, I'm just going to ask you to give us some feedback."

Speaking haltingly at first as she searched for words to fit the circumstances, she managed to articulate the ambivalence of pulling back and moving forward that team members were struggling with, of picking themselves up and dusting them-selves off. "I'm very distant," she said, "trying to hear where you guys are. I think what I'm hearing now is floundering. You're not quite sure what the next steps are. We're just kind of here . . . and I don't know, really what the purpose of this meeting is, but it sounds like it's just kind of a coming together to sort of air what you're feeling like and to kind of complain a little bit, which is fine because you know there are some problems."

I recall that meeting in a similar way. It was a time of floundering, but also of catharsis for those who voiced complaints. To some extent it was a rejuvenating moment as team members strengthened their resolve, like Sisyphus, to push the burden of proposal-writing uphill one more time.

## And Start All Over Again with More Conversations

Members of the Media design team picked themselves up earlier at the meeting of June 11 and dusted themselves off at this meeting on June 17. What struck me as extraordinary was that as soon as the "dusting off" meeting adjourned they started all over again by writing a proposal for what they referred to as "the Sophomore Pilot for the Media Academy (The Maynard High School of Communication)." Within two days Steve wrote to bring us all up-to-date on that astonishingly fast transition.

"We passed the first test and are now Stage 3B. (Don't ask what it means . . . we don't know.) . . . We have to submit a short proposal by July 15 to receive $30,000 in planning money for the academic year 2002-03. We have to be approved for recommendation to the school board next year [spring, 2003] before we will be allowed to open as a new small school on the Fremont campus [fall, 2003]. The Architecture team and Mandela team are in the same situation. The SMART [PE] team is delayed until 2004. [He failed to mention Business or YES.]"

I wasn't part of the team when the July 15 proposal was written and submitted because I was in Denmark finishing a research project on the diagnosis and treatment of back pain. However, when I read the proposal on my return it showed the benefits of their added work, and it did the trick. They got their $30,000.

Shortly before the new school year began, and by then substantially recommitted, the Media team used part of their summer planning money to fund a long three-day conversation as an August retreat at Lake Tahoe. Later Mike told me they made good progress in planning but the big benefit was that they all came out of it feeling bonded as a team. Unfortunately, I had to give up sharing that experience in order to spend a couple of weeks with Edna, who had moved into an apartment in the United Arab Emirates, where she was a visiting professor for the year. When I flew back for the beginning of the fall semester at Fremont and at Mills I thought the Media team would continue to be consistently upbeat the way they had been during the previous year, but I was wrong. It was to be a turbulent time of highs and lows, like bouncing back and forth between the Middle East and East Oakland, between war and peace, which is what I was doing that year.

## The SLAM School Year

Slogans always seemed to splash down unexpectedly from some mysterious cloud chamber high above. RRR as an unanticipated slogan (Renewal, Reading, Results) sounded inspirational at the beginning of the previous year, but turned out to be meaningless. "Renewal" ended up being postponed for at least another year and "Results" on the whole stagnated, even for "Reading" and literacy. Perhaps that's why RRR was scarcely mentioned after the first few weeks and was quite forgotten by the end of that year. Would a new slogan succeed this year where the old one had failed?

The new slogan was SLAM (Smallness, Literacy, Accountability, Mastery). Principal McKibben announced in September that he expected to complete the implementation process by the end of the current year, in time to open five new small schools the following September [2003]. But, after all we had been through since the year 2000, none of us took that kind of a promise at face value. "To that end, he added, 'Our school wide focus this year is SLAM.'"

**Smallness**. The first goal for the SLAM year was Smallness, the purpose being to have "most classes in the same location this year." In other words, as a first effort, and to the extent possible, each leadership team was to take possession of its own separated part of the campus. Spatial integrity for a small school was considered essential if personalized relationships were to flourish. Writing about her research on the transformation of several big high schools, Mary Anne Raywid emphasized the need to adapt or renovate a large building [such as the main one at Fremont High] in order to make "it possible to reduce the *experienced size* of school, despite building size" (1996: Raywid's emphasis). There are other good reasons as well.

Those making plans for Fremont High understood that imperative. A year earlier, McKibben sent out a memo in which he wrote, "On Wednesday, a group of folks from OUSD. . . BayCES . . . Castlemont

[High School] . . . [along with] Ben Schmookler, Maureen Benson, and I made a walking tour of Fremont. The purpose of the tour was to begin to determine the capacity of Fremont for SLCs [small learning communities]. The fundamental questions were these: how many SLCs can Fremont support physically, and what would the enrollment capacity be for each SLC? Accompanying questions dealt with such things as possible reconfiguration of certain spaces, relocation and/or addition of portables, ensuring space within each SLC for 'common areas,' support staff, equipment, and storage. None of these questions were answered. Wednesday was simply an information-gathering exercise."

A month later at an early Tuesday morning meeting of the leadership teams, McKibben drew a preliminary sketch on the board of how space might be allocated. The most straight-forward way to carve out physically separated localities was to locate each school in a wing of the main building, but that was not offered as an option for Media. Instead, perhaps because one double portable had long been equipped for teaching journalism and another for radio and TV broadcasting, the decision was that a Media island would be created by completely taking over the red-painted "B" portables that had long constituted the campus heart of the Media Academy.

Having that planning behind them, the fall semester of 2002 began with an attempt to consolidate the housing of Media personnel. The Spanish teacher left her classroom in the main building to move into a red portable, as did some other teachers, but the number of rooms was less than the total number of teachers who needed to move, so the chemistry/biology teacher remained in the main building where he had his laboratory set-up. Also, one long portable in the B complex remained part of a different academy (Visual and Performing Arts) because, with hardwood floors, wall mirrors, a changing room and a small toilet room, it was equipped as a dance studio that could not be relocated. Confinement to the B portables also deprived Media of basic amenities such as student lockers and lavatories for boys, girls, and teachers, which at some future date would need to be rectified. The most serious problem, though, was that the space was too small for the proposed school. It could only accommodate 150 students.

O'Donoghue grew increasingly discouraged that September. In one conversation he told me that Media had wasted the last two years in part because the plan to build a new building across the street for Media had been jettisoned. More recently he complained that the future size of the school would have to be much greater than they thought. "For the last two years we've been told it would be 250. Now it has to be 400 because the five small interconnected schools have to distribute the entire student body [of 1800] among themselves." No one attempted to explain how 400 students could eventually be accommodated in a space only adequate for 150.

The other SLAM goals were Literacy, Accountability, and Mastery. Taken together, those three vaguely defined goals appeared to share a commitment to improve the quality of teaching.

**Literacy**. The second goal, for example, ordained a focus on "professional development for second language learners, having every child reading at or above grade level." "Professional development" is code for a program of continuing education activities designed to encourage, assist, and train teachers to become more effective in their classrooms. Based on their documentation of how schools elsewhere transformed themselves, Linda Darling-Hammond asserts that a team approach to professional development was of key importance and had to be very different from that of traditional high schools, "because creating a new school increased the need for new knowledge and skills and increased the opportunities for teachers to learn from each other" (1997: 41). It could require group planning, experimenting with new approaches, taking courses, peer-coaching, shared readings, and instruction from visiting specialists, but very little was put in place that pilot year.

In addition to teaching English and journalism, a major goal of the literacy program was to ensure that every student would become fluent in both English and Spanish. As her contribution to professional development, the Spanish teacher was asked to coach teachers so that non-speakers would at least develop minimal word and phrase recognition while those with Spanish capabilities would improve in fluency and comprehension.

Alas, that teacher failed to move efficiently on this, perhaps because she was very busy with teaching her classes, but just as likely because she was only minimally motivated to take on this enormous and probably hopeless chore. All that happened pretty much began and ended pathetically about six weeks into the year when she handed out, almost without comment, the kind of vocabulary aid commonly printed in travel books for tourists, but tailored somewhat for classroom use. A couple of my favorite phrases were "You have to do your home-work. That's life" (*Hay que hacer la tarea, Asi es la vida*) and "Talk less, work more" (*Menos hablar, más trabajar*). The most useful section, consisting of eleven words, was even helpful to those already possessed of some fluency: "Swear Words [you should recognize but] not say" (*Palabras malas: ¡Eso no se dice!).* Neither my 9th grade Spanish teacher when I was a boy nor anyone since has ever provided such intriguing information, but good manners forbid that I repeat it here.

**Accountability**. This goal expressly emphasized the importance of improving the quality of teaching insofar as "we must be accountable [note below] to each other as a team for the testing criteria as well as 'horizontal and vertical accountability'." In other words, constructive feedback should be elicited horizontally from colleagues and vertically from the principal and superintendent's office to ensure that students were learning what they needed to know for the all-important standardized tests.

Conference periods in a small school were supposed to be scheduled for the same time slot for all in order to permit and encourage teachers to collaborate on professional development and, most importantly, to dialogue on how to help every student who wasn't doing well.

The shared conference period didn't work out, mainly because Media didn't have enough autonomy to create a schedule different from that of the rest of Fremont High. Media personnel therefore agreed voluntarily to meet on Mondays in Steve's room for conversations at lunch-time, but within a month the agreement was in trouble, as became clear in an early October e-mail from Media Co-Director Jackson.

"Having attended two BayCES meetings and spending five unpaid hours listening to the yammering of the other 'integrated wannabe schools', I have a renewed sympathy for those of you who think meeting even once a week over lunch to share what we're doing is not an efficient use of your time. I propose: The Monday lunches are voluntary and for general venting and sharing BUT [they are not truly voluntary because it is required that] each of us shares, over [that is, after] the weekend, what they will do in their sophomore classes for the coming week. Sophomore class is required, others, optional. AND remember to include, starting this weekend or sooner, how you plan to use FAST FOOD NATION in your class beginning second marking period, which begins next Monday" (capital letters in the original).

All of the pilot schools had to stay on the same bell schedule. The only time they could officially meet regularly was on Wednesdays when classes school-wide were dismissed early so that teachers could attend staff meetings after lunch. I sat in on many of those fairly informal Media meetings. What follows is a conversation sampler taken from my notes on a day in mid-September.

- They talked about how to deal with a boy who just leaves the room when he feels like it.
- A girl is a problem because she walks around the class disturbing others. "She hawks up and finally spits in the waste basket."
- Another girl defied a teacher saying, "I'm damn sick of your white ass."

- [Deleted] is a really smart kid, but has a mind of her own. Schmookler: "She's late every day." Sevilla: "She cheated on a test and she addresses me by my first name." Jackson: "She's not a behavior problem in my class, but is always tardy." Hoffman: "She said, 'I wanna go to the football game', so she left."

- Mentioning another student by name one teacher said, "Her mother gave me her cell number. She wants me to call as soon as there is a problem." Looking across the table at a colleague he added, "I'll give you her cell number." The other teacher replied, "She's well behaved. No tardy problems, but I have her in second period, not first, which is better for tardy." Jackson: "Thirty-four [students] in a 90-minute class [without air conditioning]. It's hot as hell." Schmookler, still the vice principal responsible for campus-wide discipline: "If they come in late, send 'em to me."

On the formal agenda that day, Susheela Moonsamy, the academy counselor, reported that next year there would be less autonomy than promised and that the school leaders would be vice principals, not principals. O'Donoghue boiled over. "In that case, Ben [who was not present] will go somewhere else where he can be a principal. I'm pretty much ready to say 'screw you'." A few days later he told me he had a talk with Principal McKibben and told him he was fed up and planned to quit in June.

*Steve to me*: "We wasted two years of hard work – endless meetings – because what we end up doing is just fine-tuning the academy."

*Bob*: "Which is what we said we should do in the first place, Right?"

*Steve*: "Right."

**Mastery**. Mastery essentially restated the focus on accountability, but with the addition of feedback from students. It was explained as consisting of "evaluations of administration by students and faculty, of faculty by students so that we can continually improve ourselves to be masters of what we do." Everyone agreed that it was important to elicit feedback from students and their parents or guardians in addition to that gotten from colleagues and superiors, and the site management team was supposed to organize it. But it didn't work out that way that year. On Wednesday, September 25 I wrote the following in my journal:

"To Fremont for a 3:30 meeting on small schools, only to realize that it was scheduled to take place downtown, so I had to get back to Mills for my office hour and class. Mike and Steve are angry that meetings arranged by BayCES require driving into town after school. Only Mike was going to represent the Media Academy, and they want me to write a strong letter of objection to them saying they are there to help us get an autonomous interconnected small school started, yet require us to come at their convenience. Steve said today, they are supposed to turn control over to the site management teams, but he indicated skepticism, having been misled so many times."

Two days later I had a chat with Steve in Portable B-3. From my journal, "I wanted to know how the meeting with BayCES went. He told me that the intent was to turn direction over to the site management teams. It seems that they did, but that it is the SMT for the whole of Fremont that they were discussing, [not one for each pilot program]. But, Steve said, there are a lot of uncertainties, so it is not clear what that means."

What followed in my notes captures some of the flavor of how emotions fluctuated from conversation to conversation, sometimes from one moment to the next. "Whereas the day before this meeting Steve displayed a cynical attitude, today he seemed, one more time, to be on board. As we were talking, Michael Jackson came in, very excited. Addressing Steve, 'My 6th period class, your 3ed, is a great class. We just had a great time.' It was Mike who attended the BayCES meeting on Wednesday evening, so Steve was giving me feedback from what Mike had told him."

The Site Management Team (SMT2) met 15 times between October 31 and June 9. (The "2" indicates that this was the second year that Fremont was officially administered by an SMT.) The number of participants was always ten plus-or-minus two, with one or two representing each of five design teams plus Principal McKibben and Vice-Principal Moore, one or two from BayCES, and the new office manager, Sheroyne (Shey) Capdeville. Notably missing were students and parents who in theory should have projected powerful voices in making decisions affecting the school.

Heavy duty planning for the coming year was attempted, but it was burdensome. According to SMT2 minutes, Ellen Salazar of Mandela pointed out that it seemed "too much for a full-time teacher" to try to design a school. Evelyn Smith of the Art Academy agreed. "I cannot do another thing. I'm going to resign [which she did the following year] if I have to do something else. She listed all that she is doing, which is a lot." Maureen Benson of YES, "speaks her truth about work load too."

At the Fremont faculty meeting a week later the principal said, he would like to figure out a way for the funded [pilot] teams and unfunded teams to buy some released time, a day or half-a-day, to sit down together and address issues and concerns, especially as the teams move beyond conceptualization to the realities of implementation. Nonetheless, by mid-November when Mike and I were chatting after a meeting of the Media faculty, he told me, (quoting from my journal) "we're losing four new teachers. The job is too demanding on new people. They get overwhelmed by all of the administrative tasks. For example, look at the agenda for the faculty meeting this afternoon."

To return to that second SMT2 meeting, Robin Baler-Glover of Mandela confessed, "I'm blurry about the role of STT (site transition team). I am clear about SMT2, but now that both . . . exist, I'm not clear about their roles." The representative of BayCES contrasted the SMT2 as "governance" – making decisions – while that of the STT is to monitor and advise. McKibben clarified further, that the function of the STT was twofold, one is "to communicate what we are doing." The other is that "we give them a chance to ask clarifying questions . . . to give us feedback. It's another kind of filter. It needs to be a public forum for the work we are doing."

Parents were supposed to participate in the STT, but so far only YES parents were taking part. Glover of Mandela pointed out that "if we want parents at STT, then we need to be mindful about . . . the time." Working people cannot usually attend afternoon meetings. They also need to be alerted to times and places.

Personally, I wasn't told about the meetings and so I was never able to attend. Maybe it didn't matter. At the end of February O'Donoghue told me that he didn't take part anymore. "They just go over and over the same things." Jackson also told me that he "got nothing out of it," but he chose to continue attending "out of self-defense." Schmookler had no choice. He had to attend, but would leave early when he could, which may have been agreeable to the others, since he characteristically takes very straight forward and often uncompromising positions on debated issues. In an early June meeting, when they were discussing how to arrange a two-day retreat in September or October, Schmookler objected. He flatly stated that he was willing to take part on a Saturday for seven hours, but not for a whole weekend. "I need time for relaxation and rest," he insisted, "and for family." That sounded reasonable to me, but ran counter to the prevailing ethos of selfless sacrifice for a common good.

## The New Culture of Conversation at Fremont High

At the leading edge of organizational reform was a growing awareness of a need for communities to reframe the decision-making process, to encourage participation by all stakeholders, to democratize in that sense (Wagner 1997). In the words of Ernesto Cortez, "We have to replace our habit of command and control with *a culture of conversation*" (cited in Cushman 1997:3; italics added). In part, a shift away from command and control was discernable in the third year of the struggle to implement a small school policy.

The major remaining implementation challenge for that year was to work out how the new small schools would perpetuate some functions of the comprehensive school, how campus facilities would be shared. To that end, SMT2 scheduled a heavy agenda. They needed to make efficient use of their time, so with BayCES guidance they learned to dialogue in a new way that began with coming to an agreement on a "tentative calendar for decision making," as illustrated in part by the following timetable:

- Student Admission and Transfer Policy – November 21
- Shared Services and Facilities –December 5
- School Employees – January 9 and 16
- Safety and Security – January 16
- Curriculum –January 23 and 24 "and possibly another date"

In the time allotted for each meeting, they needed to work through issues and establish rules, regulations, and procedures that would limit the autonomy of each new small school by agreements in advance on concessions that would govern the interconnectedness that was inherent in sharing a single campus.

In the traditional way of handling such complex and important issues a dozen individuals with voting rights would only be able to stick to such a tight and demanding schedule if for the most part they merely rubber-stamped decisions that the principal and vice principals had reached in an inner-sanctum or, alternatively, if meetings went on seemingly forever. But the new culture of conversation in various permutations functioned both effectively and democratically (see Wagner 2002).

The tenor of these meetings was set at the start when participants were invited to articulate how they wanted to conduct polite and efficient discussions. In contrast to following Roberts Rules of Order, as is still customary in bureaucratic settings, these participants felt committed to the new rules because they emerged as explicit agreements. Written in large type and prominently displayed on a flip board at each meeting, they could be amended or elaborated any time discord or confusion made it advisable. As posted for the last meeting in June they read as follows:

## SMT-2 Meeting Norms

- Speak your truth
- Assume positive intent
- Have clarity regarding when to ask questions
- Be aware of speaking time
- Stay focused on agenda
- In order to promote team building and collaboration be intentional about building alliances across school affiliation, roles, and experience
- Acknowledge and respect interdependency

## Procedural Norms

- No cell phones unless negotiated w/ the group
- Begin and end on time

In addition to voting on their own norms, four individuals were assigned supportive roles at the beginning of each meeting. One was to function as "facilitator." The person assigned that role, which for SMT2 was always someone from BayCES, performed more like an umpire or orchestra leader than like a principal or superintendent. Her job was mainly to pass out an agreed-upon agenda, to enforce the norms, and to coordinate the discussion.

Participants sat around a large square table that facilitated a conversational tone. What a contrast to faculty meetings in which the minions sat in rows and mostly just listened to the principal as he looked down at them from on stage. Votes were taken in a somewhat different way from what is customary. Instead of voicing a "yay" or a "nay," or of raising hands, each participant showed a clenched fist with the thumb up for "yes," down for "no," and horizontal for abstention. Although the practice allowed for quick and accurate counting, it struck me as less important for efficiency than as a stylistic convention that symbolized an attitudinal change.

The agenda itself was presented in a way I had first encountered the previous year when Maureen conducted her focus groups. It indicated in advance how much time was scheduled for each topic. That eliminated or greatly diminished the tendency for participants to "yammer" on, as Mike might put it. It made it possible to get through a long agenda efficiently within the allotted two hours. The facilitator was entitled to approve additional time when more time was needed, but always an express number of minutes.

In my experience, the new culture of conversation did not unduly inhibit free expression among participants, and it did encourage speakers to get to the point so that conversations could progress. In that last meeting, for example, the agenda (much abbreviated) read as follows, with the written notations of allotted minutes in parentheses supplemented for completeness by my notations of time in square brackets:

3:30 – 3:40 Pass out notes from May 31st, assign meeting roles [10 min.]

3:40 – 4:25 [The first topic] [45 minutes]

4:25 – 5:00 [the second topic]Presentation (4 minutes)

    (a) Questions (3 minutes)

    (b) Discussion (25 minutes)

5:00 – 5:15 [The third topic]

    (a) Suggestions (5 minutes)

    (b) Discussion (10 minutes)

5:15 – 5:30 Process Observations and Appreciation [15 minutes]

The three other roles were performed by volunteers, who were usually different for each meeting. The role of the "timekeeper" was to set a clock that buzzed or sounded a bell to announce "stop." Another important role was that of "notetaker." Perhaps the most innovative role was "process observer." As exemplified in the sample agenda above, the last few minutes of every meeting were scheduled for "process observations and appreciations" as a way to reinforce the importance of abiding by the agreed upon norms. It was a time to compliment individuals or the group as a whole for performing well and to identify failures to conform.

Non-members were not welcome to attend SMT2 meetings and the distributed notes did not ordinarily record process observations, so I can only report the following two examples when they did appear in published minutes.

*One Example*: "[The] process checker . . . saw three things: We seem not to have consistent hands raised when called on . . . We were jumping out and talking. Secondly, we got off track when we were trying to gather our information. Finally, when questions were raised . . . we stopped and answered, but we didn't take time out to write down [our] concerns [on the flip chart] so that everybody can see what is being said." That last reference is to the regular use of a large sheet of paper on which comments, suggestions, lists can be written for all to see as a way to efficiently help discussants track on the conversation. Flip-chart writing is not done by the notetaker, but can be very helpful to that person.

*Another Example*: "Process observations: Noticed that 'One Voice' [at a time] policy was not adhered to. Request for facilitators to intervene when violated. Did not 'need' to start late since there were people here at 3:30."

## Introducing Media to the
## New Culture of Communication

BayCES assigned one of their coaches to teach the Media Leadership Team how to use their innovative techniques for efficiency in dialoguing. I had been waiting for the coach to come on board ever since she wrote almost a year earlier to ask if she and I could meet "to talk and see how we might be able to work together to help Media create a more high functioning culture for meetings."

She turned up for the first time at a Monday noon faculty meeting early in November. After we had all taken seats around the long table in Steve's classroom she introduced herself as our BayCES coach by explaining what her role would be. "Think of me as a supporter, as an ally at BayCES," she said. "In interfacing between here and the district I will advocate for you. We do have some influence," she added. She came across as sincere and sensitive, but also as quite young and completely lacking in experience as a school administrator or classroom teacher. She announced that she was assigned to work with us on how to accomplish four major goals that we needed to achieve:

- To conduct data-based inquiry, so that decisions could grow out of research findings.
- To train principals and teachers for instructional leadership.
- To improve school design in all of its complexity, including team teaching and professional development.
- To incorporate equity, based on talking honestly about the complex issues of race, class, gender and sexual orientation (see Bryk and Schneider 2002).

"We have developed curriculum in those four content areas," she told us, "but coaching is more than that." On Friday, she would return to review themes in our RFP, how to involve parents, and she would be looking at "the teacher-learner community." "She will also evaluate your lesson plan," Ben said to the Spanish teacher, who was under pressure to make us all bilingual.

The coach's approach was gradualist, no doubt as a compromise with an obvious lack of enthusiasm on the part of her team. The only innovation introduced a week later was to begin with a "roundtable," whereby each of us in turn took only a minute to report on something meaningful we had done since we last met. The practice served well to make us feel that we were a team of colleagues, all equally interesting and important. Every meeting was supposed to begin that way, but in Media it was never done again. In all other ways the meeting proceeded as always with up-dates on school events, planned meetings, and discussions of problem students. The Spanish teacher translated a couple of the words on her list. For some inexplicable reason she did not include English equivalents on her handout, which puzzled me.

At that meeting O'Donoghue inserted a version of his oft-repeated complaint. "They want you to be creative, to work together, to innovate. But instead you are forced to go through a check-list of hurdles: Do this! Then this! Then that!" A few weeks later Ben said, "I'm tired of our meetings where we just sit around and talk about little problems." But the coach was not within earshot when those complaints were shared with the rest of us.

At her third meeting with us, Ben announced that we would be doing something new. A timer would be used to keep us on track, but nothing came of it. Our table talk proceeded the way it always did as an informal and unpredictable mélange of gossip and announcements. In all events, the timer was never used again. There was no more discussion of Spanish vocabulary. Our meetings were almost only about the sophomore pilot. It was the same at the fourth week. The coach had gotten into the habit of just listening and taking notes. She urged us to follow the new norms that week, but no one paid any attention. In the sixth week she led us in a discussion about using collaborative methods with students and how to revise our attendance policy.

Finally, at her eighth meeting with us in February she announced that she would no longer attend on behalf of BayCES because our meetings were mostly informative and she was a coach with many more urgent things to do. After she left everyone seemed to agree that she was young, inexperienced and not qualified to tell professional teachers and administrators what to do, but the real reason, I would wager, was that they preferred the old informalities of backstage chatter. So much for conversational innovations of that sort at that time in that place.

## There Are No Villains in This Story

As I documented revolutionary changes in the process of evolving it was in the nature of autoethnography that I sacrificed any hope I might have had of being completely impartial or neutral. For one, my intense involvement with the Media design team biased me in their favor as I shared in and empathized with their exhaustion and frustration. For another, my identification as *The Cecil B. De Mille of Fremont High*, as the recorder in detail of unfolding events, at times possibly made me appear threatening to power-holders as a potential whistle-blower, given their awareness that many things were going wrong. As a consequence, it appears, I was excluded from their deliberations.

What leaders with the power to make things happen could not know was that I resisted bias and was committed to an ethical code that respected their vulnerability. As an experienced ethnographer, with all of my personal shortcomings, I always struggled to be open-minded, fair and objective (see Anderson, 2005: 217-222). In actuality, I came away with enormous respect and appreciation for their leadership. I was fully aware that it needed to be evaluated and appreciated as a well-executed confrontation with complex social, political, financial, and cultural realities. They were fearless reformers, all the more to be admired because they knew very well that they would become the inevitable targets of criticism, and even of character assassination. And they were sincerely dedicated to making schools work for inner city kids. Reporting back from one of the numerous downtown meetings convened by BayCES, Steve O'Donoghue told me, as noted in my journal,

> Steve Jubb, [the BayCES Executive Director], got so emotional that he cried. He said he remembered how hard it was when he went through this kind of major change [when he was a school teacher]. He also said that they needed to remember that if the small school movement fails for the Oakland Public Schools or for Fremont it is his failure, and the failure of BayCES as well.

Through her writing, Jacqueline Ancess let us know in advance that administrators involved in this kind of dramatic departure from traditional practices can expect intense scrutiny, set-backs, and turbulence. Transforming a failed school system is, she wrote, a "Herculean task that deserves respect and support. It needs to be looked at in the context of real not fantasized alternatives" (1997: 17).

Specifically at Fremont High, while Media Design Team members struggled with the day-to-day challenges of creating the new school culture that was beginning to emerge, the people they reported to were working on the last of the major big picture challenges: How to design a new culture of shared personnel and facilities for the Fremont campus as a whole. In the year to come, in spite of their best efforts, interconnectedness was to frustrate success and threaten survival. But their efforts were nonetheless Herculean and well-deserving of respect and support.

## School Year Surprise Ending - The Federation is Born

By mid-February, major uncertainties evaporated, only to be replaced by minor ones. The big news was that Brian's goal and Jubb's purpose were achieved: Fremont High as it had been known since 1905 was dissolved, to be replaced in the fall of 2003 by "new small autonomous interconnected schools," although the number was six. We had expected five. (It was actually seven, because Life Preparatory High School was already autonomous.)

One was The Media Academy. That puzzled me. Not that Media was finally granted autonomy, but that it wasn't named The Robert C. Maynard Media Academy. Jackson explained that, as he understood it, "the family was afraid the school would be a flop when things were uncertain and the school was given only pilot status, so they withdrew permission." Over the next two years the name of the new school varied a lot, in part because it needed to keep the term "academy" in order to continue to qualify for a state career academy subsidy. Media College Preparatory Academy High School was favored at times, but it is so cumbersome that it was tempting to fall back on the old pre-independence name, The Media Academy, which is what the circulated announcement of autonomy did.

Architecture survived as the College Preparatory and Architecture Academy. Two schools that once were told they would have to wait a year longer than Media and Architecture also gained independence at that time, even though they had started serious proposal writing much later (which suggests that proposal writing functioned, perhaps inadvertently, as a diversionary and to some extent unnecessary constraint). One was the Paul Robeson College Preparatory School of Visual and Performing Arts High School and the other was Mandela High School. the one named after a world famous African American musician and patriot and the other after Nelson Mandela, the first black president of South Africa and a world famous humanitarian. (The African American Publisher of the Oakland Tribune would have been in good company if the use of his name had been authorized for the Media Academy.) Youth Empowerment School (YES) was also approved. In spite of getting a late start it organized itself rapidly and effectively and, as was true of Health and Bioscience three years earlier, was clearly ready to take on the responsibilities of autonomy. (YES also provided yet one more reason to question the need for requiring that Media and Architecture invest three long, hard years in writing and re-writing proposals.)

Two early applicants for new school recognition dropped out of the competition: physical education and the business school. That left five new schools, the number we had been told to expect as far back as last September. At that time we didn't trust their promise for obvious reasons, but they were sincere and determined. The sixth school, Fremont in Transition (FIT), came as a total surprise, but do not be misled. It only functioned as a residual institutional category to accommodate juniors and seniors in the Business Academy who stayed on as surviving Fremont High students at large. The seniors were to graduate after the first FIT year, and the juniors, the year after that. By June, 2005, FIT was disbanded and its space became available to the other schools.

But a lot more than that took place during between 2003 and 2005. As to new uncertainties, the most imminent was that teachers who were not invited to join any of the new autonomous schools worried that they would receive "March 15 letters" informing that they no longer had jobs. Most ended up staying on at the Fremont Federation of College Preparatory High Schools and those who did not mostly transferred to other schools within the district. The big uncertainty, of course, was how the new Federation of Interconnected Schools would work out beginning in the fall. We were to experience uncertainties and surprises, achievements and disappointments, that made the final two years of the Fremont century a challenging time for the people of Fremont as well as for the anthropologist who was swimming or drowning with them.

# Chapter Seven

## Assessment: More is Better
## at the Fremont Federation

### Career Academy Policy Recap (1985-2003)

Beginning in the 1960s and persisting since then, most of the students who attended Fremont High have been academically at risk. The labyrinth of cultural complexity was over-whelming. Ethnic cultures diversified with the increasing addition of Latino, Asian, and Pacific Islander immigrants to the earlier mix of white and African American. English for many children was a language to be learned rather than a tool to be used. Family culture in East Oakland was challenged by unemployment, poverty, substance abuse, teenage pregnancy, single-parent households, uneducated adults, and violence. Neighborhood culture was disordered by civic neglect and shattered by crime. High school culture was sabotaged by youth cultural values hostile to classroom commitments and a culture of teachers and staff that was correspondingly threatened by discouragement and disengagement.

It was unrealistic to expect school reform as such to succeed for all students. The underlying cause of school failure was so deep and wide that only massive urban renewal could offer hope for the children of

East Oakland. Their happiness and success required programs to end unemployment and stamp out poverty, but programs for that purpose failed. Schools cannot compensate for "the problems of poverty, alienation, and family disintegration," as Neil Postman observed. "But schools can *respond* to them", and that is what happened (1995: 48, emphasis in the original; see also Olson, 2007; Lee & Burkham, 2002).

The career academy policy offered hope. The expectation was that every at-risk student would be motivated by long term relations with key teachers, by opportunities to pursue personal interests in focal fields (art, health, electronics, business, architecture, journalism), and that academy partnerships with business enterprises would provide guidance and inspiration from the community. In addition, as students in the comprehensive high school, they also took courses in physical education, ROTC, foreign languages, music, drama, and advanced placement college-level subjects. They had options as well to participate in organized extracurricular activities that included a wide variety of competitive sports.

Under a less is more policy – no matrix – implementation of the Media Academy and those that followed was neither tightly controlled nor systematically executed, but notable success was achieved for the first four that were established.

By the time wall-to-wall academies were in place their quality varied from one to another, but even the best of them could not rescue students who were only semi-literate when they arrived from failing elementary and middle schools. On formal assessment by the State Board of Education, Fremont High and its academies were classified as underperforming because the drop-out rate for the school as a whole was high and scholastic achievement was low. Even an excellent academy was not adequate to compensate for the anomic cultural labyrinth in which the children of East Oakland were entangled.

# The New Small Schools Policy of 2001

As a measure of desperation and determination to turn failure into success, the new district policy written into law in 2001 authorized a revolutionary dissolution of large high schools and the creation of small autonomous schools as replacements. Ironically, the new initiative essentially reaffirmed the academy model for small learning communities, mainly adding only the need for complete autonomy and better financing. It also advocated school-wide college preparatory commitments. The educational goal of every new small high school was to qualify all graduates to meet college entrance requirements. That goal previously worked for about ten percent of Fremont students by means of tracking. What could be done to make it work for every student?

Empowering autonomous high schools, a less is more policy, showed promise. But with misguided zeal, a matrix approach to implementation diverted the promise of success into a three-year quagmire. It might have been anticipated. When the idealism of a well-intentioned policy is implemented it almost inevitably contorts in response to pragmatic realities. In the words of Michael Fullan, "Those skilled in change are appreciative of its semi-unpredictable and volatile character" (1994: 12).

The matrix that was put in place to rescue Fremont High School was itself transformed into a labyrinth that discouraged and confused teachers and administrators for three years until finally the Fremont Federation of High Schools was born. And the labyrinth persisted. The seven neonate schools varied from one another in significant ways. On emerging from the womb it became clear they were not all equally endowed for rapid educational success. A promising innovative policy was not the same as a prediction of success.

• **Life** was privileged with the most autonomy in its establishment and with the best financial support when it became autonomous in the fall of 2001. It was the only new school permitted by the teachers union to select staff with complete freedom. It was able to move into its own nicely renovated building whereas the others had to make do with existing facilities on the old Fremont campus. It was well funded by outside grants additional to district funds. Laura Flaxman, principal for the first two years, concluded at the end of 2004, its third year of existence, "Life has been able to improve school culture and academic outcomes in ways that so far have eluded the other new Fremont Schools" (Flaxman 2004).

On the negative side, Life students could no longer effectively access the Fremont library, cafeteria, auditorium, gymnasium, and after-school student services programs, even though they were available to them in principle. Life students were removed from the music and excitement of spirit activities on the plaza. They no longer thought of themselves as Fremont Tigers.

Teachers, for their part, suffered from staff burnout. Beginning each day before first period, working through the lunch period, and continuing to work with students in the late afternoon required a level of enthusiasm and commitment that for some proved difficult to maintain after the first year or two, so they left.

• **YES (Youth Empowerment School)** benefited enormously by beginning with only a 9th grade class. Its school culture evolved with new freshmen, with a small total number of enrollees, and with a small initial staff of teachers motivated to get involved. YES offered the opportunity to create a school culture without the handicap of a history of academic failure and misbehavior. The school was minimally constrained by prior commitments or expectations. Yet, because the principal and core teachers had taught in Fremont academies before cutting loose, and because they had participated in the implementation program, they were experienced enough to strike out on their own.

Laura Flaxman singled YES out for special mention at the end of the first Federation year. "At the Youth Empowerment School, Principal

Maureen Benson has implemented many innovative structures and worked hard to create a positive culture and sense of community. Attendance is up and disciplinary incidents are lower than the district average. Parents are very involved in the daily life of the school; more than thirty signed up to be on the hiring committee for the next year.

"While the cultural changes are taking hold, shifts toward academic excellence aren't happening as quickly, and some students complain that the school is too easy and their teachers' expectations of them are too low. Hopes are high though that as the school grows, doubling the number of students and staff and moving to another campus, they will be better able to implement their vision of community-based, project-based learning and see gains in student achievement" (Flaxman 2004).

As was the case for Life, moving to a new campus had a downside. YES students, too, were removed from the enthusiasms of spirited activities on the plaza. They also could no longer access the Fremont library, cafeteria, and after-school shared services programs. True, they did inherit a basic physical education playground and structure. The campus had previously served a failing elementary school that was removed, but in its place the campus hosted a start-up middle school as co-tenant with YES. With older inner-city youth on the campus the two schools had to respond to complaints in the neighborhood that students were involved in local vandalism and thievery. The middle school was closed down by the District at the end of the 2006-07 school year.

## From Fremont High Principal to Campus Council

During the 2002-03 pilot year (Stage 3A), the main work of the Site Management Team for Fremont High was to establish procedures and preliminary agreements for how campus-wide governance would be coordinated to produce results for six independent schools after the principal of Fremont High School was removed and the Fremont

Federation was established. In August of 2003, with the Federation finally in place, the site management team was reincarnated as the Campus Council.

The Council was a small body made up only of the principals plus two support personnel, the one a non-voting BayCES coach who served as meeting facilitator and the other, also non-voting, an employed campus manager with oversight responsibilities for the maintenance and use of shared Federation properties, a weak and ineffectual substitute for the former Principal of Fremont High School, who was transferred to duties elsewhere in the district. In place of the former principal as institutional leader, the committee of six principals was empowered to provide campus-wide leadership. In retrospect, they should never have expected clear and decisive leadership from a hydra of six co-equal decision-makers.

Enormous importance was attached to accomplishing all of their tasks within the time constraints of meeting for a single one-hour-and-a-half period each week, so they structured meetings very tightly in the new conversational style. The responsibility of the BayCES facilitator was to make sure that every voice was heard and that the principals adhered to an agenda of strict time limits monitored by a ticking clock. The campus manager served as notetaker. A labyrinth was compelled to function as if it were a matrix.

Taylorism, the rationalization of time and movement in smokestack factories that dehumanized manual labor for earlier generations, was reincarnated in these meetings for administrative work, but rather than dehumanize, it empowered those who submitted to the new regimen. One unanticipated dehumanizing consequence, however, was that for strict time constraints to be enforced, council principals found themselves compelled to exclude the rest of the Federation community, except by specific invitation.

External service providers meeting as a group explicitly decried this practice, as noted in minutes for their meeting of February 6, 2004. "There is much concern about the decisions being made at

Campus Council without any input from students, parents or staff. Communication with Fremont Federation principals is difficult. . . . It was suggested that Campus Council provide an open forum for comments by community members, staff, parents and students so that different perspectives are heard."

Maureen Benson, Principal of YES, responded on behalf of the Council. "I know that it has been six times as difficult this year to communicate with the principals, and I for one appreciate your patience and support as we all learn how to work alone and together to serve our kids the best we can. . . . We encourage community participation and the bringing of issues to our group. We are just working through hammering out the most effective processes for us to all maintain regular communications."

After half a year of not being able to observe a council meeting directly, Principal Schmookler of Media arranged for me to sit in on a meeting as a special favor, and that was the only opportunity I had to see for myself how business was conducted. It was apparent that the council constituted an inner sanctum that practiced a form of autocratic control at odds with "the belief [of small school advocates] that those who are most affected by decisions ought to play a significant role in making those decisions" (Johnson, et al, 2002: 191).

However, in no way did the Campus Council function as a unified board of directors in which all power-holders shared common goals. On the contrary, meeting Federation needs, many of which required contributed funding from each school for shared Federation purposes, often faced principals with dilemmas of balancing Federation needs against those of their individual schools. A principal could have good reasons for wanting to protect role autonomy against control by others. Those contradictions resulted in near gridlock at times. A special education teacher who did not attend Council meetings opined, "when the six principals meet they each have separate agendas." In another conversation, a science teacher told me "the campus as a whole is out of control." A math teacher confided, "the principals can't agree. They work against each other. . . . There is confusion and frustration with no [effective] central administration." One of the six principals told me she thought they would be much better off if they didn't have to share facilities with the other schools. Principal Maureen Benson said the same and added that she hoped to move her Youth Empowerment School to a different site, which she did at the end of their first year in 2004. YES relocated to a campus five miles distant, which released them from the frustrations and intrusions of Campus Council oversight.

## Five New High Schools on the Old Campus

**Mandela** began with grades 9 and 10, and thus with approximately 200 instead of 400 students. Although they did not have the advantage YES enjoyed of beginning with students who had no earlier shared history in the failed culture of Fremont High, they did enjoy the benefits of beginning on a smaller scale.

The disadvantage was that the wing of the main building that would eventually be solely theirs and fully isolatable had to be shared during the first year. Two rooms were temporarily assigned to Architecture teachers and their students. That arrangement contributed to security problems for both schools because it permitted and required students to move between campuses and authority spheres. History teacher Craig Gordon summed up his evaluation of the first two years. "Despite the struggles and uncertainties, as my small school, Mandela High, nears the end of its second year, I can attest to amazing efforts by staff, students, and parents to create a functional and caring learning community. I feel more connected with the student body than I ever did in a large school. And despite early misgivings, most students seem to have grown attached to our school. But so far we have not seen much evidence of significant academic gains. Most of the old issues of low student achievement, behavioral problems, and teacher burnout persist" (Gordon 2005).

**Architecture,** like Life and Media, was a highly successful academy, and also like them it began with all four grades in place. The leadership aggressively enrolled many of the best students, referred to as "creaming" by other Foundation personnel. It developed a challenging college preparatory program. The strong achievement culture of the Architecture Academy carried over into the new school. In adapting to Campus Council needs and demands, Architecture had the advantage of being located in well-demarked territory located on the periphery of the campus as a whole.

Circumstances were less than ideal, however. Their campus consisted of old portables that did not fully meet their needs for space, which is why they were given temporary access to classrooms on the Mandela campus. Because the portables were lined up like boxcars in a railroad yard, separated only by narrow pathways, the atmosphere was claustrophobic. To overcome that, the school took advantage of classes in carpentry to make a student project out of constructing a raised platform that eventually was expected to serve as a place where students could hang out.

**Fremont in Transition** survived as a vestige of the failed business academy and the parent comprehensive school as a whole. It enrolled 11th and 12th grade students who chose not to move into any of the new small high schools. As planned from the start, it ceased to exist when the last FIT students graduated in 2005.

**Robeson,** like Architecture and Media, began with all four grades in place. They were assigned an upper wing of the main building that constituted a well-demarcated campus. By leaving only the main entrance open for arrivals, and by stationing a uniformed security person where the short entrance corridor right-angled with the main hallway, they created a secure campus. To take pride in their school and to make it an icon of the arts they painted and decorated.

The new small school was challenged when the Art Academy co-directors followed through on their threat to retire as soon as the Academy was reconstituted as an autonomous school. For the start-up year a first principal was hired from elsewhere in the District who had not participated in the three years of implementation and was unprepared for all of the transitional challenges. The most discouraging challenge for Robeson, moreover, was to attempt to offer a full curriculum in visual and performing arts without the necessary financial resources. They needed more music, art, drama, and dance teachers, equipment, and facilities than they could afford, since they also had to staff general education and basic college preparatory courses as did every other school. The District came down hard on them. Beginning in the fall of 2010 they were ordered not to admit new freshman ever again. Like Fremont in Transition before them, as each year graduates its current senior class Robeson is destined to fade away. It is scheduled to totally disappear in June of 2014.

**Media** was my observational platform for the design, implementation, and assessment of the small school policy after 1999. Framed as a case study based on "micro-level perspectives with an analysis of the historical and structural conditions" (Kenny 2006: 26), what I experienced at Media does not provide a basis for generalization. Remember, there is a trade-off involved in this documentation. In contrast to the big picture achieved by survey research, autoethnography necessarily sacrifices the benefits of an overview for the insights of a depth analysis (Coleman 1986: 1313-1316). What can get lost in quantitative research is what qualitative research reveals about each small school as unique in significant ways. Yes, less is more. Given the contrasting histories of each of the seven new schools, Media can only incompletely represent how the Fremont transformation unfolded. That being the case, after two years as a small college preparatory school, Media can be said to still be struggling to become a successful college preparatory school. In results published in 2009, Media ranked in the bottom ten percent of

Bay Area schools on the annual Academic Performance Index, the API. No other Federation school ranked that low, but on the other hand, not a single one ranked in the top ten percent (*San Francisco Chronicle,* May 22, 2009: A12).

## Assessment Based on Ten Features

When I showed up for the inaugural registration of Federation students in the fall of 2003 I paused on my way to ask Michael Jackson how it was going. "It's a mess," he glumly announced. "They still run it like a large high school, so people are standing in a long line, waiting."

I walked through a rear door to see for myself and to my surprise encountered the opposite of restless people trapped in line. I saw registration tables with nothing happening except for a few teachers sitting and chatting quietly. However, when I turned to look toward the front end of the building I saw what Mike called a disaster, a crowd of people bunched up at the head of a line that stretched out through the door and beyond, snaking uphill almost to the entrance gate on 47th Avenue.

The problem was that everyone had to get past a clerk at the first table who was laboriously thumbing through lists of students to identify the occasional one who might not have returned a textbook at the end of last year. Finally, someone with an authoritative voice walked up the line telling people that if they didn't have textbooks to return they could proceed immediately to the tables. With that the traffic jam broke up and students with their parents moved on to register. Media had three tables that soon got busy, so it wasn't a total mess, just a temporary glitch.

I wandered around to see how the other schools were doing. Fulton Brinkley, one of the new principals, asked my size and handed over a green and yellow (think "gold") tee shirt emblazoned with a large tiger and six stars (think six new schools) above prominent yellow lettering that read,

---

**FREMONT FEDERATION
OF
COLLEGE PREPARATORY HIGH SCHOOLS
2003-2004**

**OAKLAND UNIFIED SCHOOL DISTRICT
BAY AREA COALITION OF EQUITABLE SCHOOLS**

**SMALL HIGH SCHOOLS, BIG RESULTS**

---

At long last the splintering apart of Fremont had become a reality, and the old comprehensive high school was now divided into six separated campuses. For the Federation as a whole, most of the students were Latino and African American (48 and 30 percent for a total of 78 percent). The third largest ethnic category was Asian/Pacific Islander (18 percent) with just a few categorized as non-Hispanic white (2 percent) and "other" (2 percent).

Directors of the Bill and Melinda Gates Foundation inspired and funded the Bay Area Coalition for Equitable Schools (BayCES), which in turn, through the Oakland Unified School District (OUSD), and in alliance with the Oakland Community Organizations (OCO), spearheaded the conversion of Fremont High into small schools. The tee shirts worn by faculty and staff on registration day explicitly acknowledged the Bay Area Coalition of Equitable Schools as a school identifier equal in emphasis with the Oakland Unified School District.

As part of furnishing many kinds of valuable backup support, BayCES provided the redesign leadership at Fremont High with a treasure chest – it was literally a large chest, albeit constructed of un-pirate-like heavy cardboard – containing a valuable library of binders and books containing helpful research findings, theoretical disquisitions, and how-to-do-it manuals. One monograph that proved to have been particularly influential at Fremont High was published as *Ten Features of Good Small Schools* (Darling-Hammond, 2002). Professor Darling-Hammond personally came to Oakland to meet with Fremont High leaders during the implementation phase. Because Ten Features gave direction to deliberations during the three years of planning they are well-suited now to serve as guidelines for assessment of the first two years of Media Academy High School, as it was often called.

The Gates Foundation also provided primary support for the National High School Alliance (NHSA), which brings me to an important point. NHSA is a partnership of national organizations dedicated to "fostering high academic achievement." The Alliance identified six core principles, everyone of which "must be addressed" if failing high schools are to be salvaged.

The Six Core Principles and the Ten Features for the most part describe the same innovations but sort them out differently. In some ways they differ. Thus, real-world career experience for students and "communities of practice" for teachers are high-lighted in the Core Principles but missing from the Ten Features. Conversely, a strong emphasis in the Ten Features on teaching *Habits of Mind* and on multicultural and anti-racist teaching is absent from the Core Principles. Overall, however, the two approaches are congruous. Therefore, for assessment purposes, I have enhanced my abbreviated presentation of the Ten Features with certain strategies emphasized in the Principles. All of the ten features and six core principles were incorporated into the design of Media.

**(1) Personalization.** In reconstituting itself as an autonomous small school, Media further enhanced the small personalized learning environment it experienced as an academy by bringing all teachers and staff together on their campus archipelago. Implementation was incomplete, however. For a teacher to work more closely with students, the daily pupil load needed to be reduced to 40 students, or no more than 80. Yet daily student encounters remained at about 130 to 150, so personal involvements were inevitably truncated. Assessment: a commitment not yet fully implemented.

**(2) Continuous Relationships.** According to plan, personalization would be further enhanced by the practice of looping (enrolling students in classes that a teacher would work with for at least two years). Looping was recommended but incompletely achieved.

As an important feature and principle, a small group of 15 or 20 students were supposed to meet daily in a kind of home-room with a teacher who would remain with them on a looping schedule. Usually called an advisory, this arrangement was meant to ensure that every student would be closely mentored in an enduring relationship with an adult. Advisories were designed to provide a time and place for the mentor to get feedback from individual students on how they were doing on a day-to-day basis, for counseling, for tutoring, and above all, for confronting problems as soon as they cropped up. Unfortunately, advisories were not integrated into the schedule during the first two years. Assessment: a commitment not yet implemented.

**(3) High Standards and Performance-Based Assessment.** It was recommended as a cross-curricular practice that all teachers should do their part to inculcate a version of *Habits of Mind* first developed by Deborah Meier and the teachers she worked with (1995). "[T]hese habits may require students continuously to weigh and use evidence, address multiple perspectives, make connections among ideas, speculate on alternatives, and assess the value of the idea they have studied, as well as to present their ideas clearly and with appropriate use of conventions" (Darling-Hammond, 2002: 14). In a comparable way, a core principle emphasized the importance of acquiring skills and experience in "problem-solving, higher-order thinking, and the capacity to construct, rather than merely reproducing [*sic*] knowledge" (NHSA, 2005: 5, 9).

Unfortunately, even excellent teachers cannot succeed in teaching habits of mind (higher order thinking) if they are working with students who are not motivated; who simply don't care enough to pay attention or do homework, as was the case for most Media students. "They don't do homework."

One main strategy for improving success with low-performers is for teachers to confer regularly and collaborate on shared strategies. To that end, a shared conference period is not a luxury; it is a necessity (NHSA, 2005: 6). Yet it was not possible to put in place because the bell schedule, which sounded loudly throughout the whole campus, had to be agreed upon by all of the principals and had to accommodate a Federation-wide schedule, including physical education classes and ROTC activities. (Although the department structure as such was dismantled the Department of Physical Education and the ROTC persisted as stand-alone Federation services.)

Performance-based assessment is the requirement that all courses should contribute to "a rigorous, standards-based core academic curriculum," (NHSA 2005: 6), including "portfolios of student work that demonstrate in-depth study through research papers, scientific experiments, mathematical models, literary critiques and analyses, arts performances, and so on," (Darling-Hammond, 2002: 16). It was only minimally implemented, mostly in the form of senior projects.

Media committed itself to implement performance-based measures, but was impeded by not being able "to ensure that state-level policies for standards and accountability do not constrain," specifically, as it happened, by pressure to orient teaching to the demands of standardized tests that were imposed as district, state, and federal requirements (NHSA, 2005: 9). "Teaching to the test" left little time and energy for inquiry-based learning.

This core principle also emphasizes the need to, "Provide accelerated learning opportunities" (NHSA 2005: 9). Unfortunately, resources for staffing advanced placement courses fell victim to the financial limitations of small school budgets and the management shortcomings of the Fremont Federation Campus Council. Even so, Media did offer advanced placement classes in U. S. History, English and, beginning in year two, in calculus. (It was difficult to put calculus in place because very few students in the small school were qualified to enroll). Assessment: a commitment not yet fully implemented.

**(4) Authentic Curriculum.** This feature "engages students and challenges them to understand concepts deeply, find and integrate information, assemble evidence, weigh ideas, and develop skills of analysis and expression" (Darling-Hammond, 2002: 20; note the resemblance to Feature Nr. 3 and Core Principle Nr. 6 as well as to Theodore Sizer's less is more principle). Because most students do not complete homework and are slow to invest themselves in independent assignments, this effort to engage students remained superficial and was rarely attained. It was further undermined in math and English classes in which teachers were under pressure to drill students in test-taking skills.

An authentic curriculum involves "active learning in real-word contexts" (Darling-Hammond, 2002: 20). "Academic engagement is strengthened when educators and students co-construct learning experiences that are relevant to economic, social, and political dynamics." In accord with that principle, Media students were urged to consider the possibility of pursuing real-world careers in publishing, radio broadcasting, and television programming, even though many enrolled in the school who indicated no interest in communication of any kind. Some journalism students gained relevant hands-on experience by editing and writing for *The Green and Gold* and *Teenager Magazine*. Other students produced radio programs or video-documentaries. Adult professionals contributed through partnerships that connected the school with relevant community enterprises (newspaper publishers as well as radio and TV stations). Assessment: a commitment not yet fully implemented.

**(5) Adaptive Pedagogy.** To some extent teachers did employ multiple instructional strategies "ranging from whole class lecture and recitation to guided inquiry, small group work, discussions, independent work, projects, experiments, book and internet research." Scaffolding as a teaching strategy that leads "students through a step-by-step process, from framing a question to finding sources to taking notes to developing a thesis to outlining to writing and editing" was consciously implemented (Darling-Hammond, 2002: 27, 28). However, it was unrealistic to expect "educators and students [to] co-construct learning experiences," given a culture of the classroom as it was at that time (NHSA, 2005: 5).

Adaptive pedagogy includes the provision of extra support, especially supervised after-school and Saturday catch-up periods and volunteer tutors. To this end, Media consistently funded Saturday school.

As of June, 2005, Media had not yet succeeded in fully overcoming language and other skill deficiencies. Many students were weak in vocabulary, punctuation, spelling, grammar, and composition. School projects such as writing articles for the *Green and Gold* and *Teenager Magazine*, were often poorly done, falling far short of the quality of writing that characterized the *Flame* (the school yearbook) and the *Green and Gold* a century earlier. It should be noted that in 2004-05, over half (53.7%) of 9th graders got D's or F's in English 1. The D/F rate fell to 22.7 percent in English 2, suggesting that by the second year some 9th graders had dropped out and others had improved (Schmookler, 2006: 39). Assessment: a commitment not yet fully implemented.

**(6) Multicultural and Anti-Racist Teaching.** A first requirement for success is to counteract "the effect of low expectations," and this was achieved by advocating a policy based on the belief that every child can succeed. Although negative stereotypes of racism were explicitly minimized in classrooms, many students evidently struggled with the negative self-concepts that characterize a racist world. They also struggled with what Darling-Hammond refers to as "the effect of discrimination," including "fewer books, materials, and equipment, and more dilapidated facilities" (2002: 32).

Multicultural awareness was enhanced by "subtle and explicit norms and mores." The strategy of eliminating academic tracking was explicitly implemented. The curriculum included a multicultural studies program for the 9th grade and American History courses that highlighted racial, ethnic, and gender discrimination.

It was certainly true that on breaks for lunch and after school students tended to socialize in racial and ethnic clusters. They did the same when they were permitted to select seats in classrooms. Nevertheless, when class-work, athletics, and after-school activities required interacting across racial and ethnic lines, students typically did so easily and without apparent distress. Although ethnically based gang culture constituted a neighborhood reality, potential hostilities were mitigated by the tendency of violent youth to be truant. Assessment: a commitment substantially implemented.

**(7) Knowledgeable and Skilled Teachers.** In her assessment of the new small schools that replaced Fremont High, Laura Flaxman observed, "Successful conversions, indeed successful schools, require that the quality of teaching and learning be extremely high. Significant changes in student learning cannot be effected without a dramatic shift in teaching; therefore excellent teaching is always at the heart of an excellent school." "As for changing the pedagogy in the new schools," she reported specifically for Media, "Ben Schmookler, principal of the Media College Preparatory School, [states], 'In my experience, it's been more difficult to get experienced teachers to teach new pedagogies, while new teachers, because of their lack of experience, are reaching out to get new ideas and support for their classroom practices'" (Flaxman 2004).

The No Child Left Behind Act requires that every class be taught by a "fully qualified teacher." Although fully certified teachers were hard to recruit, by 2004-05, 15 of the 18 staff teachers were fully credentialed and the remaining three were working toward certification. In 2005 Michael Jackson earned National Board Certification. None were teaching outside of their subject areas and none were employed on the basis of emergency permits or waivers.

However, as Craig Gordon forcefully argued, drawing on a statement from the Oakland Education Association, "real reform is inseparable from a campaign for full educational funding . . . this means 'schools with the resources to offer full programs and to provide educators with respect, reasonable workloads, small classes, and adequate support, materials, facilities, and time to plan lessons *and* to run the school. Teacher teams will be empowered only [if they have] enough time during the workday to discuss and make wise policies'" (Gordon, 2005, emphasis in the original). Assessment: a commitment partially implemented.

**(8) Collaborative Planning and Professional Development.** Teachers need to be experts in three domains: subject matter, the needs of diverse learners, and how students learn (Darling-Hammond, 2002: 38). To become accomplished in those areas they need "ongoing, job-embedded professional development and support" (NHSA, 2005: 6; see Feature 7).

At one of the evening II/USP workshops in 2001, John Browne commented as an aside to us attendees that teachers need to think of themselves as "a professional learning community." He wanted us to "be up-to-date on the current concept at play" (see DuFour & Eaker, 1998; Buffum & Hinman, 2006). Core Principle Three emphasizes "communities of practice" as helping to "transform school culture by providing ongoing, job-embedded professional development and support, which teachers need to learn and apply new practices, and by fostering a sense of collective responsibility for all students' achievement" (NHSA, 2005: 6; see Feature Nr. 7).

To this end, weekly workshops were organized to teach new skills. For a teacher to be fully expert requires moving beyond the old practice of lecturing to passive students behind closed doors. Contemporary inquiry-based methods require new interactive and communicative skills. Changing old habits was initiated, but will take more time.

It was agreed that team teaching is highly desirable. Class periods lengthened by block scheduling (changing to 90 minute periods) is the recommended way to arrange for two teachers to co-teach without the need for additional hires. Unfortunately, that kind of calendar change could not be implemented because of the campus-wide bell schedule.

Leaders at all levels must ensure that quality resources are available to every student on an equitable basis. Their single most important resource is the faculty. To improve the professional quality of teachers, some national leaders recommend an increase of 50 percent in teacher salaries as soon as possible (*Education Week*, July 19, 2006). Chaconas under-stood that five years earlier when he increased salaries in Oakland by 24 percent. Unfortunately, to improve resources in that way he bankrupted the district, because California public schools are grossly under-funded. With bankruptcy Oakland teachers lost what they had gained and they have been struggling ever since to recoup. Assessment: a commitment not yet fully implemented.

**(9) Family and Community Connections**. It is important to collaborate with families because "differences between the norms and expectations of home and school can lead to serious disjunctures that cause students to fail in school" (Darling-Hammond, 2002: 46). Media was weak in implementing this feature, including capabilities in communicating with families in their primary languages. Advisory teachers were supposed to "call home frequently and meet with students' parents several times a year to strengthen relationships with families. . . ." (Darling-Hammond, 2002: 12; see Feature Nr. 2). Follow through on that strategy was spotty at best, as documented in questions addressed to teachers (Schmookler, 2006: 35).

| 2003-04 | Strongly Agree or Agree | 2004-05 |
|---|---|---|
| | Parents receive academic information about their children every month | |
| 30% | | 30% |
| | Parents' ideas have influenced school policies and practices | |
| 20% | | 8% |
| | Parents regularly participate in school leadership activities | |
| 0% | | 0% |

Students ought to "participate in decision-making that affects their [school] and [community]" (NHSA, 2005: 8), but the effort to "co-construct" the school never got off the ground. Still to be accomplished is to organize an active and committed school site council that fully involves parents and students as influential members.

Media leaders need better collaboration with community leaders. Recommended strategies include establishing partnerships, such as those that Media High School established with the city's leading newspaper, the *Oakland Tribune*. Another recommended strategy is to work with civic organizations such as the Oakland Community Organizations and BayCES, which Media has done.

The loose confederation of student service organizations known as the Fremont Collaborative (Unity Center) constitutes a potential resource for youth who want to be as involved as is possible. The Collaborative is especially committed to one major goal under Core Principle Five, which is to "organize and build youth capacity to exercise leadership."

As for "problem-solving, higher-order thinking, and the capacity to construct, rather than merely reproducing knowledge" (see Features

Nr. 3 and Nr. 4 above), I confess to serious pessimism about meeting that standard simply by creating a small school and emphasizing project-based programs designed to get "educators and students [to] co-construct learning experiences." That kind of teaching cannot be effective unless dominant peer, family, and community cultures modify values and attitudes that undermine motivation. Teachers do not in themselves possess enough cultural power to overcome those cultural barriers. Assessment: a commitment not adequately implemented.

**(10) Democratic decision-making.** An important strategy explicit in this feature is to "foster distributed leadership" as a part of developing professional learning communities (NHSA, 2005: 7). Although Media employed both a principal and a director, the extent of distributed leadership remained minimal. Parents, in particular, were not organized to maximize their input (See Feature Nr. 9).

Student, parent and teacher conversations were needed to develop a strong consensus on the values that inspire the curriculum and give it coherence. "Students [should] also lead regular town-hall meetings and participate on school-wide committees" (Darling-Hammond, 2002: 53). As integral to this goal, more needed to be accomplished in training students in leadership skills and civic engagement. To that end, the Federation failed to provide adequate support for Collaborative leadership programs. Assessment: a commitment not implemented.

## Summary: Assessment and Re-Assessment

During the first two years of the Fremont Federation, Media faculty, staff, and students committed themselves to a difficult transformation process. The inability of Media to fully implement the Ten Features and Six Core Principles, in spite of a demonstrated willingness to try as hard as they could, is consistent with what we know of the new small school movement throughout the nation, which recently led Stephen Fink and Max Silverman to conclude, "The promise of converting comprehensive high schools into small schools that better serve their students has gone largely unfulfilled" (2007: 29).

That larger reality to the contrary, measures of student achievement at Media High did improve in modest ways, as documented in a self-study submitted to the Western Association of Schools and Colleges (WASC) at the end of the second year (Schmookler, 2006). Although fewer than 45 percent of those who sat for the California High School Exit Exam (CAHSEE) achieved passing scores in English and math, the trend was upwards (Schmookler, 2006: 6).

|  | 2004 | 2005 |
|--|------|------|
| English | 39% | 44% |
| Math | 30% | 41% |

And what was the explicit goal for success? It was to prepare "all students for college, careers, and active civic participation," which is to say, for "successful post-secondary transitions" (NHSA, 2005: 2, 4). During those first two years, when it was still not required to pass the exit exam in order to graduate, it is notable that the graduation rate improved from 72 percent in 2003-04 to 80 percent in 2004-05 (Schmookler, 2006: 42). Furthermore, of 44 who graduated in June, 2005, 4 (9%) were admitted to the University of California system, 9 (20%) to the California State University system, and 27 (61%) to community colleges for a total of 90 percent of the graduating class qualified to enroll in college (Schmookler, 2006: 42).

Overall implementation was slow and in many ways discouraging, but commitment held strong. Patricia Wasley and Richard Lear have observed that, "The culture of small schools typically revolves around hard work, high aspirations, respect for others, and the expectation that all students will succeed" (2001: 24). Assessment: If we take that statement as basis for assessment, the faculty, staff, and leadership completed the first two years in an exemplary way. Looking to the future, further improvement can be expected, but it will not be easy.

## The Labyrinth and Teachers at the School Level

Cultural complexity was the confounding variable in planning for success at Fremont High. The school was located in the domain of complexity. It was trapped in a labyrinth with no Theseus string to lead to an exit. The small school policy can be thought of as a plan for how to improve the basic institutional culture of a specific school, culture being "an intricate system of claims about how to understand the world and act in it," (Perin, 2005: xii), or more simply, as "conventional understandings" accepted by all members of the community (Bidney,1967: 24). But Media culture was not at all that simple, because those definitions, stuck in the domain of homogeneity, do not factor in cultural complexity. Multiple stakeholders were involved and they were motivated by diverse and often incompatible claims about how to understand the institution and act in it.

Teachers functioned within one intricate set of understandings about how to act, that is, about how and what to teach. What is impressive about a culture in the guise of a policy is that it moves beyond describing what is, in order to plan what might be. The small school policy challenged the inherited pedagogic culture of a school such as Fremont High. It proposed a normative policy that advocated higher levels of educational attainment for every student and a technical policy that indicated how new norms could be attained. It was flawed on both normative and technical grounds because it did not adequately accommodate cultural complexity.

Not every teacher conformed to the ideal culture of the small school movement. A regularity universally observed, as Lawrence Hirschfeld has written, is that, "At any given moment the cultural environment which an individual inhabits is . . . comprised of multiple, contesting, competing subcultural environments" (2002: 615). Variable configurations of teacher culture resulted in some teachers helping to advance new policy objectives while others held back.

The policy itself was a tool kit that the leadership implemented in varying configurations. Although shot through with shared understandings, the six core principles and the ten features of good small schools taken together present a "fragmented, fluid, noisy and negotiable" culture of intent, of technical policies that fit classificatory boxes only by tearing apart a holistic reality and crushing it, nearly lifeless, into a filing cabinet of axiomatic folders and of self-defeating double binds, into a matrix.

For example, socioeconomic classes differed dramatically from one another in their shared understandings. American teachers traditionally teach values, attitudes, behaviors and goals inherent in white middle-class culture. Discordance with the laboring-class culture of many students and their families has been implicated in the high dropout rates that have characterized Fremont from the day it was founded in 1905. Class lines in East Oakland are even more dramatically diverse now, because the gap between the "haves" and the "have-nots" has deepened into a cultural chasm.

In addition to the poverty versus well-to-do gap, teachers and families tend to differ by race and ethnicity. Awareness of the value for students of having teachers with their own cultural backgrounds encouraged valiant efforts to hire non-white, non-mainstream faculty, but in 2004-05, when 98 percent of Media enrollees were students of color, 72 percent of the faculty were white (Schmookler, 2006: 44).

Ethnic cultures themselves differ significantly as Latino, African American, Asian and others. Polls indicate that Mexican American parents, for example, place a high value on education, but also on the importance of family ties. A frequent problem at Fremont Federation schools is that some Latino students are absent at times in order to provide infant care for younger siblings, to serve as translators for monolingual parents, or for a couple of weeks in the winter to return to Mexico with their families to celebrate the Christmas holidays. Faced with competing school and family values, Latino families struggle "to negotiate their own priorities with those of two or more cultures" (Poplin & Weeres, 1992: 30).

Whether for success or for failure, family, peer, and community cultures are surely implicated. Dr. Bill Cosby, who earned a doctorate in education while at the height of his acting career, argues bravely for an interpretation of educational failure that identifies black family culture as at fault in the failures of black boys and men (Clarence Page, 2006). It is a brave argument, because some African Americans, including sociologist and educator Edward Rhymes, "respectfully disagree." Rhymes insists that "all communities are in crisis," including African American but not limited to them (2004). National Public Radio Senior News Analyst Juan Williams is among those who respectfully agree with Cosby, targeting the contemporary "culture of failure" with a reminder that in the past, values of self-help, strong families, and belief in God empowered oppressed generations to survive under slavery and to succeed in the civil rights movement (Page, 2006).

Former Congressman Ron Dellums, elected Mayor of Oakland in 2006, has said the same (Fulbright, 2006), as has journalist Clarence Page, noting that "Williams, like Cosby, also calls on the black middle class, burdened as we may be by our struggles for upward mobility against institutional racism, real or perceived, to reach back through mentoring and other support to help break the culture of poverty" (Page, 2006). More recently, journalist Cynthia Tucker added that Bill Cosby "isn't the pariah in black America that his critics would have you believe. Quiet as it's kept, his emphasis on academic excellence, standard English and old-fashioned good manners is widely accepted. Those values are the subject of countless parental lectures in black middle-class homes" (2007).

Perhaps the most significant fault lines are those of diverse peer cultures, all of which cut across adult worlds and some of which are limited to cliques, genders, interest groups (including gangs or athletic teams), and ethnic coteries.

What is common for many Fremont students is their disengagement from education and a capacity for just "chilling out," being present in body but not in mind, being disruptive rather than engaged. Ted Sizer, asserting the benefits of small schools, reminds us that "it is all too easy to forget both the intense dailiness of schools – the urgency of the immediacies found in any swirl of adolescents – and the senselessness of the regimens that most students follow" (1997: xi). In spite of the "dailiness of schools," many Asian students succeeded well in their studies at the Fremont Federation. Latino and African American students had the least success. As Antoine Garibaldi and Melinda Bartley point out, if they do not drop out of school, they tend to be "pushed out" by means of suspensions and expulsions (1989: 227).

Peer culture is missing or merely implied in the cited commentaries of Cosby, Rhymes, Dellums, and Coleman, but it is effectively targeted by a controversial black politician, Rev. Al Sharpton, who says, "We have got to get out of this gangster mentality, acting as if gangsterism and blackness are synonymous." He asserts that, "we have allowed a whole generation of young people to feel that if they're focused, they're not black enough. If they speak well and act well, they're acting white, and there's nothing more racist than that."

I lifted that challenging observation from one of my favorite columnists, Chip Johnson, an African American who reports regularly on Oakland and agrees with Sharpton on that particular point. According to Johnson, "Young black men, many of them without guidance or role models in their lives, are slipping from society's grasp faster than we can catch them. But it's particularly galling to see corporate America cashing in on the carnage." By corporate America, Johnson means "the record and fashion industries, and all the other companies promoting gangster-like behavior. . . ." (Johnson, 2006).

*Robert Anderson*

# Cultural Complexity at the Urban Level

What is missing in most policy analyses relating to small schools, and specifically in the small schools policy adopted by the Oakland Board of Education, is an aggressive, comprehensive, and feasible plan to eliminate the root cause of school failure in Oakland. Beginning in the 1960s, the school culture of Fremont High was dragged down by a socioeconomic catastrophe, a political, economic, and demographic upheaval that installed massive unemployment, devastating poverty, and racist cultural attitudes and practices in the city.

Echoing Illich and Myrdal, sociological research findings by James Coleman minimized the extent to which new technical policies for schools have the capacity to turn that kind of urban failure into success. Coleman concluded that the inadequacies of schools were not as detrimental as "inequalities imposed on children by their home, neighborhood, and peer environment" (Coleman, et al, 1966). That finding was reaffirmed by Christopher Jencks, who demonstrated that changes in educational policy produced only minor improvements and that educational success was primarily impeded by family culture and non-school factors (Jencks, et al, 1972). In the more recent words of Richard Rothstein, "Equal opportunity requires a full menu of social, economic, and educational reforms: in employment policy, health care, housing, and civil rights enforcement, as well as in schools" (cited in Olson, 2007: 1).

Ron Dellums attributes failures broadly, as does Rhymes, to a complexity of social factors that impact all communities in crisis, including law enforcement, unemployment, and community breakdown. One in four black men in the United States today is unemployed and it is claimed that more are in prison than in college. One in four have not graduated from high school (Fulbright, 2006).

Anthony Cody, a National Board certified science teacher in the Oakland Unified School District speaks for many Oakland teachers in insisting that we need "a new definition of accountability."

No Child Left Behind posits that we have troubled schools because they have not been accountable. If we make teachers and schools pay a price for the failure of their students, they will bring those students up to speed.

But schools are NOT the only factor determining student success. Urban neighborhoods are plagued by poverty and violence and recent reports in The Chronicle show that as many as 30 percent of the children in these neighborhoods suffer from post-traumatic stress disorder. Fully 40 percent of our students are English learners, but these students must take the same tests as native English speakers. Moreover, a recent study provides strong evidence that family-based factors such as the quality of day care, the home vocabulary and the amount of time spent reading and watching television at home account for two-thirds of the difference in academic success for students. Nonetheless, NCLB holds only the schools accountable. (2008, emphasis in the original)

The Six Core Principles and Ten Features advocate ways to improve what can be accomplished in school for many young people, but not for all. The small school policy is a policy of amelioration, but it is inadequate to salvage all children. To serve the needs of all families and their children, we need a new New Deal. We need a policy that will transform a culture of unemployment and poverty into something akin to the modest but reliable socioeconomic stability that characterized Oakland at mid-century. In short, we need a new War on Poverty, a political-economic plan to make the city a site of humane revolution. East Oakland is a labyrinth in the domain of complexity. Developments in educational policy have achieved a lot, but ultimately the problems are economic and political on a city, state, and national level. Will we ever succeed in the labyrinth of cultural complexity?

# Part IV

## More is Better at Mills College
## (1998-2009)

# Chapter Eight

## Policy Design: Creating a Matrix

### More is Better as Educational Policy

The original purpose of college and university accreditation was simply "to establish that accredited institutions were what they said they were, had what they said they had, and did what they said they did in accordance with standards approved by the American academic community" (*Education Encyclopedia*, 2002). Accreditation in that less is more mode was beneficial and quite reasonable in terms of compliance requirements for Mills College faculty. It fully achieved its purpose, which was to differentiate Mills from degree-granting institutions that were not up to par. Other universities could be confident that a student coming from Mills was well educated. For many decades that policy served us well.

With the passage of time, however, the policy shifted to a more is better agenda. Certification that a college met "high standards of quality and effectiveness" became merely an establishment phase to demonstrate so-called "basic accountability." From that beginning, a future without end would require massive documentation of additional "*school improvement*" beyond what had been accepted as adequate six years earlier when last re-accredited. As a "principle of good practice" for assessing student learning, the American Association for Higher Education (AAHE) fully endorsed that revolutionary change, officially affirming for the new policy that, "Assessment is not an end in itself but a vehicle for *educational improvement*" (AAHE 1997, emphasis added). By 1997 the original standards for accreditation had expired and the new so-called "process-oriented protocols" were fully in place in all of the regional accreditation agencies in the United States.

Fully submitting to the new policy, Mills College began in 1998 to work toward satisfying what Ralph A. Wolff, Executive Director of WASC, described as the Commission's new accreditation model, which would,

(1) provide a more simple and efficient means of assuring *basic accountability*,
(2) permit self studies to be more aligned with institutional priorities,
(3) use processes that would contribute meaningfully to the *improvement of the institution*.

Wolff further wrote of "obligations for demonstrating both compliance with accrediting standards and the broader accountability of its commitment to self-reflection and *improvement*" (1998, letter to the Chancellor of UC San Diego, emphasis added). In that year Mills revised the College Mission Statement and in 1999 organized a task force to work on revising the General Education Requirements.

The concept of General Education requirements had been in place since 1985. I remember when they first appeared, thinking they were a bit of a nuisance, probably designed mainly to make sure that every academic division got its share of students ("satisfying divisional needs for equity" as one internal review acknowledged), but easy for advisors to cope with since a student only needed to sign up for any two courses in each division, and there were plenty to choose from. The policy of less is more was not seriously violated, and in itself it strikes me now as a step in the right direction.

A new addition to the General Education Requirement was introduced in 1996, which was also easy to accommodate. It merely required that every student take an interdisciplinary College Seminar taught by two faculty members, each from a different discipline. The expectation was that students would not only master content but would acquire sensitivity to how scholars from different fields approached topics in ways overlapping but different. As an example, Ann Metcalf from anthropology co-taught Tribal Cultures in Fact and Fiction with Christian Marouby from French literature. That course worked well for students, and the two professors enjoyed themselves. Unfortunately, it was expensive to pay two professors to co-teach no more than 20 students each in six or eight courses every semester, so the next time Tribal Cultures was offered Professor Metcalf taught it by herself, as she has been doing ever since.

Again, the policy of less is more was not seriously violated, and the new requirement turned out to be beneficial in a way not fully anticipated. It was academically beneficial for students in their freshman and sophomore years to have a seminar experience long before the culminating senior seminars of their college majors. It was not likely, of course, that one professor would have the skills it would require to demonstrate two different disciplinary mind-sets in action, which was the original goal of the new policy, so the actual benefit, a seminar experience, was somewhat serendipitous.

In all events, three years later the Task Force decided they had identified a hitherto unnoticed and unaddressed weakness in the distribution requirements. They acknowledged that selecting two courses in each academic division offered the benefit of providing "ample student choice in designing their academic experience," as they phrased it. They went on to conclude, however, that in practice those requirements did not reflect the college "commitment to an integrative and coherent approach to delivering a liberal arts education." They felt they had identified a gap between educational philosophy on the one hand and educational practice on the other, so they energetically searched for a better model, supported by a $400,000 grant. No one seemed to notice that in undertaking that search the College had succumbed to a more is better policy that would eventuate in the tyranny of a matrix. I failed to see the long-term implications of what otherwise struck me as a plan with some merit.

In hindsight, however, handwriting on the wall should have been apparent. The Task Force began by constructing a matrix. First they drew up a list of "content areas of learning experience" identified as ten "objectives." The objectives fell into three categories, which created the rows and columns of a matrix. Taking a "course-centered approach," every convergence of an objective with a category created a box in which the courses that would satisfy that requirement could be listed (not itemized below).

(1)     Skills (proficiencies)

- written communication | course choices |
- quantitative and computational reasoning | course choices |
- information literacy/technology | course choices |

(2)     Perspectives (insights)

- interdisciplinary perspectives | course choices |
- women and gender | course choices |
- multiculturalism | course choices |

(3)     Disciplines

- creation and criticism in the arts | course choices |
- historical perspectives | course choices |
- natural sciences | course choices |

- human institutions & behavior | course choices |

To comply with the matrix and to ensure at least the minimal enrollment in any one course that could stave off its cancellation, a faculty member had to take action. More students would be tempted to sign up for a course if it satisfied one or more of the General Education requirements. However, to gain that advantage for a course required drawing up and submitting a formal proposal to the Committee on General Education. In some cases it was like composing a legal brief to convince the Committee that the course would be "consistent with the Rationale and show a strong likelihood of achieving the Student Outcomes for that requirement" (capitalized letters as in the original *Guidelines for Proposal and Approval of Courses to Fulfill the General Education Requirements*, 2000). Proposals could be denied, as I know from personal experience.

The way it worked out in practice, most courses easily qualified to satisfy a Discipline requirement (category 3) as long as they were taught in the Division customary for that field. But God forbid that you would ask for a course to count in a different Division. My proposal asking that Human Evolution meet the Natural Sciences requirement was rejected, even though it satisfied a natural science requirement in universities all over the nation, including the University of California in Berkeley where I first taught. On the other hand, differing as it did from all of our other courses in cultural anthropology, it did not neatly meet "the human institutions & behavior" requirement. As a compromise it was agreed that it could serve to satisfy the Historical Perspectives disciplinary requirement, notably because that kept it in the Division of Social Sciences where the Department of History was located and the historians, with high enrollments, did not feel threatened. Not discussed were concerns of the natural science faculty that they might suffer under-enrollments in some of their classes if courses from other divisions competed with theirs. (Faculty politics can be quite byzantine.)

To meet the Perspectives requirement (category 2), one also had to navigate territorial waters (faculty politics). For example, my anthropology courses dedicated to ethnic, tribal, and regional cultures, including the traditional topics of cultural diffusion and acculturation, were denied approval to meet the multiculturalism requirement. Yet every ethnic studies course was approved for that requirement, which had the effect of virtually requiring every student to take at least one ethnic studies course in order to graduate.

For Skills (category 1) the situation was quite different again. Only a few English courses satisfied that requirement, but instructors in other disciplines could qualify a course by requiring students to submit extensive written work related to the subject. Since working on writing skills as such made a course more time consuming and difficult to teach, most of us preferred not to compete for that designation, even though it was an effective way attract students.

Following WASC directives, representatives of the faculty put hours of work into constructing the matrix, but their efforts would be wasted if they were unable to achieve buy-in from the faculty as a whole. Buy-in was a challenge, since the matrix marked a transformational change from less is more to more is better in educational policy.

To that end we were all invited to a faculty retreat early in the fall of 2000. An internal memo recalled that, "Central to the successful transformation of the GE Program was the emergence of a critical mass of faculty members who were concerned with the quality of general education, and who were willing to provide leadership to make *changes in the College's fundamental philosophy* as it related to GE" (emphasis added to highlight the control WASC had come to exercise over the Mills educational program). The administration believed buy-in was necessary, because it would prevent the matrix from being "seen as one person's agenda."

A good deal of give and take took place as professors confronted other professors on how to fine-tune that matrix, but it worked out well. "Flexibility in the nature and description of the educational goals of the Program and the method of implementation . . . contributed to the final adoption of the change." Again, "less is more" was not seriously compromised, and the change served a purpose. It tightened up the distribution requirements to ensure that every student was challenged to explore the full spectrum of academic fields more systematically and completely than had been the case before. The new General Education program was launched with the incoming class of 2003.

All seemed well and good. What I certainly did not anticipate – and probably almost all of my colleagues with me – was that a more is better policy was eventually to become a more is too much policy in which changes would become counterproductive in the extreme.

## The Strategic Plan for 2003-2007

A resolution by the Board of Trustees authorized a campus steering committee to oversee development of a new strategic plan by appointing small working groups. The overall goals were "to consider how Mills could become bigger and better." They included programs to develop bigger and better graduate programs, to increase undergraduate enrollments, and to grow the endowment. All of these goals were achieved, and will not be reviewed here. My focus is entirely on teaching at Mills.

A holistic perspective on teaching must include some outstanding achievements since 2003. For example, first year resident students are now organized into Living and Learning Communities (LLCs), each one centered on an introductory course. Professor Maggie Hunter, for example, sponsored an LLC for new students in her introductory sociology course. In addition to sharing the course, students neighbored one another in a residence hall and all of them had Professor Hunter as their academic advisor. She, with the assistance of a committed collaborator from the staff of the Dean of Students, organized group activities, including special lectures, films, exhibitions, theater evenings in San Francisco, and other field trips related to the central theme of their LLC. Learning for those students became a Sizer-kind of learning in depth, with the added benefit of bonding new students with one another, with their professor, and with the College.

A summer bridge and learning program each year now enrolls fifteen or twenty at-risk students from inner-city high schools to prepare them for the rigors of college work. Professor Bruce Williams and his colleagues make sure that those summer students are ready when fall arrives to study consistently and effectively, to write well-composed essays, and to survive difficult exams. Professor Williams also works closely with them as their academic advisor during their freshwoman year. They bond with one another. They bond with him. They end up doing well.

The College has worked hard for years, now, to create a culture that appreciates diversity and that approaches differences as learning opportunities. College forums and workshops keep social justice issues in the forefront. Solidarity Lounge for women of color provides a special place on the central campus were food and refreshments are available and students can retreat to discuss shared concerns and celebrate achievements. Affinity groups for African American and Latina groups are also active, as are other special interest clubs of all kinds.

As one example among many, for the last four years I have been faculty advisor for an official college club called Sisters Inspiring Sisters (SIS). Motivated and led by two dedicated students, one of whom, Erica García, was a Fremont High graduate, SIS was established by concerned Mills students entirely on their own initiative. As a college club it is autonomous and self-directed. I'm just there for them as back up if they need me, but I do follow their activities closely and am frankly amazed at what they accomplish. At the beginning of every academic year, each member becomes a "big sister" to a "little sister" in an inner-city charter named Oakland Unity High School. Each big sister spends at least two hours every week with her little sister to help her with homework, befriend her when troubles arise, or just to keep each other company as they both do school work.

Once every month the big sisters organize a weekend activity. The first event each year is always to organize an overnight together for the whole club, big and little sisters sharing dorm space, taking meals together, doing fun things in the evening, and attending classes on Monday with little sisters in tow to give them a taste of college life. Other monthly activities include academic workshops, museum visits, field trips to special places, and at the end of the year, visits to other colleges and universities to encourage college ambitions in the little sisters. SIS activities can be life changing for the little sisters and inspirational for their big sisters as well.

Yet another innovation is service learning, an academic program that connects courses on the Mills campus with involvements in the Oakland community. One goal of the Mills strategic plan is to encourage a sense of social responsibility, "to effect thoughtful changes in society." Many courses now offer extra credit to students who sign up to involve themselves in a service-learning component. It is done in courses of all kinds. I have already referred to students who worked with me at Fremont High for service-learning credit. Other opportunities have included assisting in an old people's home, serving as nurses aids or assisting in other ways at the Children's Hospital and Research Center in Oakland, helping out with a Meals on Wheels project, and planting bushes and trees in vacant lots as part of an urban beautification program.

## More is Better as an Academic Quagmire

It is important to acknowledge that more is better has done some great things for Mills College. But it also moved the college to expand WASC accreditation from approving or rejecting courses to fulfill specific GE requirements, as complex and time-consuming as that had become, to a comprehensive plan for evaluating educational effectiveness. On the face of it, such a plan seemed quite reasonable when first introduced, even though it would divert more faculty time from teaching and other responsibilities. It could be helpful to know how much students gain from the new distribution requirements. Since student learning has been so central to what we do at Mills it seemed reasonable to stop taking it for granted that we were successful and to move beyond anecdotal accounts of effectiveness. It seemed to make sense that the Office of Institutional Research should be reconstituted as the Office of Institutional Research, Planning and Assessment to be staffed by a "research professional" with a doctoral degree who was qualified to carry out an enlarged purpose.

The WASC commission required that Mills was to become increasingly committed to evidence-based "educational quality improvement" that would use "research data to inform teaching and learning by integrating assessments of educational effectiveness and student learning throughout the institution."

The strategy is to impose a program of assessment in the form of a matrix that compels the use of specific teaching methods and objectives. For any given subject, a teacher must teach concepts required by a matrix, even if the subject as such would otherwise require a very different teaching purpose. Academic freedom and the freedom professors need to teach well in the labyrinth of cultural complexity are challenged when a labyrinth is expected to conform to a matrix.

Teaching at Mills is now threatened by an apparently inevitable expansion of specific demands that threaten to become equally as distortive as the testing requirements imposed on high school teachers by the No Child Left Behind (NCLB) legislation of 2001 (Phillips, 2009).

That federal legislation diverted teaching from the broad, complex goals of a high school education to the narrow, specific skills needed by the twelfth grade to successfully pass multiple choice examinations in reading at a ninth grade level and in mathematical calculations at an eighth grade level. Those needs are real, but they should not come at the cost of broader educational goals: the ability to reason, solve problems, apply knowledge, understand cultural diversity, live healthy lives, function as good citizens, participate as knowledgeable voters and community contributors, and not the least, to grow throughout life in wisdom. Louis Wildman points out. referring to "what the No Child Left Behind Act is perpetrating in K – 12 education, that,

> There needs to be such an emphasis on teaching and assessing long lists of specific objectives, that the larger part of education is being set aside. Many schools have become test preparation factories, when this country needs thoughtful citizens and creative workers. Surely we don't want this factory model in higher education in the name of accountability, accreditation, or George Orwell (2004)

> Will We Do What It Takes to Improve Public Education?" Sam Chaltain asks, in *Education Week*. "Why is our public education system being aligned to create cultures of testing, as opposed to cultures of learning?" (2009)

There is now such an emphasis on teaching and assessing long lists of specific objectives, that the larger part of education is being set aside. Many schools have become test preparation

Will a similar fate befall Mills College? Will the goals of a liberal arts education bleed out through a bureaucratic takeover? Let me explain why that fear now motivates me.

# Chapter Nine

## The Struggle to Implement
## and Assess a Matrix

### Getting Lost Between
### Macro-Design and Micro-Operations

Mills has moved steadily and inexorably from a less is more accreditation process that required only a modest amount of college time, and was decidedly beneficial, to a more is better approach that will require extensive faculty and administrative investments of time and energy. It is a new approach that commits the college to unending institutional change – to moving the goal posts farther and farther in the distance, year after year, as Ben Schmookler might put it.

WASC regulations now and henceforth require Mills faculty members to function in a matrix. Complex issues must be collapsed into "process-oriented protocols." It is an approach that packages complexity in discrete little boxes as though less is more when, in reality, less is simply less. That's what typologies or classifications do, and that's what a matrix does. In the Mills case it threatens to distort and diminish the liberal arts curriculum and to abrogate academic freedom.

As an administrative technique, working in the matrix can be useful, indeed, necessary. Bureaucracy has its good side. As political scientists applying organizational theory to the California electrical grid, an exceedingly complex entity that must maintain a high level of reliability - that must not fail - Emery Roe and Paul Schulman find it useful to describe and evaluate the effectiveness of top-down management in a highly complex industry as "macro-design" (2008).

To achieve comprehensibility at Mills on the level of macro-design, we now routinely organize data by means of matrices. But it can get out of hand. As an illustration, a summary of "Educational Effectiveness Indicators" at Mills College (2007) produced a matrix that totals 5 columns, 63 rows, and 315 boxes. One of the 63 rows is devoted to my department. The columns (and boxes) provide the following small bits of information:

(1) Category? Anthropology and Sociology BA
(2) Have formal learning outcomes been developed? Yes
(3) Where are these learning outcomes published?
    Department Assessment Plan
(4) Other than GPA, what measures/indicators are used to determine that graduates have achieved the stated outcomes for the degree?
    Senior project, oral presentations, service learning experience
(5) Date of last program review for this degree program? 1996-7

Add 62 other rows to complete that total of 315 boxes and you have succinctly captured an overview in a matrix, but an overview that is very remote from the real world. And this is just one of many matrices required for WASC re-certification.

A macro-level summary of how educational effectiveness is measured can provide a useful overview, to be sure, but on the work-shop floor – on the level of teachers and students in their schools and neighborhoods or at Mills College – we need vastly more nuanced kinds of information. As Roe and Schulman point out for macro-design, at that level, "designers cannot foresee everything" (2008: 66). Educational policy needs to cope with the complexities of what they refer to as "micro-operations (specific events)."

It is essential for our most important obligation as college professors and academic advisors – which is to help students define and achieve their own goals – that we succeed in all of our wide-ranging responsibilities. Our profession requires us to conduct research or produce literary/artistic work, to publish research papers and books or to be productive in the creative arts, to participate in professional conferences as speakers, discussants, and attendees, to do our share of college administration, and to put a lot of time and energy into counseling and classroom teaching. The arena of micro-operations also involves us in interpersonal issues, exposes us to administrative surprises, tempts us with intellectual diversions, and impedes us with health emergencies and emotional intrusions. To all of that add that every student we work with is unique in capabilities, interests, and academic goals; that every class is unprecedented in the mix of students; that everyday collaboration with students to some extent is unpredictable and challenging. To be successful in our work we must function as effectively as possible in an experiential reality that is a labyrinth, not a matrix.

## Please Do Not Scream!

Every spring, a couple of weeks before classes end, we need to wind down the current academic year and anticipate the next. As head of a mercifully small department, in addition to meeting deadlines to submit annual reports on my own professional activities, on departmental affairs, and on two faculty committees that I chair, my most important task is to collaborate with other members of the department to submit the schedule of the courses we will teach in the fall (what, where, when, and who). By April 20 of this year (2009) I had completed all of those administrative chores on schedule.

That turned out to be the very day when an e-message arrived at the in-box of every teaching member of the faculty announcing that without exception every one of us must meet a new and totally unprecedented deadline. I had to read it several times and discuss it with friends down the hall to confirm how revolutionary the new requirement was. It read as follows (slightly redacted, with emphasis added in bold):

Dear Faculty,

The Provost is asking that **all courses** being taught this fall **must be revised through the new Course Approval and Revision Process (CARP) to add assessment-related information**. To get you moving on this urgent project (and to inspire you to start on this now rather than waiting until August) I have scheduled several workshops. . . .

A workshop is mostly to help you **define the criteria as they relate to student learning of the Mission, General Education requirements, and Program [departmental] goals supported by your course(s),** and also **to craft your statement regarding how you might assess learning in your course(s**). I look forward to seeing many of you over the course of the next few weeks.

All the best, Alice

[Dr. Alice Knudsen is the research professional who now heads an upgraded Office of Institutional Research, Planning and Assessment].

On receiving that message, one distinguished colleague in his office two doors from mine, rather than scream, immediately used the power of alliteration to sarcastically brand this unprecedented policy, "the CARP crap."

In retrospect, we should have seen it coming. I failed to see it, and I believe most members of the faculty failed to realize how concerned and worried we should be. The required revisions threaten the Mills liberal arts program and our academic freedom. A case study will show what I mean. It really is that serious.

# Case Example Number One - Before CARP (2004)

## Course Goals in a Syllabus

I didn't see it coming. For the last several years it has been mentioned in faculty meetings and other encounters that on the next site visit in 2010 WASC will require our course syllabi to specify learning goals for each course. We were admonished to add learning goals to our current syllabi. I wasn't sure what that meant, so I took it as a flexible requirement that didn't require much thought, nor did I expect it to significantly challenge the long-standing less is more policy. I assumed I needed only to insert simple glosses to indicate what students could expect to learn. As background to how the new WASC directives impact teaching goals, I offer my course on human evolution as a case study. Five years ago, before the new WASC demands began to nose into awareness, the course syllabus started off with the following statements.

### Anthropology 57 (Human Evolution)

### Course Goals

To provide an introduction to prehistoric archeology, paleoanthropology, and physical anthropology (also known as biological anthropology). This course is designed to complement Anthropology 58 (Cultural Anthropology), the two together constituting a general introduction to the field of anthropology as a whole.

That paragraph is straightforward and unambiguous. During the first class meeting I defined or explained what each of the subjects covered and how the discipline of anthropology is similar to and different from other academic fields. In the give and take of questions and answers students and I explored their interests, backgrounds and goals and how what they could expect to learn in this course might benefit from or contribute to what they were learning in other courses. The course description continued:

> Methods of acquiring data and the logic of developing theory will constitute pervasive themes. In this class, how you think is more important than facts you may know. Course efforts will be directed toward understanding major contemporary issues of racial, ethnic, and gender diversity to the extent that they can be based on research in the following areas of inquiry: multicultural diversity, racial biology, from apes to human beings, origins of Stone Age cultures, discovering the New World, earliest world civilizations.

In that section on course goals, two different learning achievements were promised to students who participated faithfully and studied hard. One required me to model and teach how to think like an anthropologist. Students learned as apprentices, by exploring ways in which understandings are obtained from ethnographic fieldwork, archaeological excavations, and laboratory analysis. The other learning goal was to apply what we studied to deepen and challenge beliefs about ourselves as individuals and as members of society. The course challenged misconceptions about race and intelligence, ethnicity and co-existence, and claims of civilizations as superior or inferior. In sum, what the syllabus promised was fact based and discipline oriented. It was to learn to think like an anthropologist and on that basis to interrogate one's understandings of our own lives and of important social issues in anthropological ways.

Five years later the syllabus demonstrates that my teaching goals have changed in some ways, just as they have year by year for decades in response to personal growth that incorporates developments in the profession, the community, the nation, and the world. To those goals I added "anticipated learning outcomes" as a modest effort to incorporate the new WASC inspired directives as I [mis]understood them.

# Case Example Number Two - Before CARP (2009)

## Anthropology 57 (Human Evolution)

### Course Goals

*Those who control the present control the past* (Orson Wells)

We live in a world increasingly dominated by dogmatists who strive to control how prehistory is taught. To the extent that they are successful they undermine basic human rights to individual freedom of thought and behavior; to how we define ourselves. On the world stage the biggest current threat is from ultra-conservative Islam. In the United States the biggest menace is fundamentalist Christian. In this course we will, in part, explore how creationists distort scientific research. For them, the response when you ask, "who am I?" is that you are damaged goods because of the original sin of a disobedient woman named Eve.

*Those who control the past control the future* (George Orwell)

This course offers an introduction to prehistoric archaeology, paleoanthropology, and physical anthropology (also known as biological anthropology). Scientific methods of acquiring data and the logic of developing theory will constitute pervasive themes. In this class, how you think is more important than the facts you may learn. Course efforts will be directed toward understanding major contemporary issues of racial, ethnic, and gender diversity.

Academic freedom is precious. I was not required to seek permission from the Dean of the Faculty or to engage in a course revision process to put a new slant on my course on human evolution. The basic course objectives remained unchanged, as is evident in the second paragraph. The first paragraph, however, reflects a significant shift to current events in the news, specifically for the first weeks of the semester.

As far back as the Scopes trial of 1925 in Tennessee, creationists have fought against teaching evolutionary theory in public schools, and surprisingly, that threat continues to this day. Even after I wrote my syllabus for 2004, newspapers and magazines reported on confrontations with creationist insurgents in the law courts of Pennsylvania and Georgia. Recent attacks occurred in 2008, when Governor Bobby Jindal signed the Louisiana Science Education Act into law, and in 2009, when the Texas school board set new standards for teaching evolutionary theory (Bhattacharjee, 2009: 1385). I decided that my students need to be taught what the issues are in those religion-inspired denials of the validity of good science. They need to explore the basis for insisting that human evolution is not a theory in the sense of "a conjecture," a mere guess, but is a theory in the sense of "a set of supported hypotheses," supported, that is, by an enormous body of evidence that has not been falsified (Fuentes, 2007: 374).

An equally compelling reason to introduce a revised orientation was to confront widespread public misunderstanding. Amazingly, rather close to half of all American adults reject evolutionary theory in favor of the Genesis story about the Garden of Eden. More precisely, according to a 2008 Gallup Poll, 44 percent of respondents agree with the statement that, "God created humankind in its present form almost 10,000 years ago" (which is the creationist creed). In contrast, a mere 14 percent agree that "Humans have evolved over millions of years from less-advanced forms of life, but God had no part in this process."

I feel it is critically important in teaching a course on human evolution that students study the vast body of evidence that allows scientists to state categorically that human evolution is a fact of nature. A major goal of the course is that students should acquire the competence it requires to explain evolutionary theory in a comprehensible way to others, particularly to well-educated non-scientists.

Is that the right thing for me to do as an anthropology professor? I believe it is. I see it as consistent with the College mission as explicitly spelled out when I joined the faculty in 1960. "At Mills we believe that the essence of a liberal education is learning to penetrate any specific problem or conflict to discover what basic issues lie inside it, and what human values are involved . . . [To acquire] an education for insight, which presupposes both knowledge and skills but is more difficult." I still agree with the 1968 catalog statement that the goals are to widen awareness, improve judgment, intensify creative spirit, and deepen knowledge, which in turn requires learning how to ask important questions, test underlying assumptions, challenge stereotypical answers, and sharpen perceptions of truth.

Against acquiring those life changing intellectual capacities, my effort (below) to identify "anticipated learning outcomes" lists good things to know, but they seem mundane and uninspiring, Small wonder. I presented it as a matrix. I was not converted to a less is less approach, I capitulated to it. Doing so went against a long history at Mills (and my own personal history) of luxuriating in the openness and opportunities of a labyrinth as preferable to being regimented in a matrix. It is a matter of priorities. "Mills values the well-stocked mind and the person skillful in its use," for which a matrix can be helpful. "But ours is, at its core, not an education just for information or an education just for skills" (Mills Bulletin, 1960).

**Anticipated Learning Outcomes**

**(Continuation of the 2009 Syllabus)**

*Skills*: Reasoning (research methods and testable hypotheses)

*Perspectives*: Interdisciplinary Perspectives (science, theology, history, biology); Women and Gender (culture and gender versus biology and destiny); Multicultural (stone age cultures worldwide, early civilizations)

*Disciplinary Experience*: Historical Perspectives (from 65 million to five thousand years ago); Natural Sciences (racial biology, skeletal anatomy); Human Institutions and Behavior (families, bands, tribes,complex societies)

# Case Example Number Three – After CARP (2010)

### Course Goals in a Syllabus - After CARP

A message from the Dean of the Faculty on April 13, 2009, made it clear that it was no longer enough, as a kind of *pro forma* after thought, to list mundane and uninspiring "anticipated learning outcomes" as major course goals the way I had done. I cannot fault her for that. However, I have no enthusiasm for the following rigid demand (slightly redacted with emphasis added in bold), that the henceforth hoped for course outcomes will have to be listed on syllabi as "a **new required** section for **Assessment data** . . . particularly as we undergo **review by WASC**." Specifically, we were notified, I should say ordered in no uncertain terms, that "faculty members . . . **must** . . . **define at least one**

**measurable criterion** against which each mission, program and general education goal will be **assessed as to the level of learning achieved** by students in the course. . . . Course syllabi must also be **updated with details of the mission, program, and general education goals and assessment criteria** supported by the course."

What an astonishing assault on the traditional grading system ("assessment culture") of higher education in general, and on the official records of student achievement at Mills College in particular. As required to meet WASC benchmarks, every course from now on must conform to criteria external to the course and imposed on it. Permit me to explain.

As concerns assessing the "level of learning achieved by students in [a] course," note that we have always done that. The final grade entered on a student's official record of courses completed constitutes a meaningful measure of the breadth and depth of learning achieved in any one subject area. The official record of the whole of a student's work is a matrix, and necessarily so if it is to be usable as a summary statement that can be easily evaluated as a transcript.

Since the whole accreditation process is in the matrix, why not remain satisfied with the time-honored grading system? Cheryl Fenno offers her reason for not being satisfied. "The assessment rubric goes beyond A-B-C grades and looks at how well students have grasped the learning goals set by the faculty." However, Fenno fails totally to credit college professors with sufficient creativity and sensitivity "to," as she puts it, "evaluate student learning and the effectiveness of teaching methods and the programs offered" without recourse to a new assessment matrix. It appears she assumes we only know how to use the grading system in clumsy, unimaginative ways. "A written midterm and final exam that evaluates only a student's ability to memorize and recall information is inadequate in today's educational environment" (2002). Who would disagree with that? From our own student days, we all remember how hard we studied to memorize masses of complex information in order to earn an A on a final exam. We also share the experience of having very little recall six months later, and virtually none at all as the years go by. What stayed with us, hopefully, was how facts and information were used "for insight."

Personally, I assign take-home exams that grade on how well the student has grasped concepts and can apply theories when the necessary facts are a given, since she has a week to write her essays and can access all of her books and lecture notes. I even encourage collaboration with fellow students. Remember from my syllabus for Human Evolution, "In this class, how your think is more important than facts you may know." Some of my colleagues favor open-book in-class exams, which also minimize reliance on "a student's ability to memorize and recall information" in favor of evaluating how they think. The point is, the time-honored A-B-C grading method can function quite effectively as an assessment matrix, so why advocate a new matrix to replace the old?

To answer my own question, the problem is more serious than merely to assess how well students use information. The deeper problem is that the emphasis has shifted from goals and measures of achievement specific to the subject being taught to new imposed goals and measures that are not course specific. They are college-wide and compulsory kinds of knowledge and skills in three categories, Mission Goals, Program Goals, and General Education Goals. As a teacher I am now required to add the new college-wide requirements to those of the subject matter as such. Perhaps I can justify giving administrative time to added goals that are consistent with those I already pursue. Unrelated goals, however, will divert time, effort, and course continuity in non-helpful ways, as I shall explain.

## Setting Educational Goals for Assessment

For decades, the annual College Bulletins included a "Profile" as a way to characterize the purpose of the College. It was presented as an essay, not a matrix. The 1960 Profile indicated that students would examine conflicts of values in American life. On social issues it took the position that students should investigate "independent judgments" rather than insist that there are "right answers." Importance was attached to the "critical appraisal of assumptions and of evidence." "Intellectual curiosity" was highly valued as were "self-confidence, personal responsibility, and willingness to try the unaccustomed" [whatever that means – it got out of hand in the late sixties].

In 1963, for the first time, "On the principle that a broadening of intellectual interest and an understanding of the interrelation of ideas can best be achieved when each student has the widest possible opportunity to choose among courses of the College," College Objectives were articulated as Distribution Requirements, and years later, as General Education Requirements. Whatever they were called, they functioned as a kind of statement of College Goals for many years.

In 1976 the Profile added an important justification for the distribution requirements. "The educational program at Mills is designed to give the student maximum flexibility to find and pursue her own path toward competence and mastery." I particularly appreciated then, as I do now, the value placed on the student being provided with "maximum flexibility to find and pursue her own path."

In a consistent but much more dramatic way, the Catalog for 1984-1985 offered an expanded statement on the value self direction. For some inexplicable reason, the statement appeared for the first time in that year and in that year only. It was never published again. I have no idea why it vanished so completely, but it read as follows.

Learning for Yourself

For most students, a liberal arts education is vital to a continuing development as a person who desires a rewarding life of intellectual exploration and personal engagement. Actually, the skills students can develop through a liberal education are very important in the working world as well:

219

- A firm grasp of cultural, political and historical issues
- An appreciation of the values that shape human behavior
- An understanding of how societies organize to produce goods and services
- The role of work in our culture
- The ability to express oneself, to make sure one's ideas are heard and understood, in person or on paper
- Leadership skills which help one understand other people and inspire them to help achieve mutually held goals
- Independence and a sense of integrity, even in situations which require making difficult choices between conflicting "rights" or between immediate and long-term goals
- The ability to evaluate facts and ideas from many different perspectives, and to weigh conflicting voices of authority
- The willingness to accept responsibility and take action in order to achieve positive goals

If her liberal education has been a good one, a student will know how to use her skills and intelligence to act with purpose and conviction throughout her lifetime.

Note that "Learning for Yourself" is about the knowledge and skills one should acquire as a product of four years of College work and involvement. No one class is expected to teach more than a part of that whole. Contrast that with the new explicit goals (which for my course on human evolution add up to 18 goals in three categories), every one of which must, in one way or another, be specifically addressed in every course I teach. Can a liberal education be meaningfully prepackaged in boxes?

As recently as in the Catalog for 2003, under a section titled, Academic Requirements for the Bachelor of Arts Degree, the pre-matrix way of thinking was still articulated. In that Catalog my colleague in sociology, Professor Dan Ryan, wrote on "The Mills College Philosophy of General Education in a reaffirmation of our time-tested commitment to openness and freedom."

> Done well, a liberal-arts education is a gymnasium for the mind – as opposed to a narrowly focused training program for a single sport. Fitness for citizenship, one might say, is the goal. It produces . . . citizens who value knowledge beyond their specialties, and who want to learn all the things there isn't enough time to learn, rather than asking, "Why do I need to know that?"

In spite of what Dan wrote for the Catalog, our leadership at Mills College was already in the process of cinching down on academic freedom by re-defining our educational program in terms of columns, rows, and boxes imposed as three kinds of educational goals: Mission, Program, and General Education. Again, I offer my course on Human Evolution as an example. I write in the Summer of 2009.

## (1) Mission Goals

Mission Goals are six in number. Associated assessment criteria consist of measurable learning outcomes that I reluctantly submitted for approval (after a failure to gain approval on my first try). If I had not agreed to include new assessment criteria in my course requirements I would not be authorized to teach a course I love this coming fall (2009). So, from now on I am committed to modifying how I teach the subject of human evolution in the following half-dozen ways. I found I can commit to two of the six goals without greatly compromising my teaching agenda, so let me describe them first.

Two Mission Goals I can commit to:

---

*Goal Description.* "Educating students to think critically."

*My Criterion.* The student must have learned to, "Explain the difference between theological and scientific explanations for human biological and cultural origins and development." I got this goal accepted and can live with it, but it is a very limited and pedantic way to refer to what is actually a stimulating topic for discussion.

---

*Goal Description.* "Challenging students to consider ways to effect thoughtful changes in society." My Criteria (we were encouraged to go beyond the minimum of a single criterion for each goal, so I bit the bullet on this one and offered two).

*Criterion Number One.* "Challenge racism by demonstrating that the concept of race as a biological category is unscientific and harmful." Not a problem. This has always been a major goal for me.

*Criterion Number Two.* "Oppose efforts to forbid the teaching of human evolution in public schools as unscientific." Ditto. In fact, I expect students to learn that creationism in its various guises, including that of Intelligent Design, is unscientific and inappropriate to teach in public schools where religious advocacy is against the law.

---

Four Mission Goals that are not relevant:

Although the remaining Mission Goals are not relevant for my course on human evolution, I will be required somehow to adapt to them, because the computer program stopped me cold every time I skipped typing in at least one assessment criterion for each goal. You cannot argue with an automated system that is inflexible.

*Goal Description.* "Educating students to communicate responsibly and effectively."

*My Criterion.* In every course I teach I remind students that at Mills we expect students to graduate with the ability to speak and write effectively. Therefore, I grade an exam down if the use of language is defective. However, I do not teach communication skills as such, so I decided not to enter an assessment criterion for this goal. That was when I discovered that I have no choice but to teach to every single one of the six goals. Muttering under my breath, I finally got the following accepted as my teaching commitment: Students will learn to, "Display continuity, correct grammar and spelling, with a clear statement of purpose at the beginning and the achievement of that purpose in the conclusion." It is trivial. As a criterion for educating to communicate, it fails to capture the excitement engendered in class when we talk about intelligence and skin color, ethnicity and cultural conflict, and claims of civilizations as superior or inferior, or, for that matter, God versus Darwin. Instead, my criterion offers a few words on how to organize an essay the way I have heard Mr. Jackson teach it to 10th grade high school students in his journalism class at Fremont High School.

*Goal Description.* "Developing students as leaders and innovators in their chosen endeavors." Again, had the computer program permitted, I would have passed over this goal as something I do not deal with.

*My Criterion.* "Students will challenge their prior assumptions and respond to those who query them." I was surprised the committee let me get by with this, because it is just another way of talking about the first goal on thinking critically. I freely confess, however, that I do not see myself in this introductory survey course as teaching students how to become leaders or innovators.

*Goal Description.* "Educating students to develop and realize their own creative visions across the arts and sciences."

*My Criterion.* Students will learn to, "Explore creativity in their own lives as they study the earliest archaeological evidence for art and music in human history." You have to give me credit for creativity on this one. I'm surprised the committee gave me a pass on it, because it strikes me as just plain silly. Mind you, I love introducing students to the cave art of Lascaux, and some of my students are brilliant artists and musicians, but I don't inspire them to strive to create a twenty-first century Lascaux.

*Goal Description.* "Challenging students to push the traditional boundaries of their disciplines."

*My Criterion.* "Students will recognize the relevance of prehistory to their visions of the future." Again, I was forced to this by the computer. And, again, I'm surprised the committee gave me a pass. I do think that the history of prehistory is inspirational as we learn about the earth-shaking discoveries of brilliant, open-minded scientists, and I delight in challenging students to rethink their understandings of human origins and stone age life styles. But they take this course as a diversion from what they are majoring in ("their disciplines"), and it does not provide an obvious course basis for challenging the boundaries of those disciplines.

*Conclusion.* On all six of these goals I am committed to bring students to a level identified as "Introduce" or "Practice." (Students must "master" criteria in some of the other goal categories.) To the extent that I teach two of the goals, it is on an introductory level. Frankly, I'm not sure what is meant by expecting students to learn on a "Practice" level. It makes sense to me for critical thinking, but am I supposed to require students to attack, for example, the new law in Louisiana that encourages the teaching of human origins as described in Genesis chapters one and two? Since I cannot teach to the remaining four Mission Goals that are irrelevant to the study of human evolution, it seems that I am doomed. (Of course I am not doomed. The College administration would never permit that. But as long as accreditation is dependent on meeting matrix goals, we clearly will have to have some serious talks with the WASC Commission.)

# (2) Program Goals, Department of Anthropology and Sociology

Every academic department is required to support goals specific to the discipline. For Program Goals as for Mission Goals, every course is required to identify assessment criteria for each one. Since we are a joint department meeting the needs of two disciplines, whether listed as anthropology or as sociology, every course must meet the shared anthropology-and-sociology criteria. Fortunately, the two disciplines have much in common. Although it is a stretch to require that I provide assessment goals for all eight of the Program Goals in my course on human evolution, I should have no serious problem preparing students to be examined on the following topics (although I would hope not to present them in such a boring way).

---

*Goal Description.* "Understand what it means to be a human being in different kinds of societies and cultures."

*Criterion Number One.* "Demonstrate that it constitutes an ethnocentric error to interpret behaviors in other societies as inferior merely because they are different."

*Criterion Number Two.* "Explain the principle of cultural relativity as a way to validate cultural differences in other societies."

---

*Goal Description.* "Possess knowledge of what it means to live in highly variable kinds of societies."

*My Criterion.* "Students will have the ability to describe the reconstructed sociocultural characteristics that distinguish what it meant to live in Lower Paleolithic hunting and gathering societies from what social life was like in Neolithic villages on to the first complex societies of early civilizations."

*Goal Description.* "Understand and value diversity."

*My Criterion.* "Students will be able to explain in oral and written language how race is not a valid or useful biological concept (in contrast to its explanatory value in cultural and social terms) by giving examples of the biological concept of discordant variation."

*Goal Description.* "Possess the skills necessary to document social life including skills in participant observation."

*My Criterion.* "Explain ethnographic research techniques and describe contemporary cultures as contributory to the reconstruction of prehistoric cultures that are similar in socioeconomic terms."

*Goal Description.* "Knowledge of research methodology and basic quantitative methods."

*My Criterion.* "Explain the simple quantitative methods that are used for the interpretation of genetic relationships of populations surviving solely as skeletal remains."

*Goal Description.* "The fields: History and shape of the field, its conceptual vocabulary and mental tools, race, class and gender as dimensions of inequality."

*Criterion Number One.* "Apply the shared vocabulary and concepts of sociology and anthropology to describe and interpret prehistoric cultures. What we know about the world: substantive knowledge about the world, its core institutions, and social scientific findings."

*Criterion Number Two.* "Identify shared concepts and terminology useful for reconstructing prehistoric community life in ways consistent with how contemporary societies are described."

*Goal Description.* "Attitudes and skills of empirical research: empiricism as a value, methods of empirical research, and capacity to find what is already known."

*My Criterion.* "Demonstrate how empirical evidence for enormous antiquity and slow evolutionary change fosters understandings relevant to our lives today."

## (3) General Education Goals

Because Anthropology 057 (Human Evolution) satisfies the Historical Perspectives requirement, I had to explain how I will teach to that specific requirement. As in the case of the disciplinary Program Goals, I was able to provide explicit questions that are consistent with what I will be teaching, even if they do not represent my course priorities.

*Goal Description.* "Evaluate past events and trends from political, economic, artistic, cultural, philosophical, and social perspectives."

*My criterion.* "Explain with examples how anthropology is holistic in that it is global, including societies all over the world, and historical, embracing time depth that extends back to the beginning of the Paleozoic period."

*Goal Description.* "Recognize both differences and similarities between past eras and the present."

*My criterion.* "Students must demonstrate factual knowledge and analytical skills sufficient to clearly distinguish levels of sociocultural and biological evolution. Criteria include an ability to identify differences between a Lower Paleolithic hand axe and a Neolithic polished stone axe head, as an example. Criteria also require an ability in the laboratory setting to explain differences, *inter alia*, between the skeletal remains of *Australopithecus africanus* and those of *Homo erectus*."

*Goal Description.* "Critique existing analyses of earlier eras."

*My criterion.* "Students must demonstrate a clear understanding of the differences between science as a knowledge system based on empirical observation and experience that is open to refinement based on the results of testing and experimentation in contrast to folklore based on untested and untestable premises."

*Goal Description.* "Use critical tools to assess historical source materials."

*My criterion.* "Students will demonstrate in oral and written examinations how Abrahamic claims on the origin and development of human beings and their lifeways in the Torah, the Bible, and the Qur'an fail to meet the veracity standards of scientific explanations based on paleontological and biological sciences."

## Back to Horace's Compromise

Most students do not take Human Evolution because it satisfies one of the General Education Requirements. They certainly would not sign up for it based on how it is supposed to satisfy all eighteen of the relevant College Goals. The matrix format for those goals makes the course sound tedious. But, like other members of the faculty, I work hard to teach a course of timely interest with a presentation that is lively. It constitutes an unwelcome intrusion to be required to teach to the new three-part College Goals. Yet, somewhat perversely, that is exactly what is happening.

For the first time in the spring of 2009, instructors will be graded by students on an A to F scale based on student assessments of how accurately Goal Descriptions reflect what they learned. Note that course examinations as such require students to master the subject matter of a course as explained in the syllabus, in lectures, and in assigned readings. Those goals are subject specific and very different from generic Goal Descriptions as defined in the College Mission Statement, in one or another of the college-wide General Education Requirements, and in overall departmental (Program) Goals.

The "Anthropology Evaluation" questionnaire will require students to grade my performance in the Human Evolution course next semester by filling in bubbles as they are asked to "indicate the level of learning you felt you achieved . . as a result of this course." Naturally, professors will want to earn good grades in order to feel good about ourselves, but importantly also, we will want to earn good grades because they will certainly impact our employment status. So, what do I have to do to earn good grades? I offer Mission Goals as an example of why I am upset.

I felt I could commit to two of the six Mission Goals that were relevant to the field of human evolution. But when I re-examine those two commitments I find I must either change the way I teach or risk getting failing grades in the course. Yes, we are talking about a curious reversal here. I can imagine awarding an A or B to a student who might have liked the course very much, have learned a great deal, and perhaps, as sometimes happens, even found it a life changing experience, but who might nevertheless conclude she has to give me a D or an F because I did not teach specifically what the Anthropology Evaluation requires. I will illustrate that serious criticism.

For the first Mission Goal to which I feel I can commit, note how the student will be asked to grade me:

---

*Goal Description.* "Educating students to think critically."

*Grade Question.* How well did Anderson teach "critical thinking or analysis?"

*My Criterion for Achieving that Goal.* The student will learn to "Explain the difference between theological and scientific explanations for human biological and cultural origins and development."

---

My very specific goal has to do with creationism versus the theory of evolution by means of variation and natural selection. Will students recognize critical thinking and critical analysis in that, and also in the many other ways in which "how you think" permeates the course? Will

I need to change my approach from one of exploring issues to the rather different one of teaching analysis as such, the way a language teacher might teach grammar? Will students get more excited by learning a kind of "grammar" than by discussing problems encountered in their own lives? Does it matter?

For the second Mission Goal, the student will be asked to grade me on the following basis:

*Goal Description.* "Capacity to effect thoughtful changes in a global, multicultural society."

*Grade Question.* How well did Anderson teach "capacity to effect thoughtful changes in a global, multicultural society?"

*My First Criterion for Achieving that Goal.* The student will learn to "challenge racism by demonstrating that the concept of race as a biological category is unscientific and harmful."

*My Second Criterion for Achieving that Goal.* The student will learn to "oppose efforts to forbid the teaching of human evolution in public schools as unscientific."

Perhaps students would find the first criterion unproblematic in qualifying me for a good grade, but what about the second? I will provide them with arguments that clearly identify creationism as religion and not science, and they will master the science supportive of the theory of evolution. However the grade question is not about those understandings. It is about developing a policy and achieving a political agenda adequate to implement "changes" in some sort of generic sense. I do not teach how to develop and implement new policies. Instead, in my class we evaluate data that counters racist claims (claims that differences in skin color are predictive of differences in intelligence) based on the science of biological evolution. Do I get a low grade again? Or a will students bubble in "Does Not Apply." If it is the latter I will still be in trouble, because I am committed to teach how to take the lead in implementing beneficial changes. I can imagine being called on the carpet for not meeting my goals.

My criteria for meeting the two Mission Goals are will be narrowly defined in the syllabus as opposition to the teaching of creationism in public schools (as an effort to contribute to thoughtful change) and to teach that the concept of race as a biological category is unscientific and harmful (which has implications for race relations). To earn an A or a B I can imagine how I might be tempted to state explicitly that they are learning how to bring about "thoughtful changes" by means of these explorations, because I want to earn an A. As an employee, I fear I will be tempted "to teach to the test," which will probably put everybody to sleep and kill my enthusiasm for working with students.

But no matter what I do, I cannot win on Mission Goals, because four of the six goals do not work at all for the study of biological evolution and they cannot be valid teaching goals in this course. I will surely get D's, F's, or ""Does not Apply" for the following:

---

Goal Description. "Educating students to communicate responsibly and effectively."

*Grade Question.* How well did Anderson teach, "responsible and effective communication?"

---

*Goal Description.* "Developing students as leaders and innovators in their chosen endeavors."

*Grade Question.* How well did Anderson teach, "leadership and innovation?"

---

*Goal Description.* "Educating students to develop and realize their own creative visions across the arts and sciences."

*Grade Question.* Because of this course, how well did Anderson succeed in the "development and realization of my creative visions across the arts and sciences?"

*Goal Description.* "Challenging students to push the traditional boundaries of their disciplines."

*Grade Question.* How well did this course help me improve my, "ability to push the traditional boundaries of my discipline?"

When properly done I greatly appreciate getting constructive criticism from students, and for as long as I can remember we have had a procedure at Mills to elicit meaningful feedback in every course we teach. From that we learn what we did right and what we should try to do better the next time. Also, what is most important, the feedback is relevant to the specific field of knowledge announced in the College Catalog, spelled out in the course syllabus, and backed up with assigned readings and class assignments.

In a class meeting at the end of every semester, every teacher is asked to leave the classroom so that students will feel free to write frank and honest evaluations destined as anonymous commentaries to be turned over to the Office of the Dean of the Faculty by a fellow student. Later, each of us will get a summary statement of how well we did on a bubble form. On a scales of 1 to 5 (Excellent, Very Good, Good, Fair, Poor) students evaluate in the following terms:

- Overall quality of instruction
- Quality of lectures/classroom presentations

- Quality of class discussions
- Course organization
- Explanations
- Use of examples and illustrations
- Instructor's enhancement of student interest in the subject
- Instructor's interest in the subject matter of the course
- Instructor's availability for additional help
- Value of the course to me was
- Amount I learned in this course was
- Fairness of grading practices in this course was
- Overall quality of the course was

In my experience, I find that a second form is especially helpful. It implements the less is more policy and just asks for two kinds of information, with space to write a paragraph or two: (1) What has the instructor done especially well in teaching this course? (2), Suggestions for improving the course?

The big question concerning CARP has to be, Are the required commitments to college-wide and department-wide goals an infringement of academic freedom? Lowell Barrington would apparently answer in the affirmative as he writes,

> My critique of assessment should not be interpreted as a blanket condemnation of administrators or bureaucrats . . . . At the same time, academic freedom (that is, some lack of standardization and bureaucratically imposed structure) is essential to teach students to think. Professors must be trusted to know what their strengths and weakness are and how best to examine what students have learned (2003).

Is the assessment program being introduced at Mills an infringement of academic freedom? The answer has to be that it is too soon to tell, but CARP is very alarming. Starting in the fall I will have to include Course Goals and Assessment Criteria in my syllabus (or by a link to the syllabus) for Human Evolution, even though I consider them to be a distraction. Other faculty will also find themselves boxed in this matrix.

Whether or not my academic freedom will be infringed by the new requirements depends on the wisdom and sensitivity of the administration, which extends beyond the President and Dean of the Faculty to include The Faculty Executive Committee (elected) and other administrative entities such as the General Education Committee. I know all of my colleagues to be both wise and sensitive, but that still leaves me, personally, under pressure to change what I teach. To the extent that I am grade conscious (and I was very grade conscious as a student) I may find it difficult to resist compromising my present teaching goals in order go for good grades. Likely to happen? Not very. But what about my colleagues who are still working their way through the ranks to full professor, step seven (the highest), and who strive in every other way (teaching well, getting research grants, publishing, committee work, and so on) to earn merit increases and promotions? Who knows how they will feel the imposition? That very uncertainty is scary, and not only to me. Barrington fears that ". . . it leaves professors with the unfortunate choice of either fabricating assessment data or teaching things that are easily assessed. Fabricating data is demoralizing at best, and teaching easily assessed subject matter is a direct attack on liberal arts education" (2003),

I have not noticed any enthusiasm for the new CARP assessment plan by the people I work with, including administrators. Apparently that was predictable. Sherry Lee Linkon has observed similar reactions, writing, "Faculty have many good reasons to resist and reject assessment. . . . Like other professionals, we believe that we should be trusted on the basis of our training, our continuing professional engagement, and our practice of rigorous peer review" (2005). In her own way Dorothy D. Wills , after clearly stating, "I am not against improvement or assessment," admits to her own negative reaction. "It is a perfect example of the creeping sameness that pervades all activity when everything is reduced to business to be managed" (1999).

One would think that we should just tell WASC to back off, but we can't. In their literature, WASC states clearly that submission to regional accreditation is entirely voluntary, but of course, the contrary is true. Working to achieve accreditation is absolutely compulsory because students cannot afford to enroll in a college that is not recognized by other institutions as meeting accreditation standards. Also, only accredited institutions qualify for federal and state funding. It is true that WASC "speaks softly," but it also carries "a big stick." In short, "Congress, the U.S. Department of Education, and the accreditation agencies have given colleges and universities no choice" (Barrington, 2003).

## Does Assessment Work?

For ten years Daniel M. Tobin has directed the Mellon Assessment Project for Liberal Arts Education at Hamilton College, where he serves as Distinguished Professor of Sociology. He has been a member of the Executive Committee of the Middle States Commission on Higher Education, a unit of the Middle States Association of Colleges and Schools (a WASC equivalent for the mid-Atlantic states). He is currently writing a book on assessment. I value the responses he elicited when he asked informally, "Does assessment actually work? Does it actually improve higher education?" He put those questions to attendees at a conference on assessment and their comments confirmed, "that assessment, on the face of it, doesn't appear to be working." More specifically, when he asked attendees, "As a group, are colleges with big assessment programs better institutions than those without?" The average answer was "No." He also asked, "After 20 years of assessment efforts, is American higher education noticeably better than before?" the average answer again was, "No."

Tobin concludes, "After twenty years' effort (getting rather intense in the past ten), we deserve to see some results" (unpublished manuscript courtesy of Dan Ryan, 2009). It appears that Barrington, half a dozen years earlier, had good reason to write, "There is nothing natural or logical about the plunge into assessment in American higher education. . . . It is a choice, as other countries that have begun to discard assessment approaches well understand. And for institutions that purportedly support the ideals of liberal arts education, it is a poor choice" (2003).

Why is it a poor choice? According to Sherry Lee Linkon, "Professors . . . resist assessment because we believe that learning is a complex process that cannot be easily measured" (Linkon, 2005). She cites Nine Principles of Good Practice for Assessing Student Learning issued by the American Association of Higher Education (AAHE), which states, "Learning is a complex process. It entails not only what they can do with what they know; it involves not only knowledge and abilities but values, attitudes, and habits of mind." Given that the learning mind is a labyrinth and not a matrix, it is clear that assessment should "employ a diverse array of methods" (AAHE, 1996).

Above all, WASC errs in using its position power to enforce a policy of using assessment as way to enforce continuing educational improvement. Linkon attacks that policy, noting that "some institutional assessment programs are couched in terms of 'continuous improvement,' a concept that may seem innocuous, perhaps even laudable, but that can also be interpreted as meaning that 'nothing you do will ever be good enough'" (2005), which is exactly where we are right now at Mills College, and undoubtedly at other colleges in the Western Association of Schools and Colleges.

# Part V

In Support of Teachers, More or Less

# Chapter Ten

## Theorizing the Labyrinth and the Matrix

### Why Scream?

Complex issues can be made comprehensible by taking a typological approach that extracts order out of chaos. A matrix can be indispensable on the level of macro-design, and not the least for educational institutions struggling to meet the needs of society and governments on the one hand, and the needs of large student populations on the other. Policy design and implementation would be impossible without analysis situated in a matrix.

However, educational policy at the level of macro-design needs to accommodate individuals at the level of micro-operations. On the micro-level, rules and regulations need to be flexible and responsive enough to satisfy a myriad of needs and. To succeed, teachers must be unleashed to improvise in the extremely complex world that is a labyrinth.

Why scream? Because the implementation of a matrix can itself get reconfigured as a defiant labyrinth of complexity that condemns dedicated workers to the sacrificial needs of a Minotaur. That's what happened to teachers and administrators at Fremont High School, who struggled for three years to qualify themselves as the founders of new small autonomous schools. The matrix became a labyrinth of discouragement and confusion.

Why scream? Because conversely, the successful achievements of skilled teachers and administrators at work in a labyrinth distort and collapse if they get redefined as educational goals that must fit neatly into the little boxes of a matrix of columns and rows. That's what is happening at Mills College with the imposition of an assessment policy that is attempting to transform a labyrinth of diverse course-inspired learning goals into a matrix of subject-distant examination questions. An enormous amount of information can be distorted or lost when a labyrinth gets transformed into a matrix.

When we as teachers are coerced into turning a matrix into a labyrinth, or to convert a labyrinth into a matrix, the change can fail to make us more effective as educators, but it can take up our time, consume our energy, slow us down, and demoralize us so that we give in to Horace's Compromise.

## What is Horace's Compromise?

Over 30 years ago, Theodore Sizer led a team of researchers in a five-year field study of high schools all over the United States. Based on extensive interviews and observations, they documented in detail that American schools were not working well. Sizer published their findings as a novel about a high school teacher.

*Horace's Compromise: The Dilemma of the American High School* was published just a year after the National Commission on Excellence in Education published *A Nation at Risk* in 1983. Many years later, Steven Drummond acknowledged its continuing importance for helping us see that American high schools are still at risk. He wrote that Sizer, "makes those who think they know what teachers do and how schools work see that the whole thing is a lot more complicated than they realize . . . that much of what goes on in high schools doesn't really make sense and needs to be changed – a message that rings as true today as it did 16 [now 25] years ago" (2000). The same was still true in 2008 when my book about educational failure at Fremont High School was published as *The Labyrinth of Cultural Complexity*.

Horace's Compromise was published in 1984. The publication date should make you think back to George Orwell's classic 1949 novel titled, simply, *1984*. Orwell's story took place in a fictional dystopia – very similar to Soviet Union at mid-century – a society straight-jacketed by pervasive surveillance and control. Orwell's dystopia was reflected in a non-totalitarian, thoroughly American way, in Sizer's novel.

Our public schools were and are in trouble because school policy since 1910 has imposed a rigid structure of control that was originally influenced by efficiency experts. Frank and Lillian Gilbreth as well as Frederick Taylor indirectly impacted the movement, The Gilbreths with their time and motion studies and Taylor with his concept of "scientific management" that impersonally controlled how workers did their jobs on production lines in large factories, every worker replaceable by another equally capable of being trained and indoctrinated, like spark plugs in a motor, all the same.

Franklin Bobbitt added the "social efficiency model" in adapting the factory model to public schools. It spilled over into colleges and universities. Schools were redesigned as factories that could produce educated young adults the way cars were build at the Ford Motor Company – the factory system. In the place of the one-room schoolhouse with children of different ages and abilities, students were placed in grade levels from kindergarten through twelfth grade, and on to years in college, if they made it that far. Subjects were taught in precise 50 minute periods, with ten minutes to move from one class to another, one teacher to another, one subject to another (like the frame of a car under construction on an assembly line where each worker adds only one piece to the final product).

What was Horace's compromise? Horace was a fictive teacher somewhat like Winston Smith, the fictive civil servant in Orwell's novel. Horace was well qualified, highly capable, and committed to teaching. His big compromise was to attempt to balance what he knew his students needed with what he had time and energy to provide. "He hates his compromise, but he is comfortable with the familiar routines, however inadequate" (pg. 68). His compromise was that he taught as well as he could, but was defeated by the factory system. A car is built with uniform parts. Every Ford car came off the production identical in every way with every other Ford car. But children are all different and many do not respond well to the production line approach to schooling.

The nation is still at risk in our time. As a response to Horace's compromise, the small school policy promises to modify the factory model in helpful ways, but its implementation at Fremont High School was mishandled in discouraging ways. In a different way at Mills College, we can empathize with Horace's compromise every time a WASC demand corners us in a matrix when we can only hope to succeed if we remain free agents in the labyrinth.

## Others Should Also Scream!

For personal as well as professional reasons I got involved with people working hard to rescue Fremont High School by implementing a small school policy to improve teaching and learning. In an attempt to think anthropologically about that brave effort I found that a two-system model of policy analysis was helpful. Taking Fremont High as a case study, I described bureaucratic efforts metaphorically as located in a matrix, while teachers in their classrooms struggled metaphorically in a labyrinth.

At the same time, I was professionally and personally involved as a professor and department head at Mills College. Taking that as a second case for comparative purposes, I used the same binary model of metaphors to attempt to make sense of how a well-intentioned

WASC policy in a matrix, designed to improve teaching and learning, threatened demoralizing consequences in the labyrinth.

Having found the model useful in two case studies, I want to suggest that it may be helpful in other situations where educational policy is designed and implemented. I propose to move modestly from two case studies to three, at which point I hope it is not too presumptive to speak of ethnographic theory, of cross-cultural regularities.

In the mode of applied and practicing anthropology reconfigured as autoethnography, I will characterize this third case study, facetiously, as proxy-autoethnography, because it is based on the work of Professor Edna Mitchell in Afghanistan, whom you know already as my life companion, my wife. Edna was a thread in the tapestry of this book for both Fremont High and Mills College and that thread extends as well to include headbutting in Afghanistan, which Edna has experienced and observed for the last five years (2004-2009) as an educational consultant.

## Designing a Public School System for Afghanistan

The timing was perfect for my totally new course on Educational Anthropology. Edna returned to Afghanistan in January, 2009, just before I met that class for the first time. She returned to California on May 1, just in time to meet with the class in person for our last meeting of the semester. Since Edna and I exchanged e-messages daily, and I visited her in Kabul three times, her new assignment offered a great opportunity to use Afghanistan in the class as a case study on the design of an educational policy for the creation of a national public school system in a developing nation. In class, we followed Edna's work in real time.

After the fall of the Taliban in 2001, international aid efforts made education a high priority in re-building the nation. The illiteracy rate was one of the highest in the world. The education of girls had been forbidden under the Taliban, schools were destroyed, teachers were killed, fled the country, or went into hiding. Education needed emergency infusions and strategic planning.

With the American occupation, refugees returned and enrollments grew to unmanageable numbers as schools re-opened or were freshly established. Illiterate young adults who had been denied educational opportunities during the war years were also targeted through accelerated learning programs and radio lessons. Classes were large, classrooms scarce, and teaching methods traditional, based on punishment as a learning incentive. Multiple sessions were required to accommodate the growing number of students. Classes were often held under trees, on porches, or in tents provided by the United Nations. Textbooks were unavailable and required new curricula to be written before new ones could be printed in Dari or Pashto and distributed to remote areas.

Educated individuals who could be recruited as teachers were scarce, especially in rural provinces, where it became practical to appoint anyone as a teacher who could read and write. The attention of international funders focused on teacher education and up-grading. No matter how well educated, teachers were poorly paid, often receiving no salary for months at a time as a result of failures in the distribution system as well as of corruption in the provinces.

School teachers were included in a new Civil Service Reform Act that ensured their pay by the government, yet the government had few independent sources of funding. Money for teacher salaries was dependent on international donors who, as a group, monitored the budget process. Questions about the educational levels of teachers, their subject competencies, and their pedagogical skills became central to conversations about schooling.

To be a civil servant called for being evaluated by rank on the government salary scale (a matrix). How could teachers be placed in matrix categories without evidence of their qualifications? If not ranked, they could not receive pay increases. The decision of the Ministry of Education, under pressure from international donors, was to find a way to assess teacher knowledge competencies and communication skills.

That vision of the future included designing a policy for how teachers would earn teaching credentials and rise through a series of ranks from entry level to fully professional. It was to be based on a Western notion of formal standards of professional qualifications ranked in numbered and segmented categories on a matrix or rubric.

On the advice of international advisors and a stream of consultants, the Ministry of Education tackled the issue of how to assess subject competencies and teaching skills. Despite the advice of Western teacher educators who recommended gathering multiple kinds of evidence to demonstrate effectiveness in the classroom (or lack of it), the Ministry emphasized the need to establish a national examination system. But, what would be tested? Knowledge of grade-level subject matter to be sure, but how quickly could examinations be developed that would satisfy the demands of the donors for validity, reliability, consistency, fairness, and security? Sensitivities in the psychology of teaching and learning including skills in communicating knowledge should also be measured on written examinations, but could it be done? How quickly could examinations be prepared and testing dates and sites organized?

The examination development process had to meet standards customary in technologically advanced nations. Edna's assignment was to work through a tangled maze of products and associated labyrinthine political machinations involving international as well as national power holders, to produce a testing mechanism that would enable the Afghan government to improve teacher salaries and prepare them to function on higher professional levels.

Teachers as civil servants come under a reform act referred to as "Pay and Grade," meaning that they must be located in a box on in a matrix known as a "pay scale." Placement is determined by merit and level of performance. Money to improve salaries is and would be provided by institutional donors such as the World Bank. The donor position was, Show us competent teacher or we'll show you no money. The problem was, How can one assess levels of teacher competence throughout the nation? The question was, Competent in what? Should it be teaching methods (pedagogy)? Subject knowledge (competencies)? Both? Other?

The answer was predictable, Require them to take tests. But, tests based on what? What knowledge and skills did Afghan teachers need? Who in Afghanistan had knowledge and skills to impart? And, horrors, what if all teachers failed? As if those questions and uncertainties were not enough, another question was, Is there a hidden political agenda? It appeared so. A sense of urgency was likely inspired by a need to design the program and implement it so that teachers could be tested and placed in grade before the presidential election only a few months away in August (2009). The election outcome could be influenced by success or failure in establishing a new public school system. Jobs and careers were on line. The more visionary long-range goal, to be sure, was to move forward on establishing measurable standards that would transform teaching as a profession with a clear path to the creation of a national corps of qualified teachers by means of credentialing, professional development standards, and school accreditation.

We looked over Edna's shoulder vicariously at Mills as she put her head and heart into challenging assignments that were macro-level (system-wide). Not surprisingly, her most time-consuming task was to fill in the columns, rows, and boxes of a matrix, or more precisely, of three matrices. The first was to identify necessary teacher competencies (the subject matter knowledge they should master in order to qualify to teach). Eleven separate columns were filled in for grades 1st to 3rd, 4th to 6th, and so on to grade 12. The rows in each column were laid out as subjects such as physics, chemistry, mathematics, history, Islamic studies, language (Dari or Pashto), and so on. Each of the subject competencies required filling in precisely five boxes for each specific "knowledge topic."

To illustrate for chemistry, grades 11 to 12, the specific subtopics were (1) hydrocarbons, (2) alcohols, (3) aldehydes, (4) organic acids, and (5) glucose. That pattern was repeated for every subject, always exactly five boxes for each of 11 columns. The whole catalog of what teachers needed to know and teach inspired by the geometry of a matrix that for no subject ever permitted only four subtopics or, heaven forbid, six or more. It always had to be exactly five.

The lesson from No Child Left Behind was not learned in Kabul. Teachers themselves are destined to study to pass multiple choice tests, implementing a process of less is less in which the broader goals of education tend to fall into neglect as teachers focus on test-passing strategies.

Similarly, Edna worked to finalize a second matrix of pedagogical skills (how to succeed in communicating knowledge topics to students at each grade level). For example, "Teaching strategies" in 3 columns, and 8 rows, that yielded 24 boxes (filled with explanatory sentences) for each grade level. The third matrix constituted an assessment format: the tests teachers would have to pass to demonstrate their mastery of relevant competencies and pedagogical skills. It will come as no surprise to learn that the tests themselves were in the matrix form of multiple choice questions, with four possible answers for each question. Edna had to create 25 questions for each of 55 topics. It seemed endless. As I write, she is preparing to undertake an analysis of the results of a trial run of the exam that was administered to 200 teachers. She is unequivocally working in a matrix.

## From the Capital City to a Rural Province

However, her assignment also included travel as an ethnographically-informed educator to two rural provinces in the north, Jawzjan and Sar-I-Pul. There she met with administrators, talked with teachers and sat in on some of their "Teacher Training Circles," where experienced teachers and school leaders coached others in classroom skills. When Edna visited my class at Mills, she showed and explained photographs of that involvement in a powerpoint presentation. Several of her most memorable photos pictured old, middle-aged and young teachers in a Teacher Training Circle using a microscope for the first time in their lives, looking forward to introducing laboratory extensions some day in teaching their classes on biology and botany, assuming that someday in the future they would get the necessary instruments and supplies.

In this part of her assignment Edna was working in a labyrinth. Teachers are supposed to have completed the 12$^{th}$ to 14$^{th}$ grade. A minority meet that requirement. The law only requires completion of the 9$^{th}$ grade, which qualifies many of the teachers. Others teach on the basis of a 6$^{th}$ grade education. Others only studied in religious schools (madrasses), where they read and interpret the Qur'an, and some have had no schooling at all, including some rural teachers who, it has been said, are functionally illiterate.

On those site visits, Edna was working in a labyrinth of cultural issues as well, observing schools taught in bombed out facilities. In one small town she saw how 4000 students were divided into three successive daily sessions to be taught in tents. Human rights abuses in those provinces include child marriage, child sexual abuse, children sold as servants or prostitutes, women beaten, limited schooling for girls. It is a culture of conservative elders and mullahs, many of whom do not approve of girls being educated or of children learning through play. They want children to attend madrassas, not the provincial school. The immensity of the task is overwhelming. It is a time of terrorism with a corrupt and inept government. In a labyrinth, on the level of micro-operations (specific events), the matrix seems almost irrelevant.

## Return to Kabul and Scream!

Back in Kabul, and not surprising for anthropologists and others who have worked for policy change in developing nations, the process of designing a matrix had become a labyrinth itself.

Before Edna was involved, Kabul University professors where hired to write the first drafts of competency requirements and test questions. She was not taken by surprise to discover that professors who teach at the university level are very uninformed about how their subjects need to be taught at the elementary level.

In her first year of work in Afghanistan she contributed to efforts to reorganize the system of higher education, which was almost no system at all. Each institution of higher education had its own program. Courses in different institutions of higher learning were not standardized on a basis of class hours, course credits, or curricular goals. Libraries only casually cataloged books and shelving was a hodgepodge. Professionally trained librarians were almost non-existent. Edna organized workshops, training programs, and conferences for university professors and administrators in an effort to initiate coordination, with little to show for it after months of hard work.

Edna was also asked to help with another confounding variable, the governmental structure of two ministries, the Ministry of Higher Education as distinct from the Ministry of Education, the latter alone having responsibility for teacher training. Yet, the Ministry of Higher Education had control of all education in colleges and universities, including those where teachers received their education beyond high school. The exception, and the dysfunction, was that the Teacher Training Institutions (grades 13 and 14) were under the jurisdiction of the Ministry of Education, not of the Ministry of Higher Education. The wall between the two ministries, and their inability to cooperate across it, left each ministry boxed in its own matrix. It was a mess.

At the level of President Karzai's cabinet it was agreed that education would be more efficient if the ministries were merged, but five years later it still hasn't happened. Politics? Certainly. And a significant consequence is that courses taught in the teacher training university cannot be transferred to the academic university for credit, so trained teachers cannot move on to earn academic degrees without starting all over again at the entry level.

That attitude is significant for Edna's work on identifying the competencies to be required for the accreditation of teachers. University professors under the Ministry of Higher Education were hired to write first drafts of the competency requirements and test questions for teachers who would be credentialed by the Ministry of Education. Edna's assignment was to adapt the professor's drafts to public school needs, which left her to bounce back and forth between the two ministries. University professors take pride in claiming not to know anything at all about teaching school. In the status system of academe, the two realms are worlds apart. The irony is that, like the Emperor's New Clothes, no is noticing or talking about the fact that the competencies turned over to Edna for fine-tuning were an exercise in futility. They didn't match the curriculum. Asking higher education professors to chose five topics from their fields of specialization allowed them to cherry pick what was of interest to them, not what was of importance in school curricula.

When I discussed this dilemma with one former American consultant (who shall remain nameless), his response was, "You know, it hardly matters. The outcome will, be totally flawed, close to worthless." Yet, a lot of money is spent to pay foreign experts to produce those matrices, and they are actually worth a lot in some ways. They are compiled by consultants like Edna, who are employed by contracting agencies, some of which are non-profit and altruistic, such as Save the Children, for whom Edna now works, and others that are business enterprises with good intentions. Whether non-profit or for-profit, the contracting agencies are funded by USAID, itself a well-intentioned agency of the Government of the United State. Note that each of these entities functions in a matrix. The single most important achievement for a contractor is to produce a report of successful activities and achievements so that USAID can document that the work was done and pay them. Only on that basis can contractors pay their consultants. So, big, thick volumes of statistics are the coin of the realm in development work, and the most important consideration turns out to be getting official (bureaucratic) approval of those documents. Edna performed really well in those terms. The teacher competency document was signed off as approved by the Ministry of Education a month before her deadline. On submitting that document, USAID got their funding and, in turn, could fund Save the Children, who for their part could pay Edna's salary. Conclusion: the matrix itself became a labyrinth of political machinations, conflicting goals, and individual frailties.

## Conclusion

A pilot test given in June, 2009, to 200 teachers in the provinces raised a general alarm that required press releases from the Ministry of Education. The plan to implement a national testing policy raised fears of failure among teachers and fears of corruption and incompetence in the minds of donors. A rapidly spreading rumor claimed that test questions had been leaked and were being sold in the marketplace for 40 Afghanis (less than one dollar), meaning that whole testing program had been compromised. Fortunately, the rumor was wrong. The paper being sold was merely an information pamphlet freely available to all teachers to explain the purpose, procedures, and types of tests. Yet, considerable damage was incurred. International donors blew the whistle, demanding to know how validity, reliability, fairness, and security in test settings were being managed. National testing was put on hold until after the elections scheduled for August 21, 2009. The delay may well be further extended, because Ramadan (Dari, Ramazan), which lasts for a lunar month, begins the day after the national elections. If the test ends up being administered during that month-long time of daytime fasting, nighttime feasting, and minimal sleeping, teachers failing their tests will be well-placed to complain bitterly that the test situation was unfair and un-Islamic because righteous people become very weak and tired. As I write, the fate of this complex process is still unknown. It is a labyrinth.

Ted Sizer was right. less is more when your challenge is to succeed in the labyrinth of cultural complexity. We need the matrix, but when at all possible you need to defend against the claims of more is better, because, if the matrix becomes too complex, it can transform a mechanism that should be helpful into a labyrinth itself that can defeat its own good intentions. I was there when it happened at Fremont High School. It is happening now at Mills College. Edna is experiencing it in Afghanistan. What should we do?

# Postscript for 2009 and 2010

**MILLS COLLEGE**
**OFFICE OF THE PRESIDENT**

**MEMORANDUM**

To: The Mills College Community

From: Janet L. Holmgren, President

Date: June 29, 2009

Re: WASC Reaccreditation Update

Mills College has passed another landmark in its progress through the WASC reaffirmation of accreditation review. We have received notice from the WASC Commission that our Capacity and Preparatory Review report has been accepted and that we can continue to the next step, the Educational Effectiveness Review.

This reaccreditation review began in 2007-08 with the development of our Institutional Proposal and continued in 2008-09 with the completion of our Capacity and Preparatory Review (CPR) Report. Mills submitted its CPR report to WASC in December 2008. The WASC visiting team, chaired by Dr. Kathleen O'Brien of Alverno

College, was on campus March 4-6, 2009. We received the visiting team's final report on April 30. Along with Executive Vice President Ramon Torrecilha, and Marianne Sheldon, Accreditation Liaison Officer, I met with members of the Commission on June 18 to discuss that report. The College received formal notice on June 24 that the CPR report had been accepted.

The Commission endorsed the recommendations of the visiting team and concluded that ". . . Mills is well positioned to meet the expectations for the Educational Effectiveness Review (EER)." Our EER report is due to WASC in July 2010 with a visit scheduled for fall 2010.

We have much work to do in preparation for the Educational Effectiveness Review report and visit. As our letter from the WASC Commission observes, at the time of the EER "... **Mills will be expected to document and demonstrate that student learning outcomes are being measured, assessed, and evaluated, and that the results of these assessments are leading to program improvements to ensure that educational objectives are being met at both undergraduate and graduate levels**" [emphasis added]. Our work on this task is underway at present and will continue throughout the coming academic year, under the leadership of Provost and Dean of the Faculty, Sandra Greer, and Accreditation Liaison Officer, Marianne Sheldon.

The acceptance of our CPR report represents the culmination of months of intense preparation and work by faculty, staff, and administrators who prepared the required essays and by the entire campus community that discussed and reviewed those essays. Faculty, staff, administrators, students, and trustees met with members of the visiting team that came to campus last March. The experience thus far has been positive and constructive. I thank all of you for your efforts in support of this process and I will continue to keep you informed of our activities and progress.

# References

American Association of Higher Education, 1996.
>   *Nine Principles of Good Practice for Assessing Student Learning.*
>   http://www.cord.edu/dept/assessment/nineprin.pdf

Ancess, Jacqueline, 1997.
>   *Urban Dreamcatchers: Launching and Leading new Small Schools.*
>   New York, NY: Teachers College, Columbia University.

Ancess, Jacqueline, 2003.
>   "The Request-for-Proposals Process." In video documentary,
>   *Solving the Puzzle: Redesigning Large High Schools Together.*
>   School Redesign Network at Stanford University, School
>   of Education. (Module C4: Adopting Existing Models or
>   Developing Our Own.) Stanford, CA: Stanford University

Anderson, Robert, 1971.
>   *Anthropology: A Perspective on Man.* Belmont, CA: Wadsworth
>   Publishing Company.

Anderson, Robert, 1996.
>   *Magic, Science, and Health: The Aims and Achievements of
>   Medical Anthropology.* Fort Worth, TX: Harcourt Brace College
>   Publishers.

Anderson, Robert, 2000.
>   *Alternative and Conventional Medicine in Iceland: The Diagnosis
>   and Treatment of Low Back Pain.* Public Health in Iceland,

Supplement 2000, Nr. 1. Reykjavik, Iceland: Directorate of Health.

Anderson, Robert, 2005.
*The Ghosts of Iceland*. Belmont, CA: Thomson Wadsworth.

Anderson, Robert, 2008.
*The Labyrinth of Cultural Complexity: Fremont High Teachers, The Small School Policy, and Oakland Inner-City Realities*. Bloomington, IN: iUniverse.

Barrington, Lowell, 2003.
"Less Assessment, More Learning." *Academe*, November-December.

Bartlett, Raymond "Buzz" and Claus von Zastrow, 2004.
"Academic Atrophy." *Education Week*, Vol. 23 (30): 38, 48.

Bateson, Gregory, 1972.
"Double Bind," (pp. 271-278). In Gregory Bateson, Ed., *Steps to an Ecology of Mind*. New York, NY: Ballantine Books.

Bhattacharjee, Yudhijit, 2009.
"Evolution: Authors Scramble to Make Textbooks Conform to Texas Science Standards." *Science*, Vol. 324 (5933): 1385.

Bidney, David, 1967.
*Theoretical Anthropology*, 2ed. Ed. New York, NY: Schocken Books.

Blau, Peter, 1963.
*The Dynamics of Bureaucracy*. Chicago, IL: University of Chicago Press.

Block, R., 1996.
"Cynics, Victims, and Bystanders," (221-231). In Peter Block, Ed., *Stewardship: Choosing Service over Self-Interest*. San Francisco, CA: Berrett-Kokehler Publishers.

Bryk, Anthony S. and Barbara Schneider, 20o02.
*Trust in Schools: A Core Resource for Improvement*. New York, NY: Russell Sage.

Buffum, Austin and Charles Hinman, 2006.

"Professional Learning Communities: Reigniting Passion and Purpose." *Leadership*, Vol. 35 (5): 16-19.

Chaltain, Sam, 2009.

"Will We Do What It Takes to Improve Public Education?" *Education Week*, Vol. 28 (36), June 17.

Chang, Heewon, 2008.

*Autoethnography as Method*. Walnut Creek, CA: Left Coast Press, Inc.

Chun, Eva Wells, 1987, 1988.

"Sorting Black Students for Success and Failure: The Inequality of Ability Grouping and Tracking." *Urban League Review*, Vol. 11 (1-2): 93-106.

Clinchy, Evans, 2000.

"Introduction (pp 11-13)." In Evan Clinchy, Ed., *Creating New Schools: How Small Schools Are Changing American Education*. New York, NY: Teachers College Press.

Cody, Anthony, 2008.

"We Need a New Definition of Accountability." *San Francisco Chronicle*, January 6: E5.

Coleman, James S., 1986.

"Social Theory, Social Research, and a Theory of Action." *American Journal of Sociology*, Vol. 91 (6): 1309-1335.

Coleman, James S., et al, 1966.

*Equality of Educational Opportunity*. Washington, DC: Government Printing Office.

Cooper, Robert, 1999.

"Urban School Reform: Student Responses to Detracking in a Racially Mixed High School." *Journal of Education for Students Placed at Risk*, Vol. 4 (3): 259-275.

Cuban, Larry, 2003.

*Why Is It So Hard To Get Good Schools?* New York, NY: Teachers College, Columbia University.

Cushman, Kathleen, 1994.

"Less is More: The Secret of Being Essential." *Horace*, Vol. 11 (2).

Cushman, Kathleen, 1997.

"Essential Leadership in the School Change Process." *Horace*, Vol. 14 (4): 1-8.

Darling-Hammond, Linda, 1997.

*The Right to Learn: A Blueprint for Creating Schools That Work.* San Francisco, CA: Jossey-Bass.

Darling-Hammond, Linda, 2002.

*Redesigning Schools: What Matters and What Works (10 Features of Good Small Schools).* Stanford, CA: School Redesign Network at Stanford University.

Drummond, Steven, 2000.

"Horace's Compromise." *Teacher Magazine.* April 1.

DuFour, Rick and R. Eaker, 1998.

*Professional Learning Communities at Work: Best Practice for Enhancing Student Achievement.* Bloomington, IN: National Education Service.

*Education Encyclopedia*, 2002.

"School Accreditation in the United States."

Fenno, Cheryl, 2002.

"Assessment in Higher Education." *Teaching Today Postsecondary, Education Up Close.* Web-based, New York, NY: Glencoe/ McGraw-Hill.

Fink, Stephen and Max Silverman, 2007.

"The Not-So-Inevitable Failure of High School Conversions." *Education Week*, Vol. 27 (9): 29.

Fish, Adam, 2007.

"Mining Difference for the Culture Industry: Both Borat and Anthropologists Do It." *Anthropology News*, Vol. 48 (1): 6-7.

Flaxman, Laura, 2004.

"Life Academy and Fremont High School: Lessons for Large School Conversions." *Horace*, Vol. 20 (3).

Friedkin, William, and Juan Necochea, 1988.

"School System Size and Performance: A Contingency Perspective." *Education Evaluation and Policy Analysis*, Vol. 10: 237-249.

Fuentes, Agustin, 2007.

*Core Concepts in Biological Anthropology.* Boston, MA: McGraw-Hill.

Fulbright, Leslie, 2006.

"Cosby, Others Say Black Men Still in Crisis." *San Francisco Chronicle*, July 19: A5.

Fullan, Michael, 1994.

*Change Forces: Probing the Depths of Educational Reform.* Bristol, PA: Falmer Press.

Gallup Poll, 2009.

"Evolution, Creationism, Intelligent Design." Web-based.

Garibaldi, Antoine and Melinda Bartley, 1989.

"Black School Push-Outs and Dropouts: Strategies for Reduction" (227-235). In W. D. Smith and E. W. Chun, Eds., *Black Education: A Quest for Equity and Excellence.* Brunswick, NJ: Transaction Publishers.

Goffman, Erving, 1959.

*The Presentation of Self in Everyday Life.* Garden City, NY: Doubleday Anchor Books.

Goodlad, John, 1984.

*A Place Called School: Prospects for the Future.* New York, NY:McGraw-Hill.

Goodlad, John, 1990.

*Teachers for Our Nation's Schools.* San Francisco, CA: Jossey-Bass Publishers.

Gordon, Craig, 2005.

"My Small School Journey." *Rethinking Schools*, Vol. 19 (4).

Heller, Joseph, 1999.

*Catch-22: A Novel.* New York, NY: Simon & Schuster.

Hirschfeld, Lawrence A., 2002.

"Why Don't Anthropologists Like Children?" *American Anthropologist*, Vol. 104 (2): 611-627.

Howley, Craig, 1996.

"Compounding Disadvantage: The Effects of School and District Size on Student Achievement in West Virginia." *Journal of Research in Rural Education*, Vol. 12 (1): 25-32.

Jencks, Christopher, Marshal Smith, Henry Acland, et al, 1972.

*Inequality: A Reassessment of the Effects of Family and Schooling in America.* New York, NY: Free Press.

Johnson, Chip, 2006.

"When Gangsta Rap Becomes Grim Reality." *San Francisco Chronicle*, August 22: B1, B5.

Johnson, James A., V. Dupuis, D. Musial, G. Hall, and D. Gollnick, 2002.

*Introduction to the Foundations of American Education*, 12th Ed. Boston, MA: Allyn and Bacon.

Kenny, Erin, 2006.

"Innovations in Ethnography." *Anthropology News*, Vol. 47 (9), December 26.

King, M. Bruce, K. Louis, H. Marks, and K. Peterson, 1996.

"Participatory Decision Making" (pp. 245-263). In Fred M, Newman, et al, Eds., *Authentic Achievement: Restructuring Schools for Intellectual Quality*. San Francisco, CA: Jossey-Bass.

Kubler-Ross, Elisabeth, 1969.

*On Death and Dying.* New York, NY: Macmillan.

Lambert, L., et al, 1997.

"Who Sets the Learning Agenda? Issues of Power, Authority, and Control" (pp.122-143). In *Teachers as Constructivist Leaders*. Thousand Oaks, CA: Corwin Press.

Lee, Valerie E. and David GT. Burkham, 2002.

> *Inequality at the Starting Gate: Social Background Differences in Achievement as Children Begin School.* Washington, DC: Economic Policy Institute.

Lévi-Strauss, Claude, 1966.

> *The Savage Mind.* Chicago, IL: University of Chicago Press.

Lindseth, Alfred A., 2004

> "Adequacy Lawsuits: The Wrong Answer for Our Kids." *Education Week*, Vol. 23 (39): 42, 52.

Linkon, Sherry Lee, 2005

> "How Can Assessment Work for Us?" *Academe*, July-August.

Maran, Meredith, 2001.

> *Class Dismissed: A Year in the Life of an American High School, A Glimpse into the Heart of a Nation.* New York, NY: St. Martin's Griffin.

McNeil, Linda M., 1988.

> "The Contradictions of Control, Part 3: Contradictions of Reform. *Phi Delta Kappan*, March.

May, Meredith, 2001.

> "Oakland Schools Chief Shakes the System." *San Francisco Chronicle*, March 5.

May, Meredith, 2002.

> "Oakland Schools Broke, Face Bailout." *San Francisco Chronicle*, December 8.

May, Meredith, 2003.

> "State Administrator Focused on Finances." *San Francisco Chronicle*, May 11.

Meier, Deborah, 1995.

> *The Power of Their Ideas: Lessons from a Small School in Harlem.* Boston, MA: Beacon Press.

Meyer, John and Brian Rowan, 1977.

"Institutionalized Organizations: Formal Structure as Myth and Ceremony." *American Journal of Sociology*, Vol. 83 (2): 340-363.

National Commission on Excellence in Education, 1983.

*A Nation at Risk*. Washington, DC: U.S. Government Printing Office.

National High School Alliance, 2005.

A Call to Action: Transforming High School for All Youth. Washington, DC: Institute of Educational Leadership, Inc.

Oakes, Jeannie, 1984.

"Keeping Track, Part 1: The Policy and Practice of Curriculum Inequality." *Phi Delta Kappan*, September.

Oakes, Jeannie, 1985.

*Keeping Track: How Schools Structure Inequality*. New Haven, CT: Yale University Press.

O'Brien, Robert T., 2007.

"Anthropology: Epistemology or Nothing but a J-O-B?" *Anthropology News*, Vol. 48 (1): 54.

Ogle, L. T., Alsalam, N., and Rogers, G. T., 1991.

*The Condition of Education*. Vol. 1: *Elementary and Secondary Education*. NCES 91-637. Washington, DC: National Center for Education Statistics, U.S. Department of Education.

Olson, Lynn, 2007.

"Breaking the Cycle of Poverty: Reducing the Disparities in Children's Achievement Will Require Reaching Beyond the Educational System." *Education Week*, January 4.

O'Neil, Jaime, 2006.

"Leaving Creativity Behind: Drilling for Tests Kills Curiosity and Imagination." *San Francisco Chronicle*, March 12.

Ortner, Sherry B., 2006.

*Anthropology and Social Theory: Culture, Power, and the Acting Subject*. Durham, NC: Duke University Press.

Page, Clarence, 2006.

"The Nation's Anti-Poverty Effort Begins at Home." *Oakland Tribune,* August 24: 9.

Pascopella, Angela, 2005.

"Changing Education – For Real." *District Administration,* November: 31-32.

Perin, Constance, 2005.

*Shouldering Risks: The Culture of Control in the Nuclear Power Industry.* Princeton, NJ: Princeton University Press.

Perry, Theresa, and Lisa Delpit, Eds., 1998.

*Debate: Power, Language, and the Education of African-American Children.* Boston, MA: Beacon Press.

Phillips, Gary, 2009.

"How to Fix No Child Left Behind: Creating a New and Improved Version of the Voluntary National Test." *Educational Week,* Vol. 28 (31: 28-29, 31.

Poplin, M. and J. Weeres, 1992.

*Voices from the Inside: A Report on Schooling from Inside the Classroom.* Institute for Education in Transformation., Claremont, CA: Claremont Graduate School.

Postman, Neil, 1995.

*The End of Education: Redefining the Value of School.* New York, NY: Random House (Vintage Books).

Pratt, Mary Louise, 1992.

*Imperial Eyes: Travel Writing and Transculturation.* London: Routledge.

Rappaport, Roy, 1993.

"Distinguished Lecture in General Anthropology: The Anthropology of Trouble." *American Anthropologist,* Vol. 95(2): 295-302.

Raywid, Mary Anne, 1996.

"Taking Stock: The Movement to Create Mini-Schools, Schools-Within-Schools, and Separate Small Schools." *ERIC*

Urban Diversity Series, No. 108. Eric Clearinghouse on Urban Education, Institute for Urban and Minority Education. New York, NY: Columbia University.

Reed-Danahay, Deborah, 2009
"Anthropologists, Education, and Autoethnography." *Reviews in Anthropology*, Vol. 38 (1): 28-47.

Rhymes, Edward, 2004.
"Dr. Bill Cosby, I Respectfully Disagree." June 2: A13. New Bedford, MA: *Standard-Times*.

Robelen, Erik W., 2004.
"'No Child' Law Remains at Top of Bush Record." *Education Week*, Vol 24 (5): 1, 23-24.

Roe, Emery and Paul R. Schulman, 2008.
*High Reliability Management: Operating on the Edge*. Stanford, CA: Stanford Business Books.

Sadovnik, Alan R., Peter W. Cookson, Jr., Susan F. Semel, 2001.
*Exploring Education: An Introduction to the Foundations of Education*, 2ed Ed. Boston, MA: Allyn and Bacon.

Schlosser, 2002.
*Fast Food Nation: The Dark Side of the All-American Meal*. New York, NY: HarperCollins (Perennial).

Schmookler, Benjamin, 2006.
*Focus on Learning: WASC Self-Study*. Oakland, CA: Media Academy High School.

Sizer, Theodore, 1984.
*Horace's Compromise: The Dilemma of the American High School*. New York, NY: Houghton-Mifflen.,

Sizer, Theodore, 1997.
*Horace's Compromise: The Dilemma of the American High School*, Rev. Ed. Boston, MA: Houghton-Mifflen.

Small Schools Project, 2003.
*Thinking About Conversions*. Center on Reinventing Public Education.

Song, Jason, 2009.

>"Firing Tenured Teachers Can Be a Costly and Tortuous Task." *Los Angeles Times.* http://www.latimes.com/news/local/la-me-teachers3-2009may03,0,679507.story

Spillane, James P., 2006.

>*Distributed Leadership.* San Francisco, CA: Jossey-Bass.

Steinberg, Laurence, 1997

>*Beyond the Classroom: Why School Reform Has Failed and What Parents Need To Do.* New York, NY: Simon &I Schuster (Touchstone).

Swidler, Ann, 1986.

>"Culture in Action: Symbols and Strategies." American Sociological Review Vol. 51: 273-286.

Thompson, Chris, 2003.

>"Name-Em and Shame-Em." *East Bay Express*, February 5-11: 11-12.

Toch, Thomas, 2003.

>*High Schools on a Human Scale: How Small Schools Can Transform American Education.* Boston, MA: Beacon Press.

Toffler, Alvin, 1970.

>*Future Shock.* New York, NY: Random House.

Torrance, Kelly, 2006.

>"California's English Learners: Can You Say 'Held Back?'" *Los Angeles Times*, March 21.

Tucker, Cynthia, 2007.

>"A Black Middle Class Rises, Underclass Falls Further." *San Francisco Chronicle*, December 3: D5.

Wagner, Tony, 1997.

>"The New Village Commons – Improving Schools Together." *Educational Leadership*, Vol 54 (5): 25-28.

Wagner, Tony, 1998.

> "Change as Collaborative Inquiry: A 'Constructivist' Methodology for Reinventing Schools." *Phi Delta Kappan*, Vol. 79 (7): 512-517.

Wagner, Tony, 2002.

> Facilitator's Guide for Community Members' Small Group Facilitation on the Topic of High School Graduation Requirements. *Instructional Broadcast Center*. (Distributed in the Oakland Unified School District by BayCES.) Seattle, WA: Seattle Public Schools.

Walsh, Andrew, 2005.

> "The Obvious Aspects of Ecological Underprivilege in Ankarana, Northern Madagascar." *American Anthropologist*, Vol.107 (4): 654-665.

Wasley, Patricia A. and Richard J. Lear, 2001.

> "Small Schools, Real Gains." *Educational Leadership*, Vol. 58 (6): 22-27.

Waterman, Robert H., Jr., 1992.

> *Adhocracy: The Power to Change*. New York, NY: Norton.

Weber, Max, 1979.

> *Economy and Society: An Outline of Interpretive Sociology*, 2 vols. Berkeley, CA: University of California Press.

Wehlage, G., R. Rutter, G. Smith, N. Leskok, R. Fernandez, 1989.

> *Reducing the Risk: Schools as Communities of Support*. New York, NY: The Falmer Press.

Weiss, Melford S., 2009.

> "The Anthropology of Work-Life Balance." *Anthropology News*, Vol. 50 (5): 46-47.

Wildman, Louis, 2004.

> "Assessment and Learning." *Academe*, May-June.

Wills, Dorothy D., 1999.

"Crash Test Dummies or Good Company? Cornerstones and WASC." Presentation dated February 11, on the web http://www.csupomona.edu/~ddwills/research/wasc/cornerstones.htm

Yee, Gary, 1996.

*Miracle Workers Wanted: Executive Succession and Organizational Change in an Urban School District: An Exploratory Study*. Ed.D. dissertation, School of Education, Stanford, CA: Stanford University.